Thinking
Qualitatively

Thinking Qualitatively

METHODS OF MIND

Johnny Saldaña

Arizona State University

Los Angeles | London | New Delhi
Singapore | Washington DC

Los Angeles | London | New Delhi
Singapore | Washington DC

FOR INFORMATION:

SAGE Publications, Inc.

2455 Teller Road

Thousand Oaks, California 91320

E-mail: order@sagepub.com

SAGE Publications Ltd.

1 Oliver's Yard

55 City Road

London EC1Y 1SP

United Kingdom

SAGE Publications India Pvt. Ltd.

B 1/I 1 Mohan Cooperative Industrial Area

Mathura Road, New Delhi 110 044

India

SAGE Publications Asia-Pacific Pte. Ltd.

3 Church Street

#10-04 Samsung Hub

Singapore 049483

Acquisitions Editor: Helen Salmon

Editorial Assistant: Anna Villarruel

Project Editor: Veronica Stapleton Hooper

Copy Editor: Rachel Keith

Typesetter: C&M Digitals (P) Ltd.

Proofreader: Dennis W. Webb

Indexer: Jean Casalegno

Cover Designer: Anupama Krishnan

Marketing Manager: Nicole Elliott

Printed in the United States of America

Saldana, Johnny.

Thinking qualitatively : methods of mind / Johnny Saldana.

pages cm
Includes bibliographical references and index.

ISBN 978-1-4833-4983-1 (alk. paper)

1. Qualitative research. 2. Social sciences— Methodology. I. Title.

H62.S3187 2015
001.4'2--dc23   2014014585

This book is printed on acid-free paper.

SUSTAINABLE FORESTRY INITIATIVE
Certified Chain of Custody
Promoting Sustainable Forestry
www.sfiprogram.org
SFI-01268

SFI label applies to text stock

15 16 17 18 19 10 9 8 7 6 5 4 3 2 1

Brief Contents

Detailed Contents

List of Displays

Preface

The Purpose and Goals of the Book

The purpose of this book is to profile and activate multiple ways to think for qualitative inquiry and data analysis. Its primary goals are

- to expand your knowledge base and repertoire of subtopics for social inquiry and analytic reflection;
- to provide practical methods of mind (i.e., thinking strategies) for social inquiry; and
- to accelerate your mental processes as a researcher during various components of a qualitative study (e.g., conceptual framework development, fieldwork and data collection, data analysis, write-up).

Thinking Qualitatively: Methods of Mind offers ways to examine research design, fieldwork experiences, collected data, and the writing of reports, and to mentally reflect on them in multiple ways to stimulate analytic connections, transcendence, and insight. The text focuses on how to think about and reflect on social life and qualitative data in multiple ways—through an array of analytic lenses and filters and from a variety of angles—to conceptualize and execute your study, and how to examine textual, visual, and mediated data beyond standard data analytic techniques. If you yourself are considered the primary "instrument" of an investigation, then your mind—not the data you gather or the computer software you use—provides the central process of and for rich inquiry. I frequently quote methodologist Robert E. Stake's (1995) keen observation that "good research is not about good methods as much as it is about good thinking" (p. 19).

Readerships for This Book

Thinking Qualitatively is a text intended primarily for students enrolled in undergraduate and graduate-level qualitative research/inquiry methods courses in education, health care, business, communication, and social science disciplines such as sociology, anthropology, and psychology. The book serves as a resource for novice researchers working on class projects, independent studies, theses, dissertations, and sponsored projects in their endeavor to "rise above the data." It may provide seasoned researchers a "reboot" of their current knowledge base or as a lecture/ teaching resource.

One of the musings I sometimes hear from instructors is the regret that they can teach data analytic strategies in research methods courses, but "I can't teach my students how to *think*." I understand what they mean. From my own research teaching experiences, I've observed that students can code data and construct major categories and key themes competently through basic qualitative data analysis, yet they often do not take the next steps: finding interrelationships between categories, synthesizing their initial analyses, finding new and fresher perspectives on the phenomena, formulating theory, or transcending beyond a case to higher levels of interpretation and meaning—in another word, insight.

Thinking, reading silently, and reflection are internal, private processes (Waite, 2014, pp. 276–277). Each person reading this book will get something completely different out of it and construct her or his own opinion about its utility and value. And since our brains are unique, what constitutes an effective analytic strategy for me may not necessarily work for you. We must also accept that coincidence, serendipity, idiosyncrasy, randomness, unanticipated opportunity, chance, luck, and just being in the right frame of mind at the right place at the right time, are factors that sometime play a role in thinking and discovery. I wrote this book to the best of my ability for the transfer of information, yet you as the reader are the one who ultimately determines your own learning outcomes from this experience.

The Organization of This Book

Selected information on thinking, cognition, and how the brain functions is included purposely throughout the text. If your mind is central to qualitative inquiry, then it helps to have a very basic understanding of how your mind works. Educator Pat Wolfe (2010) posits that to fail to address such knowledge when teaching and learning is like assuming that physicians don't need to understand the body in order to treat it.

Just as your central nervous system's synaptic pathways are loosely grouped into sensory, motor, emotive, attentional, decision-making, and other systems (Dubinsky, Roehrig, & Varma, 2013, p. 319), this book's chapters are loosely grouped according to major thinking systems for qualitative inquiry. The titles of Chapters 2 through 10 begin with *Thinking*, followed by the name of the particular category for discussion. These nine categories are my own constructions for organizing the contents and serve as axial terms for their constituent methods of mind (see Figure 0.1 for an example).

Each chapter begins with my intended yet ideal learning objectives for you, not phrased as "the reader will" but "your mind will . . . ." The chapters include a series of related profiles, discussed separately to make you aware of just some of the multiple lenses, filters, and angles available for inquiry. Your brain has "modules" that handle certain functions, such as navigation and shape recognition (White, 2013). Each profile within a chapter is also like a module for qualitative thinking. Chapters 2 through 10 are deliberately formatted in comparable ways to create schemata or templates for your cognitive grasp of the content. The mind generally comprehends new information best when it's presented through organized systems and recognizable

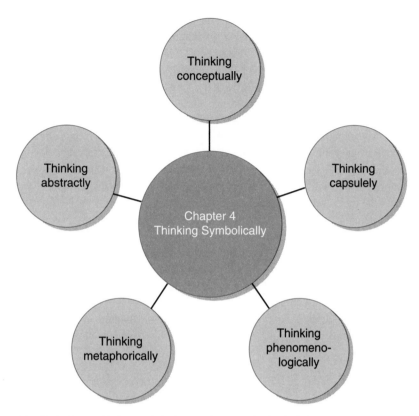

Figure 0.1. Each chapter title is an axis for its constituent methods of mind.

patterns of delivery. But there are also some intriguing facts, ideas, and visuals peppered throughout the text for occasional novelty—another deliberate tactic for maximizing attention and thus retention of information.

Chapter 1, "Introduction: Thinking About Thinking," discusses the central ideas of thinking qualitatively by providing an overview of key terminology used in the book. Chapter 2 outlines some of the more traditional forms of "Thinking Analytically." Chapter 3 segues into the epistemological realm through "Thinking Realistically." Chapter 4 approaches how we condense information by "Thinking Symbolically." Chapter 5 delves into the moral aspects of what researchers do when "Thinking Ethically."

Chapter 6, "Thinking Multidisciplinarily" (*multidisciplinarily* is an invented word), explores how various fields of knowledge can inform our work, while Chapter 7, "Thinking Artistically," profiles the aesthetic domains of knowledge construction.

Chapter 8 takes us further into the analytic process through "Thinking Summarily," followed by Chapter 9's continued analytic discussion on "Thinking Interpretively." Chapter 10 examines the writing of our research studies through "Thinking Narratively." The book concludes with a reflective "Closure: Thoughts About Thinking" in Chapter 11. A Glossary of key terms that have been bolded in Chapters 1 through 11 follows.

Each thinking profile ends with a "For Your Mental Rolodex" summary. For those unfamiliar with the device, a Rolodex is a series of small index cards that hold contact information such as names, phone numbers, and addresses (see Figure 0.2). The cards are organized and held alphabetically on a metal wheel with a knob that the user swiftly turns to access the specific card she or he needs. The term *mental rolodex* was uttered by one of my students in class one day several years ago; where he got it from I do not know, but I have used this metaphoric term ever since. When we mention a "personal mental rolodex," we are referring to the memories and knowledge store of teachers who must access various instructional methods quickly and spontaneously for in-class work with young people. Your qualitative mental rolodex is a metaphorical collection of summarized "bytes" of methods knowledge in your brain that you access on an as-needed basis for the task at hand.

Each chapter concludes with a series of recommended related exercises. Not all of them need to be undertaken in order to comprehend the chapter's main points. They are offered to students and instructors as optional extensions for in-class or independent work as available time and interest allow.

An open-access website for the book at **study.sagepub.com/Saldana** includes eflashcards of glossary terms, and full-text SAGE journal articles selected to extend the discussion in the book.

Figure 0.2.   A Rolodex, used metaphorically to refer to multiple ways of thinking.

Source: Jupiterimages/Stockbyte/Thinkstock. Image is repeated throughout the book.

Acknowledgments

Janice Morse, former director of the International Institute for Qualitative Methodology (IIQM) at the University of Alberta, coined and popularized the phrase "thinking qualitatively" for the IIQM's workshop series. I thank her for bringing that concept to the field and for its inspiration to so many researchers. (The IIQM continues to use the phrase for its programming, but this book is not based on its workshop contents.)

I thank Helen Salmon, acquisitions editor at SAGE Publications, for her nurturing support of this project and its development through production, plus the SAGE administrative and production staff: Kelly Albertelli, Sarita Sarak, Katie Guarino, Veronica Stapleton Hooper, Rachel Keith, Anna Villarruel, Anupama Krishnan, Nicole Elliott, and Dennis Webb. Thanks are extended to Liora Bresler, whose student reviews of early selected chapter drafts provided me valuable feedback for manuscript revision. Thanks as well to the SAGE reviewers, who also provided valuable feedback: Cassie F. Quigley, Clemson University; John P. Bartkowski, University of Texas at San Antonio; Michael Brown, University of Wyoming; Rachel G. Campbell, Grand Valley State University; Karrie Ann Snyder, Northwestern University; Elaine Hollensbe, University of Cincinnati; Nikki Hayfield, University of the West of England (UWE), Bristol; Liora Bresler, University of Illinois, Urbana-Champaign; Susan B. Twombly, University of Kansas; Catherine Marineau, DePaul University; Thu Suong Thi Nguyen, Purdue University—Indianapolis; and Jessica Nina Lester, Indiana University.

I extend heartfelt gratitude to my research instructors, mentors, and colleagues who significantly shaped my ways of thinking qualitatively: Tom Barone, Mary Lee Smith, Amira De la Garza, Sarah J. Tracy, Harry F. Wolcott, Laura A. McCammon, Mitch Allen, Yvonna S. Lincoln, and Norman K. Denzin.

Thanks are extended to several of my former students at Arizona State University, whose work contributed to selected contents in this text: Cody Goulter, Angie Hines, Enza Giannone Hosig, Paul Mack, Teresa Minarsich, Matt Omasta, Kathleen Arcovio Pennyway, Ebony Tucker, and Brianna Stapleton Welch. I also thank Eli Lieber, president and CEO of SocioCultural Research Consultants, for his assistance with a Dedoose software screenshot.

Final thanks go to my life partner, Jim Simpson, whose support of my work enables me to think "highdeeply."

About the Author

Johnny Saldaña is Professor Emeritus of Theatre from the Herberger Institute for Design and the Arts' School of Film, Dance, and Theatre at Arizona State University. He has been involved in the field of theatre as a teacher educator, director, playwright, and qualitative researcher.

Saldaña's research methods have been used and cited internationally for studies in K–12 and higher education, the fine arts, business, technology, the social sciences, government, social services, communication, human development, sport, health care, and medicine. He is the author of *Longitudinal Qualitative Research: Analyzing Change Through Time* (AltaMira Press, 2003), recipient of the 2004 Outstanding Book Award from the National Communication Association's Ethnography Division; *Ethnodrama: An Anthology of Reality Theatre* (AltaMira Press, 2005), an edited collection of ethnography-based plays; *The Coding Manual for Qualitative Researchers* (SAGE Publications, 2009; second edition, 2013), a handbook on qualitative data analysis; *Fundamentals of Qualitative Research* (Oxford University Press, 2011), a commissioned introductory textbook and volume one of the Understanding Qualitative Research series; *Ethnotheatre: Research From Page to Stage* (Left Coast Press, 2011), a playwriting primer for performance ethnography and recipient of the American Educational Research Association's Qualitative Research Special Interest Group's 2012 Outstanding Book Award; and *Qualitative Data Analysis: A Methods Sourcebook,* third edition (SAGE Publications, 2014), a commissioned update and revision of the second edition of the late Matthew B. Miles and A. Michael Huberman's book *Qualitative Data Analysis: An Expanded Sourcebook* (1994).

Introduction

Thinking About Thinking

LEARNING OBJECTIVES AND SUMMARY

- Your mind will reflect on what it means to "think qualitatively."
- Your mind will distinguish between and, through later rehearsal (i.e., recall, repetition, long-term memory storage, transfer), remember key terms related to qualitative inquiry.

This chapter begins with a brief overview of methods of mind for inquiry. Major terms used throughout the book are defined and clarified, particularly those that tend to be used interchangeably in qualitative research (all bolded terms appear in the Glossary). The chapter closes with some thoughts on technology and thinking recommendations for reading this text. Sections in the Introduction include

- Thinking Qualitatively
- On Epistemology
- Terminology
- On Technology
- Closure
- Exercises for Thinking About Thinking

Thinking Qualitatively

Thinking in this book refers to your mind's ways of working—that is, the mental resources you draw upon to access, organize, and analyze information; make decisions; and solve problems. David Sousa (2011), a specialist in learning and the brain, explains that

> the human brain . . . is an open, parallel-processing system continually interacting with the physical and social worlds outside. It analyzes, integrates, and synthesizes information and abstracts generalities from it. Each neuron is alive and altered by its experiences and its environment. As you read these words, neurons are interacting with each other, reforming and dissolving storage sites, and establishing different electrical patterns that correspond to your new learning. (p. 4)

If you are age thirty or younger, your brain is still maturing biologically and is not yet fully "installed" (Wolfe, 2010, pp. 84–85). But even after thirty and through middle age, the brain continues to evolve. Some cells do die off, and the brain shrinks by 2 percent every decade as we age in midlife; but myelin, the essential white matter that coats trillions of nerve fibers in your head, increases in the language region. Neuroscientists also believe that the middle-aged mind becomes more densely wired and less rigidly bifurcated, enabling more bilateral (two-hemisphere) functioning and creative thought (Strauch, 2010, pp. 51, 86, 98–99, 107).

Virtually all of us share a comparable neurology, yet each one of us thinks differently. Our unique brains have been and continue to be custom-hardwired through our personal biology, learnings, experiences, memories, habits, health, environment, and other conditioning factors that we can and cannot control. The science of understanding how the brain works has rapidly accelerated over the past few decades, providing us with new ways of changing unproductive patterns of living and working (e.g., Duhigg, 2012; Goleman, 1995; Kahneman, 2011; Strauch, 2010) and helping us to develop more innovative ways of teaching and learning (e.g., Jensen, 2001; Sousa, 2011; Wolfe, 2010). Even the classic 1950s Benjamin Bloom taxonomy of six cumulative, hierarchical levels of human thought (knowledge, comprehension, application, analysis, synthesis, and evaluation) has been revised and reprioritized for 21st century thinking as

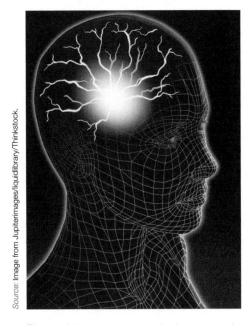

Source: Image from Jupiterimages/liquidlibrary/Thinkstock.

Figure 1.1. As you read these words, neurons are interacting with each other in your brain. (Sousa, 2011)

active cognitive processes that fluidly overlap: remember, understand, apply, analyze, evaluate, and create (Sousa, 2011, pp. 256–264).

Qualitative research is an inclusive term for a wide variety of approaches to and methods for the study of natural social life. The qualitative data collected and analyzed are primarily (but not exclusively) nonquantitative in form, consisting of textual materials (e.g., interview transcripts, field notes, documents) and visual materials (e.g., artifacts, photographs, video recordings, Internet sites) that document the human experiences of others or of oneself in social action and reflexive states (Saldaña, 2011b, pp. 3–4). Some of the most immediately recognized genres of qualitative research are ethnographies and case studies, but this category of research also includes a diverse range of methodological approaches such as grounded theory and poetic inquiry. Qualitative data analysis methods consist primarily of techniques and strategies for formatting, condensing, arraying, and constructing data, codes, categories, themes, assertions, narratives, and so on.

Thinking qualitatively means applying a particular set of thinking patterns and mental operations throughout the stages of qualitative inquiry. These thinking patterns can range from basic cognitive applications such as observation and memory to more advanced functions such as evaluation and creativity. These patterns include the canon of logical reasoning methods, such as inference-making and deduction, as well as more artistic constructions of life, such as symbolism and metaphor. There is no *one* way to think qualitatively; rather, it is a repertoire of different thinking methods, many of them consciously applied on an automatic or as-needed basis, and some of them working subconsciously and brought forward to consciousness in a serendipitous moment of connection, synthesis, or crystallization—a mental process labeled consolidation (discussed in Chapter 11).

Perhaps those first educated in quantitative methods and statistics have the most difficult time transitioning to thinking qualitatively. The process is comparable to learning a foreign language in adulthood when the brain is too "cemented" to think fluidly with new vocabulary and unfamiliar rules for grammar and syntax. Quantitative researchers have been trained to apply numbers, formulas, and a particular set of logical reasoning methods in collecting data, testing hypotheses, and drawing conclusions. The standardized, algorithmic, outcome-based functions of quantitative research methods indoctrinate its students into ways of thinking that are prescriptive, formulaic, and virtually nonnegotiable.

Qualitative inquiry, by nature, is a customized, inductive, emergent process that permits more of the researcher's personal signature in study design, implementation, and write-up. Certainly there are recommendations and guidance for the conduct of the researcher, ranging from how to construct a conceptual framework to how to ask effective interview questions. There are hundreds of methods books on how to take substantive field notes or analyze qualitative data, and even books dedicated solely to the writing of reports ranging from the traditional to creative nonfiction presentations.

But thinking qualitatively is more than methods. It is learning how to work with textual and visual languages in such ways as to use primarily (but not exclusively) words rather than numbers as the media for analysis. It is, in some approaches to qualitative inquiry, meticulously reviewing vast amounts of language-based text and condensing it into summative forms such as codes, categories, themes, concepts, assertions, and theoretical insights. In other approaches, it is creating evocative narratives that uniquely describe and comment on the facets of social life observed and studied. In still other approaches, it is using artistic modalities such as live theatre, visual art, dance, film, and music to represent the lived experiences of participants. And in other approaches, it is critically scrutinizing and critiquing the social injustices that exist in the world in hopes of generating positive change for human beings. Just as there are a panoply of thinking modalities, there are a panoply of qualitative research genres and styles.

Thinking qualitatively also means purposely adopting different lenses, filters, and angles as we view social life so as to discover new perceptions and cognitions about the facet of the world we're researching. If one of the primary goals of qualitative research is to discover what it means to be human, then we as researchers need to understand the rich diversity of human experience. It's one thing to be healthy; it's another to be a cancer survivor. It's one thing to grow up in an upper-middle-class suburb; it's another to grow up in poverty and homelessness. It's one thing to experience life as a White, heterosexual, 50-year-old male; it's another to experience life as a 25-year-old Latina lesbian. The more you can take the perspective of and empathize with your participants, the better you'll be able to understand their varied points of view.

Source: Photodisc/Photodisc/Thinkstock.

Figure 1.2.   Each of us interprets social life through various lenses, filters, and angles.

Lenses, filters, and angles refer to more than just demographic attributes. Thinking qualitatively also means acknowledging that not everyone thinks the same way you do. Thus, one of our goals is to try as best we can to think about how others might think. The sociologist will see life differently than the psychologist. The information technology specialist will experience the workplace differently than the janitor. A kindergarten teacher in an inner city school will learn about human development—if not life itself—differently than a tenured professor of biology at an Ivy League university. Since filters consist partly of an individual's value, attitude, and belief systems, the researcher must try to set aside or **bracket** his or her own worldview in order to respect and understand another's. (We don't always need to accept another person's worldview, but we should try at the very least to understand it.)

Those who attempt to manipulate our thinking through subliminal, propagandistic, repetitive, or covertly coercive tactics might succeed in changing our perspectives, cognitive scripts, and habits of mind. Sociological theories such as *differential association* posit that people's values are influenced by the groups they interact with most intensively (Rubin & Rubin, 2012, p. 132). That may readily apply to a qualitative researcher immersed in a cultural setting that seems to shake the very foundation of his or her own values system. Such moments of **cognitive dissonance** can actually be a good thing, for they signal the unbalancing of a fixed way of thinking about the world and force the acknowledgment of and possible clarity about others' points of view.

Thinking qualitatively is heightened thinking—**metacognition**—about your own mind and how it works when analyzing data and reflecting on life. Metacognition is not just thinking but knowing how to think, and knowing how to know. It is hyperawareness within social environments for observing sensory details and interpreting subtexts from people's words and actions. Thinking qualitatively is pondering the nuances of your data even when you're "off the clock" from fieldwork and data analysis. Thoughts will occur to you at the most unexpected and inopportune times—while driving, in the shower, and so on. Thinking qualitatively is purposely attempting and pushing yourself to take your thinking one step further by reflecting on the study's interrelated connections to other concepts and their implications for big-picture ideas. Thinking qualitatively is a 24/7/365 job.

And thinking itself is hard work. The brain uses glucose and oxygen at 10 times the rate of the rest of the body. The brain constitutes only about 2 percent of a human's body weight yet consumes approximately 20 percent of the body's caloric intake (Sousa, 2011, p. 15; Wolfe, 2010, p. 5). Neuroscience is still uncovering the mysteries of how the complex brain functions, so it should not be perceived as defeat when qualitative researchers feel they haven't perfectly understood the lives of people they're studying. We can only, at best, approximate through our representations and presentations what it means to be another human. Words are not all we have to communicate our social insights, but they are the most frequent mode of informing others about what we've learned.

On Epistemology

Since thinking is central to this book, a brief discussion of epistemology is merited. **Epistemology**, broadly, is a theory of knowledge construction based on the researcher's worldview—that is, how his or her lens on the world and angled ways of knowing it focus and filter his or her perception and interpretation of it (Saldaña, 2011b, p. 22).

As qualitative researchers, we construct in our minds the natural experiences we observe and the analytic connections we make with our data. There is no "truth" external to us waiting to be discovered. But I do put forth that what we perceive and interpret about life is greatly influenced and affected by the lenses, filters, and angles—constructs similar to a camera—through which we view the world. A **lens** might refer to a significant attribute such as the researcher's gender, age, ethnicity, sexual orientation, economic class, or occupation. A lens might also consist of the particular research methodology employed for a study (e.g., phenomenological, feminist, arts-based, ethnographic) or a disciplinary approach (e.g., sociological, psychological, anthropological). A **filter** could refer to your set of personal values, attitudes, and beliefs about the world, formed by your unique personal biography, learned experiences, and individual thinking patterns. Filters might also consist of particular theoretical perspectives or standpoints within a discipline, such as analysis of an interview narrative for its literary elements by one researcher and its psychological meanings by another researcher. An **angle** might function as a cultural landscape position you hold, such as insider versus outsider, intimate versus distant, emotionally invested versus objectively detached. Angles also refer to micro-, meso-, or macro-perceptions of social life—ranging from the perspectives of an individual participant to those of a national populace. These factors, in combination, contribute toward complex, multifaceted, multidimensional ways of constructing knowledge that both subconsciously and even intentionally and politically frame your observations of the world:

> Women may adopt a feminist research epistemology to explore gender- and power-related issues. Lesbians, gays, and the transgendered may adopt the tenets of what is labeled *queer theory* in their study of gay culture, heterosexism, and homophobia. Researchers of color and their personal life experiences with prejudice and discrimination from the mainstream accumulate to develop a distinctive ethnic worldview. Thus, there are no such things as "neutral," "bias-free," or "objective" lenses for qualitative researchers. (Saldaña, 2011b, p. 23)

We openly and admittedly undertake the research enterprise as *interpretivists*—people who explain social life as they construct it in their own minds. That should not suggest an "anything goes" mentality in which your own opinions supersede rigorous investigation, however. There needs to be a balance between systematic examination of evidence and personal interpretation of what the data suggest. It is unlikely that any two qualitative researchers independently exploring the same phenomenon will arrive at the same conclusions. We bring our personal signature to the inquiry, from research design to write-up. The epistemology you use is uniquely your own, since you most likely think like no one else. Cuzzort and King (2002) go so far as to claim that

> most of what we know about our social worlds is what we have been told, not what we have observed directly. At the very least, more than 90 percent of our social knowledge is what we have heard about or read about. (p. 9, emphasis in original)

Since research is an act of persuasion—the making of your case for readers—you must convince your audience that you've done your homework and carefully thought through all aspects of your study. How you think is how your signature epistemology works. Laying bare the lenses, filters, and angles you employed frames your reader for what's to come, and allows all of us to assess the credibility and trustworthiness of your account (Lincoln & Guba, 1985). Several ways of thinking described throughout these chapters hopefully will help with that task, because you can't apply what you don't know. Therefore, a major objective of this book is to first bring *cognitive awareness* of different ways of looking at and thinking about the social world, and then to stimulate *independent reflection* of these methods as well as *connection-making* between them and your own memories of experiences. After that, the ultimate objective is the *transfer and application* of these methods to your particular current and future research endeavors. For an extended discussion of epistemology (and ontology—the nature of being) in qualitative research, see *The Science of Qualitative Research* (Packer, 2011).

Terminology

There is no executive board or blue ribbon panel in the field of qualitative research mandating the standardized definitions of terms. The published literature has certainly established some commonly accepted meanings for approaches to inquiry such as grounded theory, case study, and ethnography. Some genres, however, such as phenomenology and narrative inquiry, seem open to methodological interpretation and procedural methods. As authoritative references, the dictionary and thesaurus guide us in our more precise use of terms, but even those resources can confound rather than clarify when you try to determine, for example, the difference between a *concept* and a *construct*. It is not my goal to propose any such standardization for the field in this book, but I do provide a glossary at the end of the text to offer how I conceive various terms used frequently in qualitative inquiry, purely for purposes of consistency in *Thinking Qualitatively*. In order for me to communicate with you clearly, we need to share a common understanding of the key vocabulary—the cognitive symbol systems—used in this book.

Let's review some of the most used and sometimes inconsistently interchanged terms in qualitative research. Not all of them are addressed below—just those that seem to call for a moment of clarity before we proceed further. Though I have relied on dictionaries to assist me, I have also accessed the qualitative research methods literature and my personal ways of working to synthesize these proposed meanings.

Inquiry, Research

Inquiry is a general term for, and refers broadly to, the act of investigation. **Research** is systematic exploration, usually connected with a specific study's purpose and goals. *Qualitative inquiry* and *qualitative research* will be used interchangeably throughout this book.

Thinking, Reflection, Reflexivity, Refraction

All of these terms refer to mental processes, *thinking* being the umbrella term. Many within qualitative inquiry perceive writing as thinking. And, even as you're reading this book, you're thinking. When are you *not* thinking? Even during sleep, your brain is involved in sophisticated neural activity as it dreams, including the fixing of memories and the connecting of disparate bits of information. Thinking is a given of everyday life. Thinking *in a focused manner* is a necessity for all researchers. Concentration is not cognitive—it's affective, meaning, you must feel self-motivated to think and willingly want to concentrate.

Cognitive tasks range in complexity from simple recall of information (remembering) to sense-making (understanding) to problem solving (applying), some of which may involve values systems integration. Also, the associations we make with any number of words or ideas are based on our personal experiences and memories. Add to that the emotional dimensions of memory and processing (with positive emotions enhancing engagement and negative emotions often interfering with task completion), and it becomes clear that basic mental processes and critical and creative thinking skills are unique to each individual. Analysis may seem like the ultimate thinking task, but the abilities to *evaluate* and *create* are considered higher-level modes of thought, requiring judgment and the new formulation of ideas (Sousa, 2011, pp. 256–257). Thinking is multimodal and multidimensional; there is not just one way to think, but varying levels of thinking from basic to complex. The exclusive divisions of left-brain (i.e., analytical) and right-brain (i.e., creative) functions are outdated, for both work together bilaterally to process information and generate ideas. But there are thinking "specialties" in each hemisphere, with the left handling primarily logic, sequence, and analysis and the right handling primarily synthesis, context, and the "big picture" (Pink, 2006, p. 25).

Reflection and refraction are processes related to concentrated thinking about the study at hand. **Reflection**, whether it consists of thought directed to oneself, discussed with another, or privately written, is the act of pondering various components of the research project to make sense of and gain personal understanding about their meanings. It is making sense of that which may be puzzling or confusing, and understanding the purpose or significance of something. Reflection employs your brain's "default area"—the region where internal monologues and daydreams occur (Strauch, 2010, p. 78). Talking aloud about something problematic or writing a journal entry for oneself is a way of thinking or figuring out what's going on. It is an internal, reverberative process of question-answer-question-answer-question-answer for generating better awareness and clarity. O'Dwyer and Bernauer (2014) add that **reflexivity** is researchers' "conscious awareness of . . . cognitive and emotional filters comprising their experiences, worldviews, and biases that may influence their interpretation of participants' perceptions" (p. 11).

Refraction, a recently evolved perspective, suggests tactical reflection for the purpose of deliberately making things problematic or troubling. Some use the metaphor of a broken or fun house mirror to describe refraction, which distorts an image's true appearance. Refraction is a mental implosion of sorts that prevents acceptance of the first or easiest answer. It entails relishing the complexity of an issue and diverging into multiple mental pathways to account for and ponder various alternatives and possibilities. Poverty, for example, is a phenomenon that needs to extend beyond "the poor versus the rich" in discussion and analysis. Refraction considers how multiple factors such as family history, education, race/ethnicity, gender, religion, language, culture, urbanization, socialization, community, geography, crime, employment, government, politics, social services, personal identity, individual agency, corporate power, human greed, and other factors as well as economics influence and affect the impoverished conditions of so many.

A few scholars in qualitative inquiry seem to fixate on refraction and purposely present, as their research report, summaries of unanswered questions, ambiguities, and inconclusive findings as a way of emphasizing the messiness and uncertainty of contemporary social life. I offer that this is novel postmodern scholarship, yet more of a fad for these times. I myself proclaim (through my masculinist lens, pragmatic filter, and marginalized yet assertive angle) that the purpose and outcome of research is to find answers in order to make a better world. Unanswered questions usually remain unanswered, serving no one and contributing unproductively to the social improvement goals of research. Unanswered questions in print may motivate a few selected readers to reflect. But what runs through my own mind is, "Why are you asking *me* this? Don't *you* know?"

Algorithm, Heuristic

An **algorithm**, usually connected with quantitative inquiry, is a formulaic approach to solving a problem. A **heuristic** is an open-ended method of discovery, a way of figuring out how to figure something out. As an example, consider the following equation:

$$2 + 2 = ?$$

The algorithm (formula) is *the mathematical function of addition;* the heuristics (open-ended methods of discovery) are simple *counting* and basic *logic* (if 2 is 1 and 1, then 1 and 1 and 1 and 1 is 4).

As a more complex example, how would you determine how another person is feeling? Perhaps an algorithmic solution would be to photograph the person as he or she is experiencing the emotion, then process the digital image through a sophisticated facial recognition software program installed on a computer, which might produce an answer specifying the subject's most likely emotional state as suggested by the visual data input and the calculations performed by the software. Conversely, heuristics for solving this problem might include asking the person, "How are you feeling?" and assessing the honesty of the answer you get; making inferences about the person's feelings through your interpretations of his or her facial and body language and tone of voice; accessing your own memories of comparable emotional states from your personal life experiences (generally referred to as **intuition**) and exercising your capacity for empathy so as to possibly feel as the other person does; and striking up a general conversation with the person and inductively, abductively, and deductively (explained later) concluding which state might be present based on the information and cues you receive and your own capacities for **emotional intelligence** and **social intelligence** (Goleman, 1995, 2006). Heuristics, in this case, are not only more time efficient but even more varied and reliable than algorithms.

Qualitative inquiry places great stock in heuristics. Certainly there is an evolved, published canon of recommended guidelines for participant observation, interviewing, and even data analysis, but the content- and context-specific nature of each particular qualitative research study calls for unique solutions to unique problems. There are virtually no algorithms or formulas to follow for this type of inquiry. We must rely on recommendations rather than requirements; on fluid boundaries rather than tightly defined borders; and on figuring it out as we go along rather than knowing from the beginning exactly how things must proceed. Thinking qualitatively is thinking heuristically.

Method, Methodology

A **method** is *how* you go about doing something. A **methodology** is *why* you're going about it in a particular way. Data collection might consist of methods such as interviews (and their transcription), participant observation (and the taking of field notes), and artifact review (with its digital photographing and analytic memoing). But why would you employ these particular methods? Let's take interviewing as an example.

Kvale and Brinkmann (2009) posit quite sensibly, "If you want to know how people understand their world and their lives, why not talk with them?" (p. xvii). We can infer and deduce only so much about our participants when we simply observe them as they go about their daily lives or when we examine the products they own and create. Interviewing, a purposeful conversation, enables us to ask them questions directly relevant to the research study's goals. Assuming our participants are verbally fluent and truthful, they can provide us with rich answers and insights. The *why* of interviewing *methodology* is to obtain first-person accounts that potentially provide more credible and trustworthy evidence of social meanings to support our assertions about the phenomena we're investigating. But what if our participants have difficulty articulating their perceptions? Then the *how* of interview *methods* comes into play through our strategic use of probing questions, guided conversation, elicitation techniques, and other tactics.

Methodologies also refer to particular qualitative research approaches or genres such as phenomenology, grounded theory, case study, ethnography, narrative inquiry, and so on. The reason why we may choose one genre over the others in our initial research design is because the methodology fits with and accommodates the study's goals or questions. If we are interested in documenting and describing the culture of a group of people, then **ethnography** as a methodology, with its accompanying ethnographic methods, is perhaps the most appropriate choice. If we find a particular individual an intriguing person worth investigating and writing about in depth, then **case study** methodology and compatible methods are likely the most suitable for the enterprise.

Methodology and methods are two separate yet interrelated constructs that are part of your initial research design decisions and conceptual framework development (Maxwell, 2013; Ravitch & Riggan, 2012). Several research methodologies conventionally assume that particular methods will be employed for the investigation (e.g., grounded theory methodology uses a canon of particular coding methods, but different narrative inquiry methodologists recommend their own unique data analysis and write-up methods). Ensure that your methodology and methods harmonize with each other as you plan the study, but also be prepared to change those initial choices as fieldwork proceeds and you discover that another methodology or other methods may be more appropriate to secure the data and answers you need.

Action, Reaction, Interaction

An **action** is a micro-unit of human activity consisting of a purposeful and meaningful behavior; speaking and mental activity, not just physical motion, are considered actions. **Reaction** is an individual's response to an action—either action from another person or thing or one's own action. **Interaction** is the collective back-and-forth sequences of action and reaction between individuals or between an individual and something else. All three are different yet tightly interconnected processes for observation and analysis. For example, in a classroom, a teacher may initiate an action by asking students a question. Some students react by raising their hands to answer; others react by looking puzzled and not raising their hands. A teacher calls on a student by name, and they have a brief dialogic exchange or interaction as the question is answered and the teacher verbally praises the child for the correct response. These **moments**, whether mundane, routine, conflict-laden, or impacting, are key points of interest for researchers.

Qualitative research encourages fieldworkers to pay careful attention to specific human actions and social interaction in general, yet sometimes neglects to advise attention to reactions. Stage and media actors have an adage: "Acting is *reacting*." This means that performance is not just a series of one actor's line followed by another actor's line, but a strategic series of give–take–give again–take again exchanges. Performers also know that a character's actions in a script are driven not just by what a character wants but by what a character wants other characters to do. Good actors do on stage what humans do in everyday life: we act and react in order to interact. And good researchers pay close attention not just to how humans act and interact, but how they react to the social conditions around them that influence and affect their daily and long-term lives. To quote a folk adage: "Life is 20 percent what happens to you and 80 percent how you react to it."

Code, Pattern, Category, Theme

For traditional approaches to qualitative data analysis, there are four interrelated but not interchangeable terms that require explanation, since these will be used throughout the book. Interestingly, these four aspects of analysis have parallels to the ways our minds work. We synthesize vast amounts of information into symbolic summary (code); we make sense of the world by noticing repetition and formulating regularity through cognitive schemata and scripts (pattern); we cluster similar things together through comparison and contrast to formulate bins of stored knowledge (category); and we imprint key learnings from extended experiences by creating proverblike narrative memories (theme).

First, a **code** is a word or short phrase that symbolically assigns a summative, salient, essence-capturing, and/or evocative attribute to a portion of language-based or visual data

(Saldaña, 2013, p. 3). Coding is just *one* way, not *the* way, of initially analyzing qualitative data, yet it is one of the most frequently used methods, particularly for those undertaking **grounded theory** studies. There are multiple forms of coding available, but below is just one brief example. Imagine that a male adolescent (P for Participant) is being interviewed about bullying at his school. He offers the following to the adult female interviewer (I):

P: Yeah, it's kind of hard. There's this one guy who follows me whenever he sees me in the hallway in between classes and he, he holds up his arm with a limp wrist and calls out my name in this girly way. He's a jock, so he thinks that being gay is funny, weird.

I: What do you do or say to him when that happens?

P: Nothing, I just keep walking. Otherwise it'll just get him pissed off.

The interviewer working with this transcribed data codes according to the purpose of the study and its research questions. In this case, the researcher is interviewing many young people about their experiences with bullying and needs an inventory of what kinds of bullying students encounter at one particular school, plus their strategies for dealing with it. Thus, the researcher might code her data in particular ways to serve and expedite the analysis. The codes for the above conversation are listed below in the right-hand column in capital letters; in each instance, the superscript number indicates the specific datum (*datum* is the singular form of *data*) to which the code bearing that number is assigned. The first code represents the type of bullying that occurred, and the second code represents the participant's coping strategy or tactic:

P: Yeah, it's kind of hard. [1] There's this one guy who follows me whenever he sees me in the hallway in between classes and he, he holds up his arm with a limp wrist and calls out my name in this girly way. He's a jock, so he thinks that being gay is funny, weird.   [1] HOMOPHOBIC TAUNT

I: What do you do or say to him when that happens?

P: [2] Nothing, I just keep walking. Otherwise it'll just get him pissed off.   [2] TACTIC: IGNORE

The researcher then looks for patterns of recurring, comparable codes to determine the frequency of HOMOPHOBIC TAUNTS encountered by youth. She will also cluster together the TACTIC codes to determine from their subcodes how young people deal with bullying—e.g., IGNORE, CONFRONT, NAME-CALL, TELL AN ADULT, and so on. Coding is the first step toward other analytic processes—constructing patterns, categories, and themes.

A **pattern** is repetitive, regular, or consistent occurrences of comparable actions or data. As qualitative researchers, we seek patterns as somewhat stable indicators of humans' ways of living and working in the world. They become more trustworthy as evidence for our findings, since patterns demonstrate habits and salience in people's daily lives. They help confirm our descriptions of people's "five r's": routines, rules, rituals, roles, and relationships. Discerning these trends is a way of solidifying our observations into concrete instances of meaning for further analysis. Consider the study on bullying. One of the patterns detected from coding was how prominent forms of TRASH-TALKING were among adolescent girls, and another was how infrequently TELL AN ADULT was used as a coping strategy by the teenagers.

Patterning helps transform similarly grouped codes into more subsumed categories. A **category** is a word or phrase labeling a grouped pattern of comparable codes and coded data. Categorizing becomes a way of mentally condensing and grasping larger units of social action and phenomena, again for further analytic reflection. One of the categories constructed by the researcher from the bullying study was SEXUALITY-RELATED SLURS. This category was formed by noticing how a selected pool of verbal taunts ("fag," "whore," "slut," "skank," etc.) were directed toward a teenager's sexual orientation and mannerisms, developing physical body features, or dress, makeup, and grooming styles, whether they were based on students' own observations or, as another category suggested, on RUMOR BUY-IN.

A **theme**—a term often mistakenly used to signify a code or category—is an extended phrase or sentence that identifies and functions as a way to categorize a set of data into "an implicit topic that organizes a group of repeating ideas" (Auerbach & Silverstein, 2003, p. 38). For example, a few themes that emerged from the bullying study read:

- Rumors are "confidential" forms of bullying.
- Some adolescents don't realize their actions are bullying.
- Ignoring bullying is rooted in a fear of further violence.

Themes are topic sentences, if you will, for a more extended narrative that unpacks the statement and describes or explains its constituent elements. Themes can derive from initial analytic work with codes and categories, or they may be independently constructed from a holistic review of the **data corpus** for patterns alone.

Again, the terms *code, pattern, category,* and *theme* are not interchangeable. Each one should be used deliberately and purposely during qualitative data analysis and the study's write-up. They will be discussed further in Chapter 2.

Assertion, Proposition, Hypothesis, Theory

In this book, an **assertion** is a statement of summative synthesis, supported by confirming evidence from the data corpus (Erickson, 1986). It is a way of stating interpretive observations and low- and high-level inferences about social life. Examples of assertions are: "The customers waiting farthest in line appeared frustrated at the novice employee engaging in small talk with each person at the cash register" and "The term *fast food* implies 'quick service,' yet average customer wait times and body language suggest otherwise."

A **proposition** is an evidence-based statement that puts forth a conditional event (if/then, when/then, since/that's why, etc.) of local and particular contexts. It is somewhat comparable to an assertion, but explanation or causation is purposely embedded in it. Some examples of propositions are: "When fast-food restaurant customers wait over three minutes for initial service, they will tend to speak and interact somewhat tersely with cashiers when they reach the register to order" and "To increase customers and thus sales, several fast-food restaurants often feature 'dollar menus.'"

In distinguishing the two terms, it is helpful to remember that all propositions are assertions, but not all assertions are propositions.

A **hypothesis**, used primarily in empirical research, is a predictive statement that is field-tested or put through field experimentation to assess its reliability and validity. Some examples of hypotheses are: "More than 75 % of customers will decline a cashier's offer to 'upgrade' their initial fast-food order to a larger portion" and "Indifferent attitudes by cashiers toward customers result in 'business-only' interactions with virtually no small-talk exchanges." Hypotheses may be formulated by qualitative researchers after initial observations to test the credibility and trustworthiness of their assertions, propositions, and theories in progress.

A **theory** (as it is traditionally conceived in research) is a generalizable statement with an accompanying explanatory narrative that

- predicts and controls action through an if/then logic,
- explains how and/or why something happens by stating its cause(s), and
- provides insights and guidance for improving social life.

Gobo (2008) proposes that a theory consists of a series of hypotheses that have been tested by the researcher (p. 242), but assertions and propositions can also serve as preparatory groundwork for theory development.

An example of a theory is: "A restaurant's decor and physical-aural environment subliminally influence and affect a customers' perceptions of service and food quality." The accompanying explanatory narrative of this theory might elaborate on the prediction-control criterion by describing how particular aspects of certain restaurant environments (e.g., warm colors, moderate amounts of open space, seating comfort, and so on) may lead to more strategic choices by architects and interior designers. Explanation of how and/or why a customer's perceptions are influenced and affected might cover such aspects as memory triggers and associations (e.g., the advisability of using wood materials and furnishings, rather than plastics and metals, to accompany a "homemade food" menu). And the insights and guidance portion of the theory can provide restaurant managers with specific recommendations for employee training and facilities maintenance to create a more pleasant customer dining experience and keep the business profitable and afloat.

The terms *assertion, proposition, hypothesis,* and *theory* are not interchangeable. Each one should be used deliberately and purposely during the course of a qualitative research study to meet the researcher's particular goals. These four analytic, summative methods will be discussed further in Chapter 8.

There are other terms that tend to get used interchangeably in the literature, such as *concept, construct, abstraction,* and *phenomenon,* but these will be discussed separately in later chapters. I could also spend some time defining the differences between such related items as *method, mode,* and *technique; application* and *approach;* and *strategy* and *tactic;* but these sets of terms are so similar in intent that distinguishing them does not merit an extended discussion here. (These terms might, however, informally prompt some thinking and research on your part to discern whether there are indeed any notable differences between them.)

On Technology

A current development in qualitative inquiry is the incorporation of technology and specialized software. Yet writers of CAQDAS (computer-assisted qualitative data analysis software) manuals and textbooks all posit that the software does not actually analyze the data or think for the researcher. Researchers themselves must still make sense of data arrays and outputs produced by such programs as NVivo, ATLAS.ti, Dedoose, and MAXQDA. It is the inquirer's mind, not the hardware, software, or data themselves, that formulates summaries, codes, categories, themes, assertions, theories, and the like. Nevertheless, CAQDAS programs are indispensible for extensive data storage, organization, and management. Some programs' functions and features also display your analyses as remarkable visual representations for further reflection.

If we subscribe to biosocial theory, which suggests that everything humans create is an extension of our bodies (e.g., scissors are teeth, a comb is fingers, carpeting is skin and hair, a chair is a lap with legs, a poetic iamb is a heartbeat), then the computer is a brain and the software its cell-like memory store, cognitive scripts, synapses, and other mental operations and processes. But until this technology becomes sentient, humans must still write programs and physically manipulate the hardware to make them function smoothly. (Even human brains have malfunctions equivalent to computer glitches, blue screens, and crashes.)

Technology provides some useful and fascinating apps for qualitative research projects that help with everything from memoing to recording to drawing (see Paulus, Lester, & Dempster, 2014, and http://www.nova.edu/ssss/QR/apps.html). But there is still no magic "Analyze" button we can mouse-click that produces a reliable and valid series of qualitatively formulated themes or assertions, much less a theory, from our data input. Technology supplies us with remarkable digital tools that assist us with our data collection, storage, calculations, and "noodling around." But don't let the bells and whistles of software deceive you. You, not a computer, must still feel and think.

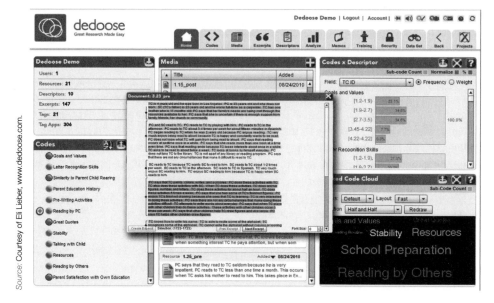

Figure 1.3.   This screen shot from Dedoose CAQDAS software demonstrates its multiple features.

CLOSURE

I could have made this book easy or hard, but I chose to write halfway between the two extremes. It's how I prefer to think and thus how I prefer to communicate. Every profile in the forthcoming chapters may not offer you specific "how-to" methods for research, but they will all offer you cognitive awareness and guidance for thinking about inquiry. Sometimes the goal is simply to make you aware of things you may not have thought of before. At other times the goal is to "retrain your brain" to think about things differently through new lenses, filters, and angles. Just reading this book itself (or any book, for that matter) will consume up to 50 percent of your body's oxygen allotment for mental activity (Strauch, 2010, p. 149) and literally change your brain's neural structure. Reflection on its contents will further activate your brain's neuroplasticity (i.e., changes in neural pathways and synaptic connections) (Dubinsky, Roehrig, & Varma, 2013).

Every twenty minutes, you brain needs to be reenergized to maintain its efficiency. Take a few minutes away from this book for a brief, refreshing break; physically move or exercise to get your blood oxygenated so that your brain functions more effectively. Drink some water to hydrate your body and, if possible, eat some fresh fruit for glucose to fuel the brain (Sousa, 2011, p. 39)—although there is still inconclusive evidence about the benefits of specific foods to enhance mental activity and brain maintenance. Research suggests that frequent aerobic exercise is the better option for birthing new neurons and enhancing your cognitive reserves (Strauch, 2010, pp. 126, 128–129).

As a teacher, I find it extremely difficult these days to meet everyone's individual needs simultaneously. What is exciting to one person may be boring to another. What is new to an undergraduate student may be old hat for a doctoral student. And what is fresh and innovative to one reader may be common sense or useless to another. "I can't read your mind" is a common rejoinder when we're frustrated with someone who believes we should know what he or she is thinking. I can't read your mind, but you can read this book. Your thinking can change from its old habits to new ones, but this requires your belief that you yourself can actively change them (Duhigg, 2012). So, keep an open mind and think for yourself. I offer various profiles in the forthcoming chapters that I hope serve as new information for you and provocative ways of looking at social life. There is no possible way to implement all of them for one particular qualitative study. They are provided here as heuristics, or methods of problem-solving and self-discovery.

EXERCISES FOR THINKING ABOUT THINKING

1. Compose a brief, one-page paper that describes the conditions necessary for you to be at your personal mental and analytic best for thinking, reflecting, and writing. Include aspects such as best time(s) of the day or night, preferred location/space/environment, necessary materials and equipment, and other motivational conditions and devices (e.g., hot coffee/tea, light

snacks, no TV/music in the background). Also discuss what distracts you from thinking and working optimally (e.g., Internet surfing, household chores, looming deadlines, personal stress, lack of sleep) and what strategies you might employ to lessen or eliminate them.

2. Generate a list of one to three people you consider to be exceptionally talented or gifted, and one to three people you consider to be geniuses. (These people do not have to be celebrities or internationally renowned; they can be people you personally know.) Write about or discuss with a peer what you believe makes these people talented, gifted, or geniuses, and what similar qualities or characteristics they may all share.

3. Access and view clips or episodes from the television program *Brain Games* on the National Geographic Channel website: http://braingames.nationalgeographic.com. Also explore the website's interactive features for additional information on topics such as perception and memory.

4. Figure 1.4 is an outline of a human brain. Trace it onto your own sheet of paper and use colored pencils, crayons, or markers to creatively draw a representation of what's inside your mind. You can use both words and illustrations, but preferably more of the latter. The contents might consist of significant elements of your identity, key memories, general emotional states or moods, important people in your life, personal values, and so on. Share your drawing with a partner who has also drawn the inside of his or her own brain, and discuss the inferences and meanings of both drawings. Also reflect on, write about, or discuss your level of ease or difficulty with representing your mind visually. (If you complete this activity, save your brain drawing for a comparative exercise described at the end of Chapter 11.)

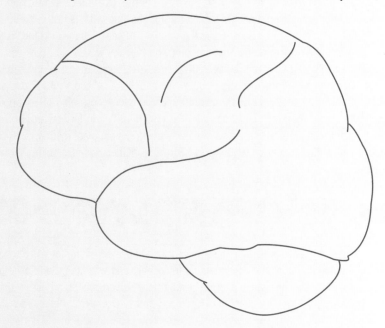

Figure 1.4.   Use this outline of a human brain to complete Exercise 4.

Thinking Analytically

LEARNING OBJECTIVES AND SUMMARY

- Your mind will identify and elaborate on basic analytic mental processes.
- Your mind will achieve metacognitive awareness of basic analytic processes and structures.

————◇ ◇ ◇————

This chapter begins the profile series by examining several "traditional"—for lack of a better term—methods of analytic thought as a foundational review. These methods of mind consist of

- Thinking Analytically
- Four "Ductions"
- Thinking Deductively
- Thinking Abductively
- Thinking Inductively
- Thinking Retroductively
- Thinking Patternly
- Thinking Categorically
- Thinking Thematically
- Thinking Hierarchically
- Thinking Causationally
- Thinking Cyclically

The purpose of this chapter is to review basic approaches to analytic thought that occur frequently during qualitative research endeavors.

Thinking Analytically

Anthropologist H. Russell Bernard (2011) succinctly states that **analysis** is "the search for patterns in data and for ideas that help explain why those patterns are there in the first place" (p. 338), while fellow anthropologist Harry F. Wolcott (1994) defines analysis as "the identification of essential features and the systematic description of interrelationships among them—in short, how things work" (p. 12). Combined, these perspectives suggest that finding patterns in our data and articulating their interrelationships are key elements of qualitative analytic work.

Analysis takes data apart and reconfigures them in new ways, but sometimes it transcends the data corpus to discuss its embedded or suggested meanings for broader applications. For example, I might conduct a case study about a fast-food worker and analytically categorize his job responsibility patterns and how he goes about carrying each of them out. But with some thought and persuasive case-making, I can extend beyond this one individual to discuss how U.S. minimum wage policies insufficiently motivate employees to do quality work and demoralize the country's core work force, comparable to what Barbara Ehrenreich (2001) learned in her autoethnographic, investigative journalistic account *Nickel and Dimed: On (Not) Getting By in America*. Also, I could eschew systematic pattern-making altogether in conducting my fieldwork and simply present a narrative account, retold primarily in the fast-food worker's own words—similar to Alison Ownings's (2002) collection of food service workers' poignant tales in *Hey, Waitress! The U.S.A. From the Other Side of the Tray*—and let the reader herself or himself extract personal, holistic meanings from the story.

How analytic you need to be with your work depends on several factors, such as the particular research methodology you adopt, the types and amounts of data requiring review, the need for demonstrating rigor for your emergent findings, and the stakes riding on the outcomes of your study. Regardless of these factors, to analyze qualitative data is to heuristically (and, some might insist, systematically) examine and reflect upon them in order to develop new insights about social phenomena. These insights can derive from and consist of condensed forms, such as codes, patterns, categories, and themes; and more statement-based forms, such as assertions, propositions, hypotheses, and theories. Some types of analytic work can generate evocative narratives such as short stories, poetry, and dramas. Generally, analysis consists of going through a massive database of primarily, but not exclusively, narrative texts, then extracting and reconstructing from them a selected number of key ideas related to your specific line of inquiry. It draws upon your ability to synthesize the various facets of what you have observed and to reconfigure them into new formulations of meaning.

We start the discovery process by carefully documenting the *whos, whens, wheres, how muches,* and—most important—the *whats* of social life. We enter an analytic realm when we pose *how* (or *in what ways*) and *why* questions about what we observe. We latch onto repetitively similar instances of participant actions, reactions, and interactions, because those suggest to us patterns of social stability that we can construct and put forth as regular ways of living. But we also need to keep an eye out for the unique and anomalous, for this triggers a rethinking of our initial or taken-for-granted patterns and how they're identified and explained.

Some methodologists have developed analogies to the qualitative data analysis process, such as a challenging picture puzzle to piece together, a mysterious crime a detective must solve, a toolkit for building a structure from the ground up, or a Rubik's Cube that must be reset to its original six-sided color configuration. My own analogy to data analysis is condensing and reorganizing the vast array of initial analytic details into a "main dish." Whimsically, I use grocery shopping and cooking as my parallel methods:

> When I grocery shop (i.e., visit a site for fieldwork), I can place up to 20 different food items (data) in my shopping cart (field note journal). When I go to the cashier's stand (computer) and get each item (datum) with a bar code scanned (First Cycle coding), the bagger (analyst) will tend to place all frozen foods in one bag (category one), fresh produce in another bag (category two), meats in another bag (category three), and so on. As I bring my food items home, I think about what I might prepare (reflection and analytic memo writing). I unpack the food items (Second Cycle coding), and organize them appropriately in the kitchen's refrigerator (concept one), pantry (concept two), freezer (concept three) and so on. And when I'm ready to make that one special dish (a key assertion or theory), I take out only what I need (the essence and essentials of the data corpus) out of everything I bought (analyzed) to cook it (write-up). (Saldaña, 2013, pp. 208–209)

Thinking analytically refers to the interaction of the researcher's background knowledge, experiences, and mental capacities for discovery with the collected data corpus to create study-specific, summative meanings with possible applications to broader social contexts. In other words, when you're analyzing qualitative data, you're hopefully learning something new about life and passing on those revelations to others who may not yet know what you've discovered. Your readers may not always be informed of or even be concerned about the analytic processes it took you to get to your findings. The products of your thinking are what you most often reveal, and you must ethically and genuinely present them in good faith—and only after a lot of work—to your audiences. Creativity scholar Sir Ken Robinson is credited with offering this cautionary advice about making a convincing argument: "Without data, you're just another person with an opinion."

I have been involved with qualitative research for over two decades, so let me assure you that analytic work does indeed get easier as you continue practicing it. Ultimately, analytic thinking becomes part of your brain's procedural memory—your **schemata**, or routines. But memory is not a thing—it's a process (Wolfe, 2010, p. 108). This suggests that experience plays a vital and cumulative role in your development, and that data analysis is not some elusive art form only for a gifted few, but a craft that can be taught and learned (Miles, Huberman, & Saldaña, 2014).

What separates a competent analysis from a brilliant one, however, is for readers, not the researcher, to decide. I've discovered that when I myself experience "Aha!" moments in the course of data analysis that transcend a typical "Whatever" feeling about what I've done so far, this signals a finding that may be considered significant by someone else as well.

Thinking analytically is a necessary method of mind that serves several purposes:

- It adheres to well-established principles of reasoning to ensure a more rigorous and robust set of summative findings.
- It reaches beyond basic description of social action to construct and present patterned regularities of social life.
- It synthesizes vast amounts of data into more manageable units for reflection and heuristic discovery of meaning.
- It pursues the construction of possible interconnections between phenomena to suggest interrelationship, causation, and explanation.
- It stimulates reflection on the local as well as generalizable meanings and implications of the study.

The following methods of mind profile other modalities of analytic thinking for qualitative inquiry: *thinking deductively, abductively, inductively, retroductively, patternly* (an invented word), *categorically, thematically, hierarchically, causationally,* and *cyclically.*

For your mental Rolodex: As you investigate social life, stay attuned to social patterns and their possible interrelationships. Consider how the particulars of what you study can apply to the general. Thinking is analysis and analysis is thinking.

Four "Ductions"

First, let me explain the differences between four "ductions," or different forms of problem-solving, before they're discussed separately: deduction, abduction, induction, and retroduction.

As you noticed above, I've found grocery shopping and cooking to be appropriate analogies for explaining several principles of qualitative inquiry. Imagine that you need a bag of apples to make a homemade pie. Here's how that need sets into motion four "ductions":

Deduction: You enter the grocery store knowing exactly what you're looking for. You walk directly to the produce section and find the apples. After all, your ultimate goal is to bake an apple pie.

Abduction: When you enter the produce section, you discover that there's more than one kind of apple. You see arrangements of Red Delicious, Granny Smith, Rome, Jonathan, McIntosh, Honeycrisp, and so on. You have several apple options available to you and must choose the one that best fits your recipe and individual tastes. Granny Smith apples will create a tart flavor and crisp texture, but Red Delicious apples will produce a sweeter dessert. You conclude (deduce) that Red Delicious would be the better choice.

Induction: After you've made the appropriate apple choice, you walk through several aisles. As you pass the spices section, it occurs to you that you might need some fresher ground cinnamon than what you have at home, so you pick up a small tin. Then you discover that the store also sells fresh cinnamon sticks you can grate, so you make that choice instead. As you pass the frozen foods section, you debate whether you should buy a ready-made pie crust to save time or make your own at home as you originally intended. You decide to make the pie crust from scratch, but suddenly remember that you may need more shortening to do so. As you start walking to the checkout stand, you wonder if you should also buy a carton of vanilla ice cream so you can serve apple pie à la mode.

Retroduction: You serve the homemade apple pie to your guest. She's impressed with it and asks for the recipe. You think back in your memory and recall all the ingredients and measurements needed, then describe the steps of preparation and baking.

This homemade apple pie story has been used to explain the differences between four "ductions" of thinking. Briefly, before they're explained separately below, let me introduce these terms. Deduction is stating, "I know what I'm looking for and how this will end"—that is, entering the research study with a very specific purpose and agenda, and reaching a conclusive goal. Abduction is determining, "Of all the possible reasons, here's the most likely one"—that is, examining an array of possibilities or explanations and selecting (i.e., deducing) the most reasonable and credible one. Induction is asking, "What's going on here?"—an open-ended investigation with minimal assumptions, leaving the researcher open to emergent leads and new ideas. Retroduction is stating, "Here's what happened"—a reconstruction of past events that describes and explains the history of a case (Bazeley, 2013).

All four "ductions" during your inquiry will be used iteratively, reverberatively, and serendipitously (e.g., again and again, back and forth, here and there, as needed, by chance, sometimes this one/sometimes that one, when the opportunity arises, and so on). It's not important that you know what specific form of thinking you're using at any given time, but it is necessary that you possess metacognitive awareness of each of these four so that you can better formulate your research design and conduct your investigation and analysis.

Let me conclude this preface with another "ductions" analogy. If you want to use lenses and angles for looking at things in your research

- Thinking deductively is looking at things from the top down.
- Thinking abductively is looking across at things in front of you.
- Thinking inductively is looking at things from the bottom up.
- Thinking retroductively is looking backward at things behind you.

And now, the individual profiles of the four "ductions."

Thinking Deductively

Though it may seem odd to start the "ductions" profiles with how you conclude rather than how you begin, the order is deliberate. Deduction is a thinking *goal;* abduction, induction, and retroducton are thinking *processes.* Thus, I first need to discuss the destination, and then I will discuss the journey. Deduction is reaching a conclusion based on an analysis of evidence. This thinking modality utilizes the other three "ductions" to get there, so it's a culminating product, if you will, of an analytic process. Most of us have been taught that the famous fictional detective Sherlock Holmes used his powers of deduction to examine clues, construct answers, and solve crimes, but rarely does anyone also refer to Holmes's abductive, inductive, and retroductive thinking. Qualitative researchers do something comparable with their data. The scene of the crime is our field site, and the suspects are our participants. However, our goal is not to solve a "whodunit" but to formulate a "what-of-it." Since the crime scene analogy casts our work in a negative light, let's try a different approach.

Thinking deductively is actually two ways of working in qualitative inquiry. The first way means going into an investigation with a very specific agenda, such as setting out to do a phenomenological study to examine acts of "politeness." From the beginning, the researcher enters various settings to document only those actions and their immediate contexts that demonstrate how humans are polite to one another (as the researcher interprets "politeness"). The second way of thinking deductively happens during and throughout the entire project whenever a conclusion of some type must be drawn. It can take many forms, from an assessment of the efficacy of previous research as part of a literature review to a discovery about the motivations behind a participant's actions to analytic summations of data, perhaps in the form of major categories, prominent themes, or a theory. Deduction is conclusion-making from evidence and your reflections on it.

But remember that three other "ductions" precede deduction. Therefore, it's important to utilize those other forms of thinking lest you reach a deductive conclusion too hastily and in error. There are times when we might put forth a conclusion based on minimal data or questionable sources of evidence or even because we're just too tired to think

Source: Thinkstock/Stockbyte/Thinkstock.

Figure 2.1.   Sherlock Holmes used his powers of deduction, abduction, induction, and retroduction.

anymore. Thinking deductively carries with it some risk of being wrong, so you must be confident in any assertions you put forth. Abduction becomes especially critical here, for that thinking process encourages you to look at several possibilities before making the most likely choice. It's the rare event that is absolutely conclusive, but anything we propose should have, at the very least, a strong probability or plausibility of being a fairly accurate "conclusion" (see Chapter 8's "Thinking Conclusively" section).

> ***For your mental Rolodex:*** As you investigate social life, remain highly conscious of your deduction-making processes and products. Back up any probable or plausible conclusions you draw with evidentiary support from the database.

Thinking Abductively

Abduction, as it is used here, does not mean to take away by force, but to spread out and to see the array before you. Abduction is good thinking for inquiry because it asks you to consider multiple possibilities before you reach a deductive conclusion. Abduction also explores the possible links and causation between phenomena—or, what plausibly leads to what.

Thinking abductively happens throughout the study. During your literature review and research design stages, you may learn about different approaches you might take toward your investigation—for example, deciding whether to situate your work as a case study, an ethnography, a grounded theory exploration, or a phenomenological study. And as you're observing social life, you may be wondering why certain participants do the things they do. Your mind might reflect on several possible motivations behind their actions, but perhaps you won't be able to confirm until you conduct interviews with them which one of your ideas was correct—assuming you even thought of that option at all.

During qualitative data analysis, abductive thinking comes into play, for example, when you're thinking of what particular code to apply to which particular datum, which code combinations and groupings work best for constructing and labeling categories, or how a set of related assertions might come together in a particular way to form a key assertion or new theory. The qualitative data analysis process is a highly abductive (and inductive) one, because there are virtually no algorithmic/formulaic methods to follow, just heuristics—self-initiated methods of discovery. Futurists and inventors pose three questions when they think about their visions for the world, which also apply to the abductive thinking process: What is possible? What is plausible? What is preferable? Abduction is considering the choices and options available to you before making that "final" decision.

> ***For your mental Rolodex:*** As you investigate social life, remain open to the multiple possibilities, plausibilities, preferabilities, and probabilities of social action, and the consequent analysis of those actions, before drawing deductive conclusions.

Thinking Inductively

Inductive thinking is the stock-in-trade of the qualitative researcher and perhaps the most used thinking approach of all four "ductions." It is the primary way to facilitate everything from research design to write-up. Induction is an exploratory and emergent enterprise, consisting of making decisions and discoveries as you go along. You cannot begin fieldwork as a completely blank slate, but you do enter the study with an open mind intending to learn as you go along. *Thinking inductively* is a willingness to have a minimalist agenda beforehand so that the investigative experience itself is like on-the-job training. You observe life unfolding before you and construct meanings as they happen and later during your private reflections and writing. Each successive fieldwork experience, literally day by day, gives you increased awareness of the participants' world and what it's like to live in it. Your cumulative learnings provide evidence and build a case for your abductive thinking and deductive conclusions about "What's happening here?"

Analytic induction is the process by which answers to research questions are emergently constructed as more and more data are collected and systematically examined. These answers can take various forms, ranging from, say, three to seven major categories or themes that seem prominent in the data to an extended narrative explanation of why things happened as they did. You do not necessarily enter a qualitative research study with predetermined hypotheses to test, but you do enter with a general topical agenda for inquiry that may evolve and even change completely as the study continues.

Thinking inductively also means you're open to continual revision of your ideas in progress. You leave yourself open to investigating the idiosyncratic event, the chance opportunity, the random happening, and the surprise twist that seems to throw things off balance. Perhaps midway through your study you will learn that your initial choices for data collection or even the methodology itself are not yielding the outcomes you had hoped for. Thus, plans are changed and new strategies are set in motion. This should not be perceived as an "I got it wrong" maneuver, but rather an "I'm making it better" tactic.

Just as there is no one central, hemispheric, or regional location for the information stored in our brains, the data corpus is a vast array of information gathered from various sources that needs emergent organization in our documentation and in our mental reflection. We can purposely arrange the qualitative and quantitative input into digital files and folders as we collect them, but our brain's internal synaptic connections and networks happen of their own accord. Nevertheless, we can make better sense of our data as we experience them when we have reference points for comparison. We might not be able to make total sense of our first day of fieldwork because we're feeling emotionally overwhelmed by the sensory bombardment of a new setting. But after a week or so, meaning or understanding of the field site and its participants' ways of working in it will become gradually clearer through our willingness to learn a little more about them each day as we engage in inductive thinking. The observations from, say, day five will seem purposeful rather than elusive because we have four previous days for comparison and context.

Our brains can make connections to previous experiences if we permit ourselves to learn as we go. Inductive thinking is giving yourself permission to wait for answers to formulate in your mind. As the folk saying goes, "What the head does not understand today, the heart will understand tomorrow."

For your mental Rolodex: As you investigate social life, stay open to emergent and inductive ways of thinking. Construct your knowledge of the setting and database in a cumulative manner to build sense and meaning, paving the way for larger ideas to formulate.

Thinking Retroductively

Thinking retroductively is imaginatively yet logically reconstructing how a particular outcome may have come about. It requires you to be part historian and part detective as you reflect on why things are as they are when you enter the field site and examine the data you have collected. You begin at an entry baseline of sorts and attempt to get up to speed with what local participants already know. That background research and knowledge of the past helps you place the present conditions into context.

Apply retroductive thinking when you're intrigued or puzzled by why things are as they are. Also apply this method when you critically wonder when or why things seem to happen without question. We are not able to witness most origins and geneses of artifacts, ideologies, actions, programs, policies, and such that have now become traditional, accepted, ritualistic, hegemonic, and ubiquitous in our world. Critically examining the motives that drove the current status or existence of things develops creation stories for analysis.

As an example of how thinking retroductively can take you to larger questions, above my desktop computer is a decorative wall hanging. I think back, in reverse order, to how that particular space on the wall was chosen for the hanging; where, when, how, and why the hanging was originally purchased; and even how the hanging may have been originally manufactured and by whom or with what technology and where. I think even deeper for motives and purposes: Why do we decorate walls with paintings, objects, photographs, printed wallpaper, and so forth, when there is no functional necessity to do so? I latch onto what may be a human need or impulse to display or exhibit to fulfill aesthetic satisfaction, to honor accomplishments, and to preserve memories. Everything we own has a story (or stories) behind it.

Interviews and document reviews are excellent methods for learning about the histories of your site. Your carefully dated and archived database also provides records of past fieldwork experiences that may provide insight into the current trajectory of the study's observations. Though your mental energies may be engrossed with what's happening here and now, your participants are historic beings whose presents have been profoundly shaped by their pasts. See Stilgoe's book *Outside Lies Magic* (1998) for insightful historical and sociological reflections on how outdoor environments, like town squares and parking lot arrangements, came to be.

 For your mental Rolodex: As you investigate social life, document not only what you observe but also reflect on how the assemblage of key artifacts and this particular group of participants came about.

Thinking Patternly

Popular films like *A Beautiful Mind, Contact,* and π *[Pi]* show their characters in analytic dilemmas, and what they all have in common is the relentless search for a pattern. Their searches are mathematical, not qualitative, but the principles are the same. They are attempting to find patterns within a mysterious assemblage of data to decode their meaning or significance. Their quests take time and they struggle at first. But in their own ways they eventually discover *how things newly fit together after they take the data apart and construct patterns out of them.*

Source: Jupiterimages/Photos.com/Thinkstock.

Figure 2.2.   A pattern in social inquiry occurs more than twice in the data.

This is one of the key heuristics of qualitative analysis. Patterns of human action are important foundations for creating codes, categories, themes, concepts, assertions, propositions, hypotheses, and theories. And thinking deductively, thinking inductively, thinking abductively, and thinking retroductively are just some of the ways to get you there. Pink (2006) purports that the ability to detect patterns is not just a researcher's job but a high-concept skill for 21st-century living (p. 2). The good thing is that our brains are hardwired for pattern detection and pattern-making.

A pattern in social inquiry is an action, phenomenon, or content arrangement that occurs more than twice in the data and that the researcher establishes as repeated and thus as possessing regularity. The more repetitions, the more stable the pattern. These researcher-constructed patterns serve as meaningful representations of participants' ways or habits of living. The magnitude of these human habits can range from the mundane to the destructive, yet it is the researcher, in his or her write-up, that most often interprets the banality or significance of the repetition and the sequences. Simply put, what do you observe people doing over and over again and why are they doing it, or what do you observe appearing over and over again and why is it reappearing?

Thinking patternly (*patternly* being an invented word) does not assign some artificial sense of order to the complexly detailed and seemingly idiosyncratic nature of social life, but assembles collections of those things that seem to consistently occur. These semi-fixed regularities suggest cultivated and established ways of living and working that are relevant to, sometimes routinely taken for granted by, and/or critically important to the participant. We look for patterns in what we observe during fieldwork, in interview transcripts, and in documents and artifacts. Identifying patterns and labeling them are the qualitative researcher's heuristics for detecting, describing, and further analyzing the established routines and habits of individuals as well as the organization of small-group and larger social life.

As a qualitative researcher, I generally look for patterns among the "five r's": routines, rules, rituals, roles, and relationships. Think first about your own habits or repeated actions every morning. What tends to be your typical *routine* from the moment you wake up through the first 60 to 90 minutes of the day? This would be an example of an action pattern. Think next about your ventures outside your home and in public spaces. There are formal and social *rules* (e.g., for driving, for riding the bus, for walking, for class attendance and participation, for eating in fast-food restaurants) that you voluntarily adhere to. These are examples of compliance or socialized patterns.

The difference between a routine and a *ritual* is the subjective significance attributed to the action or event. In many Western cultures, birthdays are recognized by accompanying actions that are repeated: typically presents, cake, and a song. This is an annual pattern for many individuals. Though you yourself might not graduate from a school at the end of every academic year, the periodic ritual of graduation is a cultural, social, and institutional pattern. Yet, a ritual has subjective significance—thus, a morning yoga class may be a routine you participate in regularly, but it may also have personal ritualistic significance for its cleansing of the body and mind.

Roles and *relationships* are two other categories in which patterns can be found. Most roles include regular patterns of specific actions to fulfill a purpose. A parental role usually consists of caretaking actions, teaching actions, disciplinary actions, and so forth, plus qualitative attributes that characterize the actions, such as "nurturing," "indifferent," or "controlling." Relationships include understood or underlying actions, reactions, and interactions between people in their roles. Friendships as relationships may consist of actions, reactions, and interactions such as listening, supporting, and arguing, plus their qualitative attributes that characterize aspects such as status and meaning—for example, a platonic friendship, an abusive relationship, or a "bromance."

Our brains are synergistically hardwired and socialized to look for, construct, and replicate patterns in the ways we create and act. If the material things we produce are extensions of ourselves, then notice how the objects we design and manufacture are infused with patterns: brick arrangements on a building's exterior, buttons on a shirt or blouse, icons on a monitor screen, shreds of lettuce in a salad. Even the natural world is filled with patterns: leaves on a tree, petals on a flower, individual blades of grass on a lawn. The human body is regulated through biological patterns: heartbeats, breathing, blinking, and so on. And our daily actions—our routines, rules, rituals, roles, and relationships—are patterned activities. Patterns don't "exist"—they are human constructions. But simply look around your environment and notice the astounding number of them.

The brain carries out pattern-making and association-making by design, and it gets better at it during middle age when experience enables adults to formulate the "gist" of a matter, or thematic, big-picture essences of meaning (Strauch, 2010, pp. 48–50). The mind's propensities for pattern construction and pattern recognition follow us into our qualitative research endeavors. It is through awareness of the repetitive and regularly occurring that we formulate the idea that a pattern exists. Our next step is to analyze—that is, attribute meaning to—the pattern we identified by explaining its properties, causes, and significance.

No one may really care that one of my patterned routines—perhaps a ritual—consists of drinking four to five cups of coffee each day. Why do I do it? Because I need an energy boost from the caffeine. And I love the taste of good coffee with cream. And drinking it comforts me. And perhaps I'm addicted to it. And even if I am addicted to it, I don't really care; I enjoy my habit. But a recent TV news story profiled a study suggesting that people who drink more than four cups of coffee a day may be at risk for a shorter lifespan—a finding that contradicts previous research on coffee consumption. So, what seemed like nothing more than a mundane routine to me now suddenly possesses life-changing impact. Research has provided me with an observed pattern that could literally affect my well-being and longevity. (I learned later that this quantitative study did not control for such factors in participants as obesity and preexisting health conditions. So I went back to my routine of drinking four to five cups of coffee a day with no worry. But that item reinforced another pattern I've observed: the media promoting a groundbreaking research news story without giving necessary details.)

Four to five cups of coffee each day is a quantity. Drinking them each day is the pattern of action. Now pay attention to the reasons or *qualities* of why I drink—the *purposes* of the pattern:

energy, enjoyment, comfort, and addiction. These are the rationale, outcomes, and consequences of the action pattern—the "payoff" or meaning for me. The greater the personal meaning, the greater the personal payoff; the greater the personal payoff, the greater the personal value (Saldaña, 2013, p. 111). By noticing my simple routine of drinking coffee four to five times a day, you've observed and constructed a pattern, which then leads you to investigate its significance or meaning. Substitute "drinking coffee" for some other repetitive social action, such as "smiling in the face of adversity," "psychologically manipulating others," or "exploiting with impunity," and you're delving into the qualitative domain. Construction of patterns constitutes the foundational heuristics for data analysis. "Patternly" is how we think and thus how we act and how we perceive the world.

> ***For your mental Rolodex:*** As you investigate social life, observe and construct patterns of action, reaction, and interaction, and analyze their meanings or significance for the participants.

Thinking Categorically

A category is a collection of similar or comparable elements that constitute or form some type of pattern. A category name is the label you attribute to the collection. Each room in a house is like a category in which relevant artifacts are contained and in which relevant patterns of human action occur. The category of the kitchen is designated for food storage and preparation; a closet contains clothing that the wearer peruses to select appropriate attire; a bathroom holds products and plumbing equipment for hygiene, bodily functions, and grooming. The room names are category labels for action, much like schools are places for learning, clinics are places for health care, and theaters are places for entertainment. But even the actions themselves are categories: learning, health care, entertainment. These three each contain their own constituent elements of actions and artifacts that, collectively, form the category (e.g., *health care* consists of physicians, nurses, medical equipment, patients, diagnoses, billing, compassion, treatment, etc.).

Like patterns, categories don't exist; we construct them in our minds. This is yet another function of our brain—it organizes and classifies experiences into similar, subsumed memory "chunks" of information. If I were to ask you to "list all the movie titles you can think of," your mind does not have to access extraneous details such as whether you actually saw the movie or not, or whom you might have gone with to see the film, or whether you saw it in a theater or at home or on a mobile device. Yes, those memories might be jogged through association, but they are irrelevant to the task. My prompt was both general and specific—specific in that you know to exclude television series, live plays, and rock concerts because they don't fit the category of movie titles.

Unfortunately, we can't always rely on our brains to automatically categorize all the qualitative data we collect. The movie title prompt above asked you primarily to think deductively, so answers should have emerged fairly quickly from your mind's long-term memory store. But qualitative inquiry and analysis demand that you think primarily in inductive, abductive, and retroductive ways—and that takes much more time for your brain to process because the categories are not usually predetermined but emergently constructed as you sort through the data. In other words, unless you know ahead of time what you're looking for, you're starting from scratch with category construction. And you really can't (or shouldn't) create a category until you first determine comparable patterns of social action at work.

Thinking categorically reorganizes the vast array of qualitative data into their most appropriate groupings based on similarity or comparability. In fact, each chapter of this book is a particular category of thinking processes, as determined by me. Chapter 1 briefly introduced codes and coding as heuristics for labeling each individual datum for purposes of pattern detection and categorizing. Remember that codes are not *the* way but just *one* way of analyzing data. They serve as prompts or triggers for reflection through analytic memo writing, but they also serve as the constituent pieces of a pattern in progress. For example, examine the following list of codes, which represent individual chunks of data from an interview transcript (Saldaña, 2014). These "process codes" (gerund-based phrases denoting action) were applied to a man's narrative about managing his personal budget and expenses during the difficult national economy. Some codes are deliberately listed more than once, and they appear in the order in which they were originally noted on the transcript:

BUYING BARGAINS

QUESTIONING A PURCHASE

THINKING TWICE

STOCKING UP

REFUSING SACRIFICE

THINKING TWICE

PRIORITIZING

FINDING ALTERNATIVES

LIVING CHEAPLY

NOTICING CHANGES

STAYING INFORMED

MAINTAINING HEALTH

MAINTAINING HEALTH

PICKING UP THE TAB

APPRECIATING WHAT YOU'VE GOT

The qualitative analyst's task is now to cluster these 15 codes into sets based on their similarity and comparability. Each new set of codes will then be labeled so as to represent the group as a category. The labels for these categories emerge from the purpose of the study, which is to explore the strategies people use to deal with personal finances. Therefore, each category name is a type of strategy the researcher interprets the participant as using:

Category 1: Thinking Strategically

Codes:

THINKING TWICE

THINKING TWICE

STAYING INFORMED

NOTICING CHANGES

QUESTIONING A PURCHASE

Category 2: Spending Strategically

Codes:

PICKING UP THE TAB

BUYING BARGAINS

STOCKING UP

Category 3: Living Strategically

Codes:

MAINTAINING HEALTH

MAINTAINING HEALTH

REFUSING SACRIFICE

PRIORITIZING

FINDING ALTERNATIVES

LIVING CHEAPLY

APPRECIATING WHAT YOU'VE GOT

Developing categories from our initial coding of data is one way of condensing the corpus into more manageable units for further reflection and analysis. Coding does not always have to precede category construction, for there are other ways of formulating categories. But with just three major units to explore ("Thinking Strategically," "Spending Strategically," and "Living Strategically"), the mind can now more easily grasp the essential qualities of the phenomenon of interest, especially when reflecting on how the three categories interrelate. Separate categories are not always isolated topics or bins—they should connect in some way, thus generating mental exercises in thinking propositionally, hierarchically, causationally, and so on as the data and study suggest.

Different numbers of categories are appropriate for different kinds of studies. Some studies, due to the magnitude of the data or the complexity of the research question, may produce up to 30 or more categories. But don't forget that, just as there are patterns of patterns, there are categories of categories, suggesting that condensation can continue even further for richer synthesis. Methodologists vary in their recommendations for a final number of categories to develop for a study after analytic work, ranging from three to seven.

Category construction is a heuristic of traditional qualitative data analysis. But it continues to have relevance and staying power for more progressive forms of inquiry, because categorizing (i.e., classifying) is what our minds do of their own accord. This heuristic is not appropriate for every study, however, because themes (discussed next) and narratives (discussed in Chapter 10) are additional options for analyses and write-ups.

For your mental Rolodex: As you investigate social life, organize the patterns of action into major categories of interest for the study. Explore how the categories interrelate through various forms of connectivity.

Thinking Thematically

The research methods literature offers various definitions of and analytic approaches to constructing a theme. Chapter 1 clarified that, in this book, a theme is a sentence or extended phrase that identifies and functions as a way to categorize a set of data into a topic that emerges from a pattern of ideas. The topics generate extended narratives that unpack the statements and describe or explain their constituent elements. Themes can derive from initial analytic work with codes and categories, or they may be independently constructed from a holistic review of the data corpus for patterns of recurring ideas.

Thinking thematically means scouting the data for main *ideas*—not just content—suggested by continuous review. It helps if you frame your analyst's lens, filter, and angle with the proper question. If you go looking for themes by asking, "What are the participants talking about?" you'll more than likely develop nothing more than a topical index, which will not move you toward thematic analysis. Instead, as you look at the data, go "looking for trouble" by asking yourself

- What worries or concerns are the participants expressing?
- What unresolved issues are the participants raising?
- What do the participants find intriguing, surprising, or disturbing? (Sunstein & Chiseri-Strater, 2012, p. 115)
- What types of tensions, problems, or conflicts are the participants experiencing?
- What kinds of trouble are the participants in?

These prompts may generate more evocative ideas for thematic structures.

As an example, here is a set of themes the analyst generated from the interview transcript coded above under "Thinking Categorically" (Saldaña, 2014). Instead of words and short phrases, however, the themes below are extended phrases or complete sentences. The codes and categories above represent the participant's processes exclusively; the themes below will also reflect some of his or her processes plus a few new general ideas. Bigger-picture ideas will emerge after the themes have been categorized or "themed" even further in this section.

The researcher looks for participants' "economic intelligence" (EI), a conceptual idea that embodies people's strategies for managing their personal budgets and expenses during difficult economic times. The use of either "is" or "means" after "EI" is deliberate. "Is" refers to specific actions the participant takes; "means" refers to more general actions or ideas. Here is a list of themes the analyst constructed from the interview:

EI IS TAKING ADVANTAGE OF UNEXPECTED OPPORTUNITY

EI MEANS THINKING BEFORE YOU ACT

EI IS BUYING CHEAP

EI MEANS SACRIFICE

EI IS SAVING A FEW DOLLARS NOW AND THEN

EI MEANS KNOWING YOUR FLAWS

EI MEANS THINKING BEFORE YOU ACT

EI IS SETTING PRIORITIES

EI IS FINDING CHEAPER FORMS OF ENTERTAINMENT

EI MEANS LIVING AN INEXPENSIVE LIFESTYLE

EI IS NOTICING PERSONAL AND NATIONAL ECONOMIC TRENDS

EI MEANS YOU CANNOT CONTROL EVERYTHING

EI IS TAKING CARE OF ONE'S OWN HEALTH

EI MEANS KNOWING YOUR LUCK

Just as codes are categorized for further analysis, themes can be categorized into theoretical constructs (Auerbach & Silverstein, 2003), or phrases that serve as a category-like, abstract summation of a set of related themes. Since one of the goals of theming the data is to get to ideas, not topics, theoretical constructs better ensure an analytic leap into bigger-picture meanings. From the example above, the analyst cut and pasted the themes into clusters that suggested similarity or comparability—that is, patterns. Three different clusters emerged, and the researcher reflected on what each set of themes had in common as an idea. "EI is" and "EI means" were retained as unifying phrases for the three constructs, with variations of "fortune" as a motif to connect them even further:

Theoretical Construct 1: EI Means Knowing the Unfortunate Present

Supporting themes:

EI MEANS YOU CANNOT CONTROL EVERYTHING

EI IS SETTING PRIORITIES

EI MEANS KNOWING YOUR FLAWS

EI MEANS SACRIFICE

Theoretical Construct 2: EI Is Cultivating a Small Fortune

Supporting themes:

EI MEANS LIVING AN INEXPENSIVE LIFESTYLE

EI MEANS THINKING BEFORE YOU ACT

EI IS BUYING CHEAP

EI IS FINDING CHEAPER FORMS OF ENTERTAINMENT

EI IS SAVING A FEW DOLLARS NOW AND THEN

Theoretical Construct 3: EI Means a Fortunate Future

Supporting themes:

EI IS NOTICING PERSONAL AND NATIONAL ECONOMIC TRENDS

EI MEANS THINKING BEFORE YOU ACT

EI IS TAKING ADVANTAGE OF UNEXPECTED OPPORTUNITY

EI IS TAKING CARE OF ONE'S OWN HEALTH

EI MEANS KNOWING YOUR LUCK

The three themes of economic intelligence now serve as prompts for an extended narrative on how "Knowing the Unfortunate Present," "Cultivating a Small Fortune," and working toward "a Fortunate Future" for oneself help the participants (and others) survive financially during tough economic times.

Thematic statements get you into the conceptual scheme of things by helping you to look beyond case-specific data and work toward broader meanings for more general populations and applications. If you find the highly condensed format of codes too reductive for your ways of thinking, or categorization a too artificial approach to organizing topics, themes may be more to your mind's way of exploring the ideas inherent in your data. Themes are particularly helpful if your research study's methodology is phenomenological or ethnographic.

For your mental Rolodex: As you investigate social life, explore the ideas suggested by the data by constructing themes. Use themes as a way of developing higher-level theoretical constructs.

Thinking Hierarchically

Some animals' instinct is to remain perfectly still so as not to draw attention and thus danger from predators in the wild. Human eyes in everyday life tend to gravitate toward that which moves, but we can occasionally become fixated on a still image or object when it arrests our interest. Our minds will also prioritize among competing sensory inputs, determining what takes precedence at any given time. Some of that decision-making is cognitive in function, and some of it is even automatic, such as when we hear an unexpected loud noise. But what takes priority is also affective, arising from our values system—what's important to us at the moment. We develop individual hierarchies of needs and wants; after basic human necessities have been met (water, food, shelter, etc.), we make choices to assign an order of importance to things in our lives. To some, family comes first; to others, career is more important. To some, a job is not as important as personal happiness; to others, happiness can only be achieved through financial wealth. Thus, what is extremely important to one person may be of lesser priority or even of negligible concern to another.

Not everything we investigate and document as qualitative data can be objectively ranked from the most important to the least relevant. Those are subjective interpretations and judgment calls by the researcher for each particular project. But there are times when some type of issue **hierarchy** is in place or assumedly constructed by participants. And there will be some data in the corpus that seem relevant or salient for analysis, while the rest must fall to the wayside. *Thinking hierarchically* is carefully considering which matters seem to be of prime importance to the study's participants, and which data merit analytic exploration. A researcher engaged in this type of thinking makes active choices about what his or her lens needs to focus on and what needs to be filtered out from the vast array of social actions.

Frustratingly, frequency can either be a strong indicator of what counts, or a poor indicator of what is qualitatively significant. In one of my mixed methods studies, in which adults recalled their high school theatre and speech experiences (McCammon, Saldaña, Hines, & Omasta, 2012), "confidence" emerged as the most frequently cited outcome among the 234 survey respondents, and this construct became the key variable in our process mapping of students' experiences. But one of my educational ethnographies (Saldaña, 1997) included the word "survival" only four times in over two and a half years of field notes and interview transcripts, yet the construct was central to my case study participant's teaching philosophy for her inner city school placement. The lesson: Sometimes, less is more.

Frequencies play a central role in traditional content analysis studies (Krippendorff & Bock, 2009; Kuckartz, 2014; Schreier, 2012), but qualitative inquiry most often examines the nuances of language rather than the magnitude of word counts. Nevertheless, an exploratory venture into frequencies is worthwhile, particularly since selected CAQDAS programs and online tools such as www.wordle.net make the task simple and quick. For instance, Figure 2.3 shows a Wordle diagram of this chapter's contents. The larger the size of the word, the more often it appears in the text; you can also get a chart of the number of times each word appears in the array. It is up to the researcher to interpret the figure and word counts to infer any possible meanings.

Hierarchies might also appear in our data analyses if we interpret one code, category, theme, or assertion as being more prominent than others, whether according to number or inferred impact. One participant might seem to stand out from the rest due to an exceptionality or difference that intrigues us. One issue might seem to override all others as participants wrestle with it. Since all of us have individual value, attitude, and belief systems, we each have our own agendas, we each have our own causes to fight for, and we each have our own axes to grind. Sometimes we are unified by an issue that brings us closer together as a community; other times we are highly divided over an issue because of our multiple and conflicting opinions. Hierarchies may be erroneously assumed when we arrogantly think that others should feel and think the same

Source: www.wordle.net.

Figure 2.3.　A Wordle image of the contents of Chapter 2.

way we do. Hierarchies may be correctly assumed when an outsider enters a situation and offers a fresh perspective that clarifies what the "real" problem is.

This profile serves as cautionary advice when it comes to thinking about hierarchies. We are often conditioned to look for the single right answer, the root problem, the main cause, the most of, the best of, the only way, the core category, the key assertion, the grand theory, and so on. Sometimes it will be just one thing above all others; other times it may be a lot of little things operating together in intricate complexity. A wide panoramic view is just as important as a tightly focused close-up for a researcher's lens and angle. And remember that filters both let things in and keep things out. Our minds can fixate obsessively on one idea, neglecting all other options and clouding our judgment. Get as many perspectives as possible during your study as a reality check of what's really important and what's probably not.

For your mental Rolodex: As you investigate social life, carefully assess whether or not some type of hierarchy may exist in the phenomena you study. Acknowledge that the variety of issues examined may be central or peripheral to the research endeavor, and that frequencies are not always a trustworthy indicator of importance.

Thinking Causationally

"Why?" is one of the most complex questions humans can tackle. Asking *why* is a search for explanation, purpose, sense, and meaning. It is an intuitive cry for understanding after a tragic loss. It is also a playful drive to satisfy childlike curiosity. We seek rationales and reasons because our minds need awareness, security, and a sense of completion for daily living and moving forward. Things need to make sense, and asking and answering *why* questions is our mind's way of sense-making. Answers to most *why* questions start with "Because." It is the "because" that takes us into the phenomenon of causation or *attribution* (the reasons we assign to those happenings).

O'Dwyer and Bernauer (2014) posit that true experimental research in the classic tradition is perhaps the quantitative empiricist's only valid and reliable way to assert cause and effect (p. 59). But I propose that, for qualitative inquiry, the concept of cause and effect is better reconceptualized as influences and affects—meaning that there is not just a Point A and Point B connection between a treatment and its outcome, but a possible multitude of factors that interrelate in complex combinations from an origin baseline through their evolutionary journey across time (Saldaña, 2003). Thus, the qualitative equation is not A → B. In qualitative constructions, the process is something like 1A + 2A + 3A → 1B → 1C + 2C. Yet even that process appears to be too linear and formulaic, since causation can be two- and three-dimensionally networked. Things don't just differ; they change. And if "participant change" doesn't seem like the correct term to apply to our observations, then "short-term impact" or "long-term impact" might be an appropriate substitute.

Causation is a slippery issue in qualitative (and quantitative) inquiry because there can be multiple attributions—reasons—for *why* something happens (Morrison, 2009; Munton, Silvester, Stratton, & Hanks, 1999). "Why?" is a research question we sometimes skirt around, preferring to preface our investigations with "what" and "how" to build a stronger case. I offer that we should not be afraid to ask others why they think something is as it is, or be afraid ourselves to formulate and propose why something happens, based on the evidence we accumulate. Qualitative inquiry is a method that can insightfully explore people's motivations, values systems, histories, and, from their perspectives, explanations of causality in their lives (Maxwell, 2012).

For example, if I were to ask you a deliberately open-ended question such as, "How did you get to where you are today?" your mind might first think of your career path, or perhaps your personal identity development, or maybe remembrances of influential people in your life. And if I were to pose the question, "What's the one single thing that got you where you are today?" you might be able to speculate and even tentatively propose a particular personality trait or significant individual or major life event that made that happen. But upon further reflection, you'd probably come to realize that how you got to where you are today is the product of multiple factors interacting in complex ways—some of them planned, some of them random, some of them through socialization, some of them through individual drive, some of them from bad choices, some of them from good people, some of them from a host of other influences.

Thinking causationally extends beyond an if/then, when/then, since/that's why, or Point A/Point B heuristic, and develops intersecting trails or webbed storylines of causation. This type of thinking entails careful examination of action, reaction, and interaction to map a minimum of three links in a chain (→ means "lead to"):

1. antecedent conditions → 2. mediating variables → 3. outcomes

This is more than just "before and after"; it's "before, and then, and then, and then, and afterward." We don't know where someone's going or where she ended up until we first know where she's been and, most important, how she got to where she ended up. Thinking causationally is not just map reading but mapmaking to plot an origin, the journey, and the destination of our participants and the phenomenon of interest. A fascinating mental exercise is to wear a *why* filter as you conduct participant observation fieldwork. As you watch and listen to people in everyday social interaction, don't just document the *what* or *how;* ask yourself *why* they are doing and saying the things they are. This is an opportunity to retroductively infer causal chains and to think about a participant's objectives, motives, drives, needs, wants, desires, agendas, subtexts, shortcomings, and so on.

People, however, do not always tell us their stories in linear form, and sometimes they are at a loss to explain why something happened the way it did. When we attempt to determine causation, we are truly exploring it jointly and collaboratively with our participants through strategic questions and verification of their answers. Imagine an interview with questions that begin this way:

- "What happened when . . . ?"
- "What's the reason for . . . ?"
- "Why do you suppose . . . ?"
- "What caused you to . . . ?"
- "What happened between [A] and [C]? What's [B]?"

Questions such as these extend beyond qualitative description and get deeper to the roots of causation and attribution. In other words, we are working toward explanation.

The metaphor of a billiard ball striking a cluster of other balls that then go off in different linear directions has been a standard yet faulty analogy for the principle of causation. It assumes that one ball (i.e., action) is all it takes to set things in motion, when in real life it is most often multiple influences that affect outcome(s). But imagine in your mind's eye that same billiards game, and envision it happening in reverse: multiple colored and striped balls (i.e., influences) coming toward and striking the single white billiard ball (i.e., the participant), which then rolls away, impacted by the collective forces. It hits the point of the pool cue and stops in a moment of reflection about what courses of reaction to take. The billiards game is then run forward, with the white ball moving toward the setup of billiard balls to strike them, creating reactive affects. Now imagine this reversed and fowarded visual storyline looped so that it plays over and over again. That streaming image is a more appropriate analogy for causation.

Source: Jupiterimages/Photos.com/Thinkstock.

Figure 2.4.   A billiards game is a popular yet only partial metaphor for causation.

> *For your mental Rolodex:* As you investigate social life, discern the influences and affects on current conditions and which actions, reactions, and interactions set things into motion.

Thinking Cyclically

Last, thinking analytically means thinking about the patterns inherent in the research project itself. Qualitative research is a cyclical process, but there are several synonymous words to use here, such as *cumulatively, successively, spirally, iteratively, recursively, reverberatively,* and *synergistically.* I choose *cyclically* because the term implies repetition with concurrent forward movement.

If we remain sharply aware of our surroundings and experiences, our instincts develop through the capacity to recall previous conditions and to sense comparability between past and present contexts (Kahneman, 2011). This cyclical thinking enables us to recount the past while moving forward and averting danger. The childhood lesson of knowing not to touch something that's hot (but touching it anyway and getting a painful burn) cautions us as we grow up to be wary of hot things—literally and metaphorically—lest we harm ourselves in the process. Some people, unfortunately, do not know how to break the cycle and end up frequently burned in the same types of painful situations.

A pattern happens again and again; a cycle happens again and again, and then again and again, and then again and again, and so on. In other words, a cycle is a pattern of patterns—a meta-pattern, if you will. And let me briefly explain the differences between the terms *phase, stage,* and *cycle.* Phases are successive and loosely bounded time periods of action. Stages are like phases but with cumulative effects across time. Cycles are repetitive and sometimes cumulative sequences of an action series (such as phases and stages) within generally bounded time periods. For example, an adolescent may go through occasional fashion *phases* in which he experiments with various clothing styles to appear a certain way to others. Adolescents also go through developmental *stages* in mental, social, physical, and other domains on their way toward adult maturity. Assuming average and healthy development, there should be cumulative improvement or growth through each stage. Some youth studies specialists attest that adolescence is not a transitional stage but a *cyclical* struggle between childhood and adulthood in which the young person reverberatively draws from and enacts both stages of human development while growing up. Phases, stages, and cycles are three time-based units of measurement at the qualitative researcher's disposal for allocation to observed series of human actions. We demarcate action into these general time periods to analyze longitudinal patterns, themes, trends, and through-lines in our lives (Saldaña, 2003). Often we need to know the long-term trajectories, not just the short-term forecasts, to plan ahead and project the journey's possible pathways.

Thinking cyclically means retrieving the past to put present conditions into context and plan for future endeavors. Fieldwork is not just one new day of observations followed by another and then another, but a collection of successive experiences that cyclically accumulate to bring a larger picture into focus or to create a picture with richer details—that is, emergent, inductive thinking. For example, if you interview a participant a second time, you cycle back to her first interview to put the second one in context and to prepare possible follow-up questions; that same process happens between the second and third interviews (Seidman, 2013).

Thinking cyclically also means reviewing your database with purposeful intent. Most methodologists concur that repeated readings of your data create intimate familiarity with them (Miles et al., 2014). Assuming you're not fatigued, each review of the corpus should add new thoughts and hopefully new connections and insights in your mind to move your analysis forward. Thinking cyclically is also going back in your mind's memories to previous aspects of your research to bring them forward and to blend them with your most recent ventures. For example, when you observe participants or analyze data, you may cycle back to your initial literature reviews and conceptual framework to determine how previous research or theory might inform your current perspectives on today's matters.

Participatory action research is a methodology in which process cycles such as investigation, formulation, implementation, and evaluation of solution strategies are continually put to the test as a social or organizational problem is tackled (Coghlan & Brannick, 2010; Hacker, 2013; Stringer, 2014). Participants may be going through unproductive cyclical patterns of action that they themselves may not be aware of. As a counseling folk saying goes, "You can't see the frame when you're in the picture." The action researcher's lens, filter, and angle might offer stakeholders a perspective on the issue that can raise constituent awareness of core problems and their root causes, plus possible problem-solving tactics for breaking from habitual, problem-sustaining patterns (Duhigg, 2012).

Renowned British educator Dorothy Heathcote was once asked by an American teacher what she thought of the late-20th-century back-to-basics movement in the U.S. school curriculum. Ms. Heathcote bristled at the term and replied, "Nonsense. You don't go 'back' to basics; you go *forward* to basics once you've reevaluated what those new basics are." I adapted that viewpoint for another matter years later. Just a few days after the September 11, 2001, terrorist attacks in the United States, one of my university students was either fatigued with discussing the tragedy or in emotional denial about its magnitude, and he shared with the class, "I just want to put it behind me and move on." I replied gently, "You don't put something like 9/11 'behind you and move on.' You keep it in *front* of you at all times, and you move on." Cycles don't just mean returning to the past; cycles mean moving forward in the present, recalling past experiences while accumulating new ones, yet remembering them all for reference as comparable situations arise in the future.

Historians, anthropologists, sociologists, political scientists, and elders may be more attuned to cyclical social patterns of action through time. Yet digital technology's ability to archive and rapidly access documents and video from decades past offers us sometimes surprising findings of parallels between the past and present. The folk sayings "Some things never change," "Everything old is new again," "It's the same but different," and "The more things change, the more they stay the same" do have a grain of truth to them. Thinking cyclically involves doing your homework to research whether what you're observing now has already happened before. I am a bit amused in my sixties when I hear someone in his or her twenties "discover" something new in fieldwork, only to be informed of a research study from several decades ago that already published the same findings. But I am comforted to know that these same discoveries have held constant for many years, affirming their currency and longevity. I am also comforted to know that a new generation of young professors are bringing to their classrooms an exciting new way of looking at life and are teaching about it with 21st-century passion. Life goes on. It has to.

> ***For your mental Rolodex:*** As you investigate social life, look for cycles—patterns of patterns of human action. Periodically review your own prior work for a research study to cumulatively build a stronger understanding of the participants and the phenomena.

CLOSURE

This chapter profiled fairly standard heuristics for working with qualitative data, and the next chapters will describe other traditional methods as well as more progressive modes of thought. There's something to be said for learning how to follow the rules before you break them. One of choreographer Twyla Tharp's most memorable quotes is, "Before you can think out of the box, you have to start with a box." I feel it is good practice for all qualitative researchers to know the conventional forms of analysis before they explore more recently developed approaches. And, every analytic act your mind rehearses hopefully leads to better mastery and the possible transfer of those skills from deliberative to automatic mental processes (Dubinsky, Roehrig, & Varma, 2013, p. 319).

Thinking analytically is metacognitive awareness of how the mind analyzes. It is also critical awareness of your own barriers to effective thinking and problem-solving. Pink (2006) puts forth that analysis (primarily a left-brained activity) takes things apart, but synthesis (primarily a right-brained activity) puts things together into a new whole (p. 22). The term Pink has coined for this conceptual way of thinking is *symphony,* that is,

> the ability to put together the pieces. [Symphony] is the capacity to synthesize rather than to analyze; to see relationships between seemingly unrelated fields; to detect broad patterns rather than to deliver specific answers; and to invent something new by combining elements nobody else thought to pair. (p. 130)

The remaining chapters hope to build on this concept by encouraging you to symphonically synthesize additional ways of thinking qualitatively.

EXERCISES FOR THINKING ANALYTICALLY

1. Think deductively, abductively, inductively, and retroductively about why people generally applaud after a performance or after a climactic conclusion in nonperformative contexts (e.g., after singing a national anthem, to congratulate someone else's accomplishment).

2. Look around your immediate environment and note all the patterns, both functional and decorative, that you observe in the physical space (e.g., patterns of keys on a computer's or handheld device's keyboard, patterns of design on clothing). Then list the patterns of actions in your own life you've experienced thus far today (e.g., not just what happened more than once today, but what series of actions happened today that were repeated from previous days). Formulate categories or themes to appropriately cluster and label these patterns.

3. Define addiction. Then brainstorm a list of things that people can become addicted to. Take two vastly different types of addiction (e.g., to the Internet versus to smoking, or to food versus to methamphetamines) and note their similarities or comparable properties that make

them addictive (e.g., what do alcohol and running have in common that satisfy their respective users' addictions?). Discuss the categorical, thematic, hierarchical, causational, and/or cyclical properties of addiction.

4. Take a one-participant interview transcript and review it to construct the major themes of the narrative. Based on the contents of the interview, reorganize and analyze the themes into a smaller number of theoretical constructs.

Thinking Realistically

LEARNING OBJECTIVES AND SUMMARY

- Your mind will reflect on selected epistemological processes.
- Your mind will reflect on the fluidity and variability of reality and truth.

This chapter discusses some of the traditional epistemologies of thinking with a segue into subjective and critical reflection. These methods of mind consist of

- Thinking Realistically
- Thinking Inferentially
- Thinking Intuitively
- Thinking Quantitatively
- Thinking Subjectively
- Thinking Critically

This chapter examines some of the types of epistemological lenses, filters, and angles we use for perceiving and interpreting social life.

Thinking Realistically

Realism, depending on how it's used, can refer to a literary genre, an artistic approach, or a mental conception of existence. It differs from *naturalism,* which suggests the verbatim and even mundane experiences of everyday life. Realism is lifelike, as in "like life," but not exactly life itself—it is a *selective representation* of everyday life through words and images used for qualitative reporting. *Thinking realistically* portrays, in appropriate forms, particular descriptions of the actual experiences of humans. Notice that "appropriate" is used here to describe the forms, for sometimes genres such as surrealism can be the most evocative way to depict realism. The often chaotic and erratic thought processes of people who are severely addicted to alcohol and drugs, for example, can be represented through rapid-fire, nonsensical, and nonnormative texts and images, for this is their reality (Caswell, 2011).

Realism does not suggest neutrality, detached objectivity, or unbiased decision-making. On the contrary, everyday life is filled with subjective perspectives, emotional drives, occasional irrationality, and actions based not just on logic but on personal values, attitudes, and beliefs. When we plead with others to "be realistic" about an issue, we are admonishing them for what we interpret as implausible (i.e., unrealistic) behavior or expectations on their part. But remember that imagining, daydreaming, and fantasizing are a part of daily reality. They simply take place in our minds along with the rest of the reality that we're experiencing and constructing.

Qualitatively, realism remains grounded in the participants' world and what it's like to live in it. It is a razor-sharp focused lens, an unobstructed filter, and an angled position that observes both ethereally overhead and omnisciently inside the participant's mind. Realism is rich description with telling details about the field site (van Maanen, 2011), as in this unadulterated portrait of an inner city apartment and its residents:

> The small apartment kitchen smelled from three days of leftover food decaying on assorted sizes of chipped white plates strewn along the counters. The peeling linoleum floor was dirty from spilled juices, muddy shoeprints, and yellowing with age. Only one bulb glowed from four light sockets in the ceiling. The thirty year-old refrigerator made a rattling sound from behind, suggesting it could break down at any minute. From adjoining apartments, you could hear the sounds of babies crying, TV shows, and men and women shouting at each other: "Don't talk to me like that, you bastard!" "I'll talk to you any goddamn way I want!"

Realism is also honesty about what humans think, feel, and do. It is an unabashed portrait of people's truths as they construct them. The narrative passage below (adapted from an anonymous source to protect confidentiality) employs an omniscient point of view to reveal the participant's stark and secret thoughts:

> Sarah watched her boyfriend Mark, high on meth, masturbate to pornography on TV. She wondered how her own life had come to this—a high school teacher from a middle-class Catholic family, working with young people by day and living with an addict by night. She no longer

cared about the illegality of it all, for it was done secretly behind closed doors and she kept herself clean. Sarah was so desperate for companionship that she was willing to put up with Mark's habitual insanity. "Look at me," she thought as she saw her thirty-one-year-old, plus-sized body in the smoke-hazed mirror. "Who else is going to love me?"

Realism also connotes a research paradigm. Some methodologists are catalyzing a resurgence in qualitative inquiry toward a "realist's stance" (Maxwell, 2012; Morgan, 2014). According to this perspective, research should be purposeful and serve pragmatic ends. The inquiry has utility, meaning that it contributes productively to improving social life. To newcomers to the field, these may appear to be admirable if not commonsense goals. But several others, primarily in academia, have advocated investigation motivated by and laden with theory to such excess that their write-ups consist of obtuse content with little potential for transferability for the public good, drawing audiences of mostly like-minded theoreticians. A small body of scholars seem to place great stock in matters such as ontology (the study of the nature of being), conceptualization, paradigms (e.g., **postpositivism**, **poststructuralism**), and other philosophical and methodological topics of intellectual interest. This scholarship also seems to draw a readership of like-minded academics. (One of my history colleagues with a doctorate once quipped, "PhDs are paid to think of a lot of useless stuff.")

There is a noticeable disconnect, however, between researchers in academia and researchers in nonuniversity settings. The latter must most often devote themselves to research projects that address immediate concerns such as health care, social services, and public education. In this arena, answers to questions and solutions to problems are needed fairly quickly, and thus the inquiry is usually well focused and streamlined to yield specific types of outcomes. To illustrate, a professional conference of psychologists, therapists, and counselors may consist mainly of grumblings among selected attendees to the effect that the "highbrow intellectuals" look down on and have little to offer professionals working "in the trenches." (There's an old joke about a mother bragging of her PhD child, "My son's a doctor—but not the kind that helps people.")

I do not intend to demean those working toward or with a PhD degree, but teaching in academia for thirty-five years without a doctorate has given me an outsider status that permits me to observe the scholarly discourse within the ivory tower. Most of my colleagues' projects are noteworthy and address topics of immediate need and relevance for the social condition, and they are indeed making the world a better place to live. There are just a handful of scholars who seem to have "lost touch with reality," if you will—meaning, their intellectual pursuits and writings are esoteric, far too theoretical, and of little practical value for the general public. Far worse may be the arrogant elitism that often accompanies members of this closed system. "Keep it real" is a folk saying offered to others when honesty, straightforwardness, and unpretentiousness are desired. This advice should be well heeded by those with advanced degrees and college/university careers.

One person's epistemological trash is another person's epistemological treasure. Audiences may hold different perspectives about the value of the same peer-reviewed journal article. Some may never venture further than the work's abstract or even its title, while others will read the piece thoroughly since its contents contain relevance and meaning for them. My reality is not your reality, and your reality is not my reality. This is not to say that we can never find common ground, but we should acknowledge that we will each have our own unique experiences, agendas, priorities, and baggage. The personal, social, and cultural ideologies we formulate will, at several points in time, clash with those of others. Through perspective-taking we might come to know another person's point of view, but only through empathy will we truly be able to feel and understand the reality of someone else's world.

Truth, like reality, is not always as clear-cut as we would like it to be. Did the World War II holocaust of over 6 million lives happen in Europe? According to reputable historians, survivor accounts, and even photographic and filmic evidence, it did indeed happen. Yet there are some in the world who deny that the atrocity ever occurred. There are also people who firmly believe that President Barack Obama was not born in the United States, people who firmly believe that man has never set foot on the surface of the moon, and people who firmly believe that humans were created in God's image about 6,000 years ago and did not evolve over millions of years from lower species. So, are holocaust deniers, birthers, conspiracy theorists, and creationists right or wrong (or somewhere in between) if what they genuinely believe is the truth as they construct it? Even an insane street character in Jane Wagner's (1986) play *The Search for Signs of Intelligent Life in the Universe* reflects, "After all, what is reality anyway? Nothin' but a collective hunch" (p. 18). Many gays and lesbians and their allies perceive the right to legally wed a same-sex partner as a "marriage equality" and "human rights" issue, while opposing perspectives might perceive the movement as "an attack on traditional Christian values" and "advancement of the homosexual agenda." Reality is not just a collective hunch; it's a strongly opinioned perspective.

At the time of this writing, a major discount U.S. retailer found itself in hot water with some of its customers and gained national media attention because it classified the Holy Bible on its price label as "fiction." To some Christians, the Bible is not fiction—but what is it then? Nonfiction? Literature? Devotional reading? The controversy did not address *how* the book should have been categorized, merely claiming that it was incorrectly categorized. The classification of the Bible as fiction generated a range of public responses varying from offended to amused to affirmative. If we assume fiction to be a written work that is imaginatively and creatively invented by an author, rather than the documentation of events that actually happened, then we find ourselves in an epistemological dilemma of nonconsensus when we label the Holy Bible fiction. Fiction, or "not truthful," is now just as slippery a concept as nonfiction/truth itself.

A popular rejoinder often heard during televised debates is, "You're entitled to your own opinions, but not your own facts." Truth—the product of facts—seems to be a precious commodity these days and something that can be deceptively packaged and even socially manufactured by those in power for their own ideological ends. Truth seems to be no longer a bullet-pointed list of verified facts as much as it is an opinion poll in which the majority's outcome determines prevailing sentiment. Qualitative inquiry presents the truth as our participants construct it, but they do not have the final word. The researcher layers his or her own analysis and interpretation not just to supply an account of truth but also to give the report a sense of trustworthiness (Lincoln & Guba, 1985). I've been taught that research is an act of persuasion. If this is so, your representation and presentation depend on how well you can convince your audiences that your eyewitness and earwitness accounts are accurate or, at the very least, plausible.

This profile is not meant to serve as the be-all and end-all of ontology and epistemology. I offer it as an introduction to the other modalities of thought described below. Realism encompasses an array of thinking processes and perspectives that deal with the here and now. It addresses immediate, everyday needs and concerns itself with practical matters. While it is important to contemplate the philosophical foundations of knowledge production when planning research, the direct value return of such ponderings for the general public and problem-solving is extremely low. Besides, if you're too engrossed in theorizing about the nature of reality and being, you may be spending far too much time on elusive matters. Are you reading this? Are you comprehending this? Then it's happening and it's real. Now move on to more important questions and problems.

Thinking realistically is a necessary method of mind that serves several purposes:

- It keeps you as a researcher grounded in matters of immediate concern and public relevance.
- It expands your thinking beyond consideration of the apparent to pursuit of an understanding of the subjectivities of the social world.
- It challenges you to find varying methods of depicting reality in credible, vivid, and persuasive ways.
- It generates contributions to scholarship that are more accessible and meaningful for readers.

The following methods of mind profile other modalities of thinking realistically for qualitative inquiry: *thinking inferentially, intuitively, quantitatively, subjectively,* and *critically.*

> **For your mental Rolodex:** As you investigate social life, keep it real. Investigate the accuracy or plausibility of what is deemed factual. Continually reflect on the purpose, value, and utility of your inquiry project for others in your discipline.

Thinking Inferentially

Our brains are designed to *infer,* that is, to make reasoned assumptions about people or conditions based on partial evidence. "Confabulation" and "refabrication" are the mental processes of embellishing on bits and pieces of facts, filling in the gaps when we have incomplete information or insufficient memories (Sousa, 2011, pp. 122–123; Wolfe, 2010, pp. 145–146). We infer how someone is feeling by looking carefully at his facial expressions and listening to the nuances of his voice. We infer the quality of a relationship between two people when we watch and hear them speak to each other. We infer someone's lifestyle when we walk into her home and assess its decor, cleanliness, and odors. We infer (i.e., predict) what might happen when certain conditions are present in an environment and our instincts alert us to possible forthcoming actions and events.

Inference-making could be likened to mind reading, for it consists of assuming what may be going through a person's mind. Inference-making could also be likened to time traveling, for it involves assuming what has happened before and what could happen in the future. Inference-making could be likened to detective work, for it entails reading visual cues and clues to deduce the current state of affairs. And inference-making could be likened to puzzle-solving in which we fill in the blanks, connect the dots, or fill in empty crossword squares. Inferring is one of the most frequently used mental operations during qualitative inquiry, since we not only document what we see and hear but also extrapolate such things as people's emotions, motives, values, attitudes, beliefs, goals, identities, statuses, and relationships from their actions and from the data by consulting comparable aspects of our own lives.

Don't confuse making an inference with rendering a judgment. The latter refers to a subjective opinion we formulate about someone's actions—actions we may or may not agree with (discussed later under "Thinking Subjectively"). **Inference** consists of applying inductive, abductive, deductive, and retroductive thinking to determine or embellish what's currently happening, has happened, or may happen. We may vehemently disapprove of what participants say and do, but those researcher reactions are separated from our straightforward reportage in analytic documentation. The primary goal of inference-making is to attempt to understand what's going through someone's mind, or to examine physical artifacts and environments to assess what they suggest about the participants and how they impact social dynamics.

Thinking inferentially is a critical attribute of the qualitative researcher, particularly during participant observation and document and artifact review. We cannot learn everything there is to know during fieldwork, and participants may not always be as forthcoming as we would like. Researchers need to fill in the blanks to uncover or construct the possible hidden meanings at play, and to read the meaning-laden nuances of social interactions. We need to exercise caution and restraint, however, lest our speculations go too far off the mark. Whenever possible, we should confirm our inferences through follow-up interview

Source: Jupiterimages/Photos.com/Thinkstock.

Figure 3.1.   Inference-making could be likened to puzzle-solving.

questions with participants, or through additional observations in the field to detect consistent patterns of action.

Bogdan and Biklen (2007) advocate the use of *observer's comments,* or *OCs,* in field notes. OCs are opportunities for the researcher to make inferences about the action just described. They are personal responses that embellish the realistic portrayal of social life. The example below illustrates an observation at a university weight room of a young man in his twenties (identified as WORK BOOTS, since these were a prominent feature of his workout clothing) and his exercise routine. The first section is an attempt to objectively document the physical actions observed. The second, italicized section is the OC, which makes inferences and attributes additional meanings to the scene and its participants:

> WORK BOOTS is still seated at the bench but the weights are on the floor. He leans back, his hands interlocked behind his head, his legs spread apart. He looks at himself in the mirror. He then looks to the side, breathes in, stretches his arms, stands, and talks to a THIN MAN next to him. WORK BOOTS picks up the same weights as before and continues his arm curls for approximately twenty "reps" (repetitions). Throughout this he looks at himself in the mirror, smiles, then grimaces his face, looks down, then looks at himself in the mirror.
>
> *OC: The man thinks he's hot. That classic leaning-back-with-your-arms-behind-your-head-legs-spread-apart pose is just too suggestive of stereotypical male sexuality ("I'm a fuckin' man"). He was checking out his muscles—the breathing in to expand his chest was a personal pleasure sensation to feel himself. The continuous looks and smiles he gives himself in the mirror make him look like an arrogant S.O.B. His self-esteem seems very high and he seems pleased with his own physical appearance.* (Saldaña, 2013, pp. 275–276)

Inference-making helps us break the surface of the reality that appears around us to delve deeper into participants' minds and the social contexts of their interactions. Through this process, we transcend the manifest (apparent) to construct and reveal the latent (hidden). It is a way of reading subtexts, decoding covert messages, and interpreting the bigger picture. Inferences are plausible attributions of meaning to actions and data for a more complete rendering of social life.

> ***For your mental Rolodex:*** As you investigate social life, infer what is hidden or implied beneath the surface of apparent words and actions.

Thinking Intuitively

Intuition is a self-perception or feeling—a seemingly unexplainable cognition of that which is hidden or of something that is about to happen. Intuition differs from instinct. The latter usually refers to some inherent trait, while the former refers to judgment based on experience.

Kahneman (2011) explains that human intuition is a "recognition" skill that is developed over time: "Valid intuitions develop when experts have learned to recognize familiar elements in a new situation and act in a manner that is appropriate to it" (p. 12). Many of us have experienced the feeling that "something isn't right," that "something's about to happen," or that "my gut is trying to tell me something." That "something" is the result of your intuition at work. And intuition is an epistemology—a way of knowing.

Intuition is all too easily discounted as a biased and unreliable researcher trait because it seems subjective and unscientific. But if intuition emerges from lived experiences and the ability to recognize familiar patterns in new contexts, it would seem to be an admirable quality necessary for investigation rather than a flawed attribute. *Thinking intuitively* is a sixth sense of sorts— the power of perceptive inference-making, coupled with the ability to reasonably predict future action based on those inferences. This is a prized skill for fieldwork—but what about intuition as a methodology?

Intuitive inquiry, as described by Rosemarie Anderson (in Wertz et al., 2011), is a five-part cyclical, **hermeneutic** process of investigation in which the inner monologic thinking and deep reflections of the researcher are documented as the data are continually reviewed. Initially, free-flowing and exploratory thoughts, ideas, daydreams, conversations, impressions, visions, memories, images, and intuitions about the phenomenon (p. 251) lead to an internal "imaginal dialogue" within the researcher. There is a holistic blending of the investigator's prior knowledge about the topic, the literature on relevant subjects, the particular data at hand, and the researcher's reflexive interplay with his or her imagination. An intuitive inquirer is urged to creatively "follow your enthusiasm and intuition. Notice what attracts your attention again and again" as cyclical analyses progress and major themes are developed (p. 253). Anderson places not just great faith but gentle validity in the researcher's ability to trust his or her impulses without being locked into or stymied by traditionally systematic qualitative approaches.

Readers of your research may be unlikely to accept your findings if you claim, "I just know" or "It just 'feels right.'" Well-documented evidence makes a strong and compelling case. But qualitative researchers use their intuition in myriad ways throughout the research endeavor; we simply don't admit it very often. We think intuitively as we reflect on an inquiry topic that hopefully will excite us, and if we're lucky enough to call the shots on what we can investigate, our final selection feels right. As we compose our preliminary questions for participant interviews, we intuitively ponder what their responses might be. When we observe social action in the field, we may intuitively predict now and then what might happen next. As we analyze our data, our minds work in systematic and strategic ways, but sometimes unexplainable impulses emerge within us—intuitive prompts that encourage us to go back to something we read earlier, to rethink and reword a category label or theme until it feels right, to reorganize our data set into a new array because our gut tells us something different might happen if we do. And as we write the report, analytic thinking continues with our intuition guiding us to the most appropriate word choices and sentence structures and predicting our readers' potential response to our work. Even audience members listening to someone's presentation will rely on their instincts and intuition to assess the credibility and trustworthiness of the speaker and the account.

Intuition has usually been categorized as a right-brain function that relies more on the impulsive hemisphere than on the logical left side. But more contemporary neurological studies may modify that belief, since research has uncovered more bilateral functions of the brain than earlier hypothesized. When it comes to relying on our own intuition, Kahneman (2011) advises us not to completely trust it, but not to dismiss it either (p. 232). Like trusting our gut, it's a process that's not difficult to explain, but difficult to rationalize to others, if not to ourselves.

> **For your mental Rolodex:** As you investigate social life, attend to your intuitive thoughts and hunches as they arise during the inquiry process. Whenever possible, assess their credibility through confirmation.

Thinking Quantitatively

We've been socialized to think quantitatively since infancy. If you held up an appropriate number of fingers when an adult asked, "How old are you?" or watched during early childhood the educational TV program *Sesame Street* with its sketches on numbers and counting, you learned numeric representation. The ubiquity of mathematics persists growing up, for the subject is taught virtually every day during the elementary and secondary education years, culminating periodically in high-stakes tests and their consequent scores. We continue with numbers and quantification throughout adulthood in our daily exchanges of money and digital transactions, in our accounting of income and expenses, and through our use of symbolic representations such as clothing sizes, phone numbers, and government-issued ID numbers.

Popular films like π [*Pi*] tout that "mathematics is the language of nature"; in *Contact,* alien cultures initially communicate with each other through numbers since mathematics is the only true "universal language."

To some social scientists who embrace **positivism**, numbers exemplify a realistic perspective. The proposed objectivity of a statistic, assuming the behavior or phenomenon it represents has been reliably and validly measured, asserts that it is an evidence-based fact. But our interpretations of those facts are laden with judgments. For example, according to a 2010 Harvard and Asian Development Bank report, 6.7% of the world's population has earned a college degree (Wilson,

Source: Medioimages/Photodisc/Thinkstock.

Figure 3.2.   Qualitative research cannot escape the occasional quantitative indicator.

2010). How you interpret that fact or infer its implications depends on your lens, filter, and angle. You might perceive it as a human capital factor that can influence the progress of a global economy, or you might perceive it as chilling evidence of the world's primarily undereducated populace. Just as reality is not always truth, numbers are not always neutral. Darrell Huff's (1954) classic text, *How to Lie With Statistics,* illustrates how numbers can be manipulated to slant the truth.

Researchers first educated in quantitative reasoning and statistical operations usually find it a bit difficult to learn about and transition into qualitative methods. Likewise, a qualitative researcher may feel somewhat intimidated by the mathematical knowledge required for the quantitative analysis of social life, often preferring language or even images as the sole media for documenting observations about human experiences. But notice how much quantification is referenced or inferred through selective word choices in the first two sentences of this paragraph: *first, usually, a bit, somewhat, often, sole.* Try as we might, qualitative research cannot escape the occasional quantitative indicator. Just as quantitative researchers rely on language to interpret the results of their statistical tests to readers, qualitative researchers, sometimes unconsciously, will suggest an amount, frequency, or magnitude now and then in their prosaic write-ups. Even our backstage fieldwork generates statistics, from the number of clock hours we spent observing to the number and length of interviews we held with a specific number of participants on specific calendar dates, all culminating in a specific number of pages of field notes and transcripts.

Mixed methods research (Creswell & Plano-Clark, 2011; Tashakkori & Teddlie, 2010) is the deliberate blending (or synthesis, comingling, integration, etc.—the field is still split on what to call it) of quantitative and qualitative methods. This research approach has an ever-growing following. Some methodologists perceive it as a natural evolutionary stage beyond the previous "paradigm wars" between opposing camps firmly entrenched in their ontological and epistemological ideologies. Others perceive it as a win-win approach with the best features of both worlds at a researcher's fingertips. And still others perceive it as an available methodology to be used on an as-needed basis when appropriate for a particular research study.

This section's purpose is not to outline mixed methods principles but to offer how to *think quantitatively* for a qualitative study. First, don't shy away from numbers or quantification in your fieldwork and write-up just because you think that qualitative research automatically discounts counting. Qualitative researchers are malleably eclectic and use a variety of techniques for their inquiries. As noted educational researcher Elliot W. Eisner said to reassure his arts-inclined audiences, "Numbers are OK." A revealing statistical fact now and then—such as Wolcott's (1973) observation that 50 to 70 cups of coffee were consumed on a typical day in the faculty lounge of an elementary school (p. 21)—can add texture to your account. McIntyre (2009) poignantly highlights the cost disparity for meals at a nursing home for the elderly through ironic comparison: "I realize that what I've paid—$4.65 with tax, for my grande tazo chai crème, my Saturday after shopping treat—is 16 cents more than our per day resident food budget." And telling me that a case study subject is "a very tall man" is not as revealing as informing me that "he stands six feet, four inches barefoot."

Second, rather than collecting statistics at the field site as a researcher, spend some time observing how the participants themselves engage with and use numbers on a daily basis. Some professions, such as education, business, and health, rely heavily on numbers in day-to-day work. Occasionally attend to the things participants count, measure, calculate, apportion, rate, rank, record, and encounter (time is a particularly critical variable for many). A very revealing statistic, if you have permission to access it, is the hourly wage or annual salary of a participant and how that influences and affects his or her lifestyle. If this information is too personal, investigate the general types of budgets participants have for work-related or life-related matters.

Third, employ magnitude coding (Miles, Huberman, & Saldaña, 2014; Saldaña, 2013), when appropriate, in your qualitative data analyses. A magnitude code is a supplemental alphanumeric or symbolic code or subcode added to an existing coded datum or category to indicate its intensity, frequency, direction, presence, or evaluative content. Magnitude codes can be qualitative, quantitative, or nominal indicators to enhance description and serve as one way of transforming or "quantitizing" qualitative data. They may consist of numbers in lieu of descriptive words to indicate intensity or frequency of a phenomenon or placement on a continuum such as weight or importance. A simple example is

3 = high, strong, excellent, etc.

2 = medium, moderate, satisfactory, etc.

1 = low, weak, poor, etc.

0 = none or not applicable

If a participant assessing her dental care provider during an interview offered the following description, the researcher might assign magnitude codes according to the 3 to 0 scale described above.

The hygienist is OK. She makes cleaning teeth as painless as possible, but there's always that scraping, which is annoying. And I have TMJ, so it hurts to have my mouth open that long for a cleaning. But, it's gotta be done, so it gets done.	CLEANING—2 [SATISFACTORY]
I knew it was necessary, but it *hurt*. No matter how much anesthetic the oral surgeon put into me, it hurt like hell. There was this infection between my two upper middle teeth, and the doctor said he could only put so much anesthetic in me to work on it. I was in agony; I wish I would have been knocked out for the procedure.	PAIN—3 [HIGH]

(Continued)

(Continued)

They gave me Peridex and this thing they nicknamed a "Christmas tree" to poke in between my teeth instead of floss-ing. I also have to use this special toothpaste which is prescrip-tion—Clinpro 5000, I think? It costs a lot, but you use just a little amount each time. I have an electric toothbrush now, and that cleans a lot better than a manual one. So, they want me to make sure I take care of my teeth this time around.

DENTAL HYGIENE—3 [EXCELLENT]

As another example, people may hold different opinions about something, but the magni-tude of each of these different opinions can vary from extremely strong to moderately con-cerned to undecided. A phone survey I once took asked me to rate the quality of service I received for a home appliance repair. The caller asked me to assign a value of 1 to 10 to my level of satisfaction with each aspect of the service she mentioned, with 10 being the highest satisfaction and 1 the lowest satisfaction. Any number equal to or less than 8 prompted the caller to ask me why I assigned that rating. Thus, the quantitative responses were cues for qualitative follow-up—a responsible way for this repair business to evaluate the quality of its services.

Now, imagine this in reverse. What if I had had an open-ended conversation as a survey and had given the caller a narrative account of my perceptions of the repair technician's service? A less-than-stellar opinion statement might have cued her to inquire, "OK, you said the appliance breakdown caused some water damage to the drywall that we did not repair, and that upset you. On a scale of one to ten, with ten being the highest satisfaction and one being the lowest satis-faction, how would you rate that part of your service?" Though the number might seem moot after my concern was verbally stated, I actually would have rated my satisfaction *lower* than I did in the first scenario because my qualitative narrative came first, framing me for a more "accurate" (from my perspective) numeric assignment. There would have been better **paradig-matic corroboration**, or, a more reliable match between the qualitative assessment and my quantitative justification for it.

Numbers are not only "OK"; numbers are critical to research. Without positivist approaches to science, we would not have the advancements in medicine and technology that we have today. As a pragmatist, I advocate researcher fluency in both qualitative and quantitative research. Knowing and practicing both is like the ability to speak two languages. But rather than being bilingual, we are **biparadigmatic**—competent to communicate using the fields' respective vocabularies and heuristic and algorithmic grammars. Qualitative researchers needn't know how to conduct sophisticated statistical processes such as multiple regression or factor and path analyses, but it is important to understand what those procedures are and how they may have qualitative equivalents (Miles et al., 2014). After all, one paradigm uses primar-ily numbers while the other uses primarily words. Just as quantitative measures and statistics are numeric, symbolic summaries of meaning (e.g., 87%, a mean score of 93.5, $p < .01$), qualitative codes, categories, and themes are language-based, symbolic summaries of textual or visual data. Both approaches seek answers in their respective ways to what are often comparable research agendas. If you're not well versed in quantitative research design and statistics, see *Quantitative Research for the Qualitative Researcher* (O'Dwyer & Bernauer, 2014) and *Statistics for People Who (Think They) Hate Statistics* (Salkind, 2013) for introductory, reader-friendly guidance.

> **For your mental Rolodex:** As you investigate social life, occasionally attend to the numbers in the field. Explore how quantitative measures and statistics play a role in participants' daily lives.

Thinking Subjectively

I've often pondered whether research is really nothing more than just getting the facts straight. But as an HLN cable TV news network promotion for its documentaries declares, "There's so much more to the story than just the facts." Subjectivity is nothing to be leery of in social research endeavors. Total objectivity is nearly impossible to achieve anyway (that's why there's no profile in this chapter labeled *Thinking Objectively*). Human beings are, well, human after all. So it seems only logical that if we wish to study the subjective world, we need to understand what **subjectivity** is all about. *Thinking subjectively* is not just pondering your participants' subjectivities, but cognizance of when your own personal feelings, opinions, biases, preferences, values, and so on, are influencing and affecting the inquiry. It is not something to be avoided completely, but it is necessary to know when it's present and, more importantly, when it's appropriate.

Subjectivity alone does not make for credible and trustworthy research. Our personal field notes can be filled with unadulterated and uncensored impressions about participants and the phenomenon under investigation. And the write-up can also reflect those first-person reactions and interpretations to some degree. Yet, depending on the research goals, readers may doubt the authority of the researcher if a too-skewed perspective, biased slant, or emotionally driven agenda emerges from the report. *Thinking critically* (see below) permits this point of view and the taking of sides after sound investigation of the facts. But subjectivity generally gives rise to wrestling over disagreement—your opinion versus the participant's.

For example, I once observed a beginning elementary school teacher and vehemently took issue with her pedagogy (Saldaña, 1997). She was a White teacher of an elective course, and her students were primarily Hispanic, inner city youth. I felt she was "dumbing down" her curriculum, as often happens at these sites, and not challenging the children and holding them to higher standards of excellence. My field notes reflected that anger when the thought first occurred to me, and my write-up initially focused on the substandard education I was witnessing. But as I continued observing this teacher's classes, my subjective reaction to her teaching clashed with the emerging facts I was documenting in my jottings. I realized that this teacher, given her novice status, the non-English-speaking children in her classroom, the gang subculture in the neighborhood, and the constraints placed upon her by the school staff, was doing the best she could in a less-than-ideal situation. In a self-confrontational and revelatory moment, I asked myself, "Could I do any better than her? If this was my class, could I reach the standards I'm expecting of her?" My subjective judgment of her ineffectiveness was my first response, but as my observations continued and my reflexivity became more honest, I realized that I had been looking at this social world through my eyes, not hers. When I acknowledged and prioritized my participants' values, attitudes, and beliefs over mine, I began seeing what was working well in the classroom—the small victories—rather than simply what was going wrong.

If you disagree with any issues arising from your study and find yourself conflicted about what you see and hear, ask yourself why. Subjectivities are not just variable—they are personal and thus reflect the identity of the individual. Just as teachers should be aware of how their subjectivities influence and affect their identities, pedagogy, and relationships with students (Wales, 2009), so too should researchers be aware of how their subjectivities influence and affect how they perceive and interact with participants and how they sway their interpretations of what they observe in the field.

Sousa (2011) differentiates between *sense* and *meaning*. Sense is what we understand; meaning is what we find relevant. If this is so, then subjective individuals will each construct their own meanings of what they personally experience. But meaning is still a slippery term to reconcile, perhaps because it is particular to each person. Noted anthropologist Claude Lévi-Strauss (1978) explains that "'to mean' means the ability of any kind of data to be translated [into] a different language" (p. 9), or rather, to use mental rules to create out of chaos a sense of order—a form of mental harmony in languages (textual, visual, symbolic, musical, etc.) that we can comprehend. Charon (2013), addressing religion's role in people's lives, proposes that to find meaning is "to *understand oneself* in relation to the universe, to find *importance* in what one is and does, and to *believe that life matters* in some way" (p. 225, emphasis in original). But that definition refers to grander concepts rooted in religion rather than daily meaning-making.

I've struggled for a long time trying to answer, "What does 'making meaning' mean?," and when I have posed that question to some rather brilliant people, even they have had trouble articulating a satisfactory response. Put simply, I define **meaning-making** as the individual's intertwined cognitive and emotional mental processing of something (a text, a piece of art, an experience, etc.) that stimulates personal interpretive relevance and generates personal understanding. Even then, I find that definition only satisfactory at best. But I take comfort in musical composer Philip Glass's anecdotal response to audiences who were mesmerized yet nonetheless confused by director Robert Wilson's staging of his landmark opera, *Einstein on the Beach:* "It's not important that you understand what something means; what's important is that you understand that something has meaning" (Obenhaus, 1985). That quote both makes sense and makes meaning for me.

As mentioned earlier, the write-up of research is an act of persuasion. And readers can be persuaded (i.e., convinced) that your report is a credible one with a proper balance of realism and subjectivity. Facts alone can make a case, but facts and feelings can make a stronger impact on a reader's meaning-making. In a way, all research is subjective, for it is developed from a particular person's point of view. The obligation for researchers, then, is to conduct themselves and their work in such a way as to persuade their audiences that they have undertaken their jobs in good faith. Trustworthy researchers will, yes, present the facts, but they will also tell their readers through confessional narratives about the ethical and moral dilemmas they faced during the project and how or whether they've been reconciled.

For your mental Rolodex: As you investigate social life, reflect on your subjectivities as a researcher, particularly when disagreement arises between you and the participants' actions. Investigate participants' subjectivities to understand how they make sense and how the participants make meaning of their experiences.

Thinking Critically

Thinking critically does not mean complaining about something, but rather exposing a social inequity or injustice that merits public knowledge and action for righting the wrong. Thinking critically is deliberately taking sides on a social and moral issue. It is investigation into the conditions that currently exist and questioning why they aren't or couldn't be better for the general population or for a marginalized, oppressed group of people. Critical thinking examines the status quo from multiple lenses, filters, and angles to ask *how come, what if,* and *why not.*

Some of the key figures of qualitative research have recently adopted not just a scientific but a moral and emancipatory stance toward inquiry (Denzin & Lincoln, 2011). The projects we undertake are no longer about objective, dispassionate fieldwork and neutral reportage, but about making social life better through constructive and positive change by, with, and for participants (Stringer, 2014). Researchers become engaged with the communities they study and adopt a collaborative rather than authoritative stance with their members. Participatory action research empowers constituents with agency over their social environment, for their "street science" knowledge is just as valid as an academician's theories (Hacker, 2013).

Thinking critically doesn't access particular sections of the brain, but it does depend on the thinker's ability to recognize unproductive patterns of action, to infer people's agendas and motives, to reflect on personal morals in relationship to others, and to sympathize and empathize with people in distress. A broad base of human experiences, coupled with aptitudes for skepticism, resistance, and a sense of justice, help trigger the awareness necessary for formulating alternative plans of thought and action. Thinking critically is a higher-level cognitive function because it taps into the *evaluative* dimension of interpreting life around us. Though all researchers should employ critical thinking, it is a particularly essential filter for feminist research, discourse analysis, queer theory, multicultural research, action research projects, and, of course, critical theory.

The development of critical thinking skills in young students is touted in many educational programs as a highly desired outcome, though various definitions of and approaches to critical thinking skills exist. Yet, even this seemingly admirable goal has its detractors. The conservative 2012 Texas Republican Party platform issued a statement on a forthcoming *Knowledge-Based Education* program in its schools:

> We oppose the teaching of Higher Order Thinking Skills (HOTS) (values clarification), critical thinking skills and similar programs that are simply a relabeling of Outcome-Based Education (OBE) (mastery learning) which focus on behavior modification and have the purpose of challenging the student's fixed beliefs and undermining parental authority.

Ironically, this position set off a volley of critical thinking reactions from selected respondents who took issue with the party's "mind control" tactics. (It was later reported by the Texas Republican Party that their statement was taken out of context, which generated even more critical thinking toward the follow-up.) Though we want students to be competent enough to critically examine literature and the arts, the most fertile disciplines for enhancing critical thought are hot button areas such as politics and government, religion, the social order (economics, poverty, violence, etc.), and multicultural issues centered on gender, race and ethnicity, sexual orientation, and so on. Even the most basic of dyadic relationships (e.g., best friends, spouses, parent and child) can trigger critical thinking about interpersonal issues of power, status, and negotiation.

Thinking critically also involves playing the devil's advocate for yourself and your analyses. Once you've formulated an inference, assertion, proposition, or theory, you interrogate the claim by rigorously seeking disconfirming evidence or thinking through another plausible, alternative explanation. Thinking critically also entails maintaining a critical stance toward what you read from colleagues as you evaluate the credibility and trustworthiness of the researcher's work. I recall a vignette about a university program that brought in distinguished guest speakers each week for a particular class. Students were instructed to read the key writings of the presenter and to be prepared to ask questions and debate the speaker by giving reasons why his or her work was "totally wrong." Though this may have been a tough exchange for the guest, I could understand the purpose of the exercise: to help students avoid being clouded by others' celebrity status and encourage them to critically interrogate what they were reading.

Be cautious of knee-jerk and first-impression reactions to an issue. This is particularly critical if we use the Internet as a primary source for our information. As a democratic forum for people's voices, the Internet gives virtually everyone who has electronic access the ability to post content. But some of that information may be inaccurate or falsified. One of the most amusing memes in recent years has been a mock quote:

> These days, it's hard to trust the credibility of anything posted on the Internet.
>
> —Abraham Lincoln

Even televised media admit that initial broadcast reports of breaking news stories may contain factual errors because their sources of information are incomplete and sometimes speculative. There are also intentional slants toward particular ideologies and political parties in selected U.S. cable news networks, rendering the concept of "objective reportage" an outdated notion.

The best critical thinking arises from sound and thorough research of the "facts" (and I set the word in quotation marks because there are different conceptions of truth out there). Barbara Ehrenreich's (2001) book *Nickel and Dimed: On (Not) Getting By in America* remains one of the best examples of investigative reporting on the social and economic fallout of a minimum wage workforce in the United States. Ehrenreich relies not just on government statistics and sociological theories, but on carefully documented personal experiences of living and working as a minimum wage earner herself for several months. The poignant accounts of her financial and emotional struggles lay a solid foundation for her insightful critical analysis in the final chapter. Her case rests on compelling and convincing evidence, according her the right to harshly judge the avaricious actions of big business and an indifferent government and their impact on society.

Critical thinking can result in not just a report but a manifesto—an extended narrative about one's opinions, policies, and goals. The academic journal article is no longer just a social scientific description of the facts but an op-ed piece, an autoethnographic confession, a social satire, and even a rant. Though there's still much value in answering *how, what,* and *why,* sometimes there is an urgent need to address issues and solve problems by asking *how come, what if,* and *why not* questions. Thinking critically is thinking twice: The first time, it's decoding what your senses interpret; the second time, it's evaluating your mental responses to the stimuli. Andrew Abbott (2004) proposes this heuristic for thinking critically: "Every argument, every generalization, every background assumption that you run into, should be scanned with this simple check: Is that really true? Could I get somewhere by regarding this as a problem rather than as something taken for granted?" (p. 126).

For your mental Rolodex: As you investigate social life, maintain a critical lens, filter, and angle on what you observe at all times. Assess truth value cautiously and propose alternative ways of improving the world.

CLOSURE

The lenses, filters, and angles discussed in this chapter encourage you not to accept everything at face value. The thinking modalities profiled above deal with truth in its various manifestations. To some, truth is what we sensorially experience. To others, it's what we infer and interpret about the reality we experience. Some place more truth value on numbers, while others prioritize subjective feelings and intuitions as inescapably genuine and meaningful. Facts, truth, sense, and meaning, though, are mental and social constructions. Thus, each person and each culture will employ its own heuristics and maintain its own standards for determining what is real and true. You needn't spend sleepless nights puzzled by ontological and epistemological mysteries. There are more immediate and important things to worry about. Keep it real.

EXERCISES FOR THINKING REALISTICALLY

1. Define and discuss the following concepts separately: *reality, truth, meaning, fact,* and *number.*

2. Review an interview transcript and mark those passages where you believe the participant may have been insincere, lying, in denial, "performing," putting up a false front, or hiding something from the interviewer. Document what you infer may actually have been going through the participant's mind during those passages.

3. Observe a general-purpose public setting (e.g., a mall, a park, a bus, a street with foot traffic; not a purpose-specific setting such as a restaurant, office, or school classroom), and infer why people are there, what they may be thinking, their biographical backgrounds, and so on.

4. Write out on a sheet of paper a list of numbers in descending order, with 10 at the top and 1 at the bottom. Assign words or phrases to the numbers that qualitatively correlate with each value in regard to one of these constructs: *happiness, love,* or *pain.* For example, if a 10 is "agonizing" pain and a 1 is "barely noticeable" pain, what words will you assign to numbers 2 through 9? Use a thesaurus and dictionary for guidance, and see Hakel's article "How Often Is Often?" (1968) for a short yet intriguing discourse about the slipperiness of language when it comes to describing quantities.

5. Select a hot button social issue (e.g., abortion, gay marriage, immigration). Compose a one- to two-page manifesto or rant expressing your genuine opinions on the issue. Then write a one- to two-page manifesto or rant as someone with an opposing perspective on the same issue might compose it.

Thinking Symbolically

LEARNING OBJECTIVES AND SUMMARY

- Your mind will reflect on ways to condense and consolidate information.
- Your mind will transcend from realistic to symbolic modes of thought.

This chapter explores deeper thinking by reflecting on representational modes for social life. These methods of mind consist of

- Thinking Symbolically
- Thinking Conceptually
- Thinking Abstractly
- Thinking Capsulely
- Thinking Metaphorically
- Thinking Phenomenologically

The purpose of this chapter is not to discuss the multifaceted details of symbolic representation or their utilization in, for example, semiotics, but to heighten your awareness of their possible applications for qualitative inquiry.

Thinking Symbolically

Symbols and their related variants (concepts, metaphors, etc.) are human constructions and condensed attributions of specific associations, memories, and meanings. They consolidate various properties into a single representative entity. The function of a symbol can range from practical utility (e.g., shorthand) to maintenance (of customs and traditions) to aesthetic achievement (in literature and the arts). Symbolizing may be our brain's way of creating order and making meaning from disparate pieces of information. It consolidates various parts into a significant whole. If the symbol is a tangible object, something we can actually see, it is retained longer in our memory store. But the symbol is meaningless without some type of association to it—for example, a memory, an analogy, a person, or a story.

A symbol is an essentialized "something" that represents something else larger. A flag may represent or symbolize a nation. In Nathaniel Hawthorne's masterwork, *The Scarlet Letter,* Hester Prynne's symbolic "A" on her bosom represents the stigma of adultery. A dangerous carnival ride in a dream may symbolize the dreamer's sense of chaos and lack of control in daily life. Science relies on symbols such as Fe and Cu for iron and copper, respectively, on the periodic table of elements. Mathematics employs numerals and other figures such as β and $\leq$. And don't forget that words themselves are symbols. Every sentence we read and write is an intricate symbol system of meaning.

Symbolic representations imbue qualitative research. One- or two-word codes symbolize the meanings of larger passages of data. A matrix of qualitative data contains condensed analytic summaries in its cells, representing or symbolizing the patterns and larger phenomena of social life observed during fieldwork. And Angrosino (1994) learned that a developmentally disabled adult male's drawing of a heart (replicated from a logo painted on the side of a city bus) symbolized for the participant not love but aspiration, independence, and status. Riding the bus represented luxurious freedom from walking all the time. The lessons here are that symbolic attributions can be particular to each person, that symbols contain significant and meaningful memories and stories, and that symbolism is contextual. The white rose, for example, means something different depending on whether it's used at a wedding, at a funeral, on Mother's Day, in *The Hunger Games* films, or as a Valentine's Day gift (see Figure 4.1).

From technology, the visual icon has become a prominent feature of most people's lives. The "f" of Facebook, the "t" and bird of Twitter, and the "swoosh" of Nike are well recognized globally. They are eye-catching and ubiquitous symbols of something greater. Imagine if your field site or

Source: Polka Dot Images/Polka Dot/Thinkstock.

Figure 4.1.   The white rose evokes various symbolic meanings.

even key participants had their own customized icons. How would you represent or symbolize them visually? Which emoticon best symbolizes their general temperament? Your ability to capture the totality of something into an essentialized form is a higher-level analytic if not creative act.

Thinking symbolically is a necessary method of mind that serves several purposes:

- It enhances your ability to distill, condense, and summarize the massive qualitative and quantitative databases you accumulate into more manageable and salient representations.
- It stimulates your creativity by making analogous connections between social life and other domains of experience.
- It encourages you to transcend the reality of your observations to develop more evocative presentational forms.
- It represents and presents the salient features of your research study in more elegant and accessible ways for your readership.
- It permits possible transferability of your specific and local fieldwork observations to more general applications.

The following methods of mind profile other modalities of symbolic representation for qualitative inquiry: *thinking conceptually, abstractly, capsulely* (an invented word), *metaphorically,* and *phenomenologically.*

> **For your mental Rolodex:** As you investigate social life, look for actions, artifacts, roles, routines, rituals, and so on that seem to symbolize something larger, either to you or to your participants. Attribute symbolic properties to core items in your study, or generate original symbolic representations of selected key aspects.

Thinking Conceptually

A **concept** is word or short phrase that symbolically represents a suggested meaning broader than a single item or action—a bigger-picture idea beyond the tangible and apparent. A concept is something you literally cannot touch; thus, it suggests an idea rather than an object. For example, a wristwatch is something you can touch, but its higher-level or bigger-picture meaning is the concept of *time*. The "touch test" is a heuristic for transcending the reality of what you can experience with your senses to develop an entity with more magnitude. For example, I can touch a church building, but I cannot touch the concept of *religion*. I can touch and smell a red rose, but I cannot touch (or smell) the concept of *romance*. And I can internally think and feel assured that a good friend will repay a small loan I gave him, but I cannot physically touch my *trust*. A smartphone is a handheld device, but it's also *technology*. McDonald's is not just a fast-food restaurant; its building and golden arches represent a *corporation*. Note that these concepts are nouns.

Concepts also refer to observable actions—processes—and their bigger-picture or broader meanings. For example, you can see me brushing my teeth and gargling with mouthwash, but in the bigger scheme of things I'm *maintaining oral health*. I can watch a pianist pressing down white and black keys expertly on a keyboard, but what she's also doing is *making music*. I could take it a step further by saying she's *expressing her artistic sensibilities* or *creating art*. I once bought a $25 gift card for an eight-year-old girl's birthday, and I jokingly mused that I wasn't just buying her a birthday present (the observable action), but *indoctrinating youth into consumer culture* (the concept). For some, visiting Starbucks five mornings a week isn't just about purchasing coffee (an observable action), but a means of *performing a morning ritual, maintaining a workday habit,* or *feeding an addiction*. Note that these concept phrases begin with gerunds— "-ing" words—to describe broader processes at work.

Some use the terms *concept* and *construct* (as nouns) interchangeably, yet to others there are subtle differences between the two. For example, is the human soul a concept or a construct? What about consciousness? To some individuals, the soul and consciousness are constructs because they are ideas or phenomena whose constituent elements cannot be observed and thus proven to exist. I won't split hairs here or develop artificial and fluid differentiations between the two terms. I will simply use *concept* as my term of choice for this modality of thinking. Familiar concepts these days include *emotional labor, fighting terrorism,* and *legislating morality.*

Thinking conceptually in qualitative research means inferring how single or patterned instances of social action, or a field site's architecture (in its broadest sense) and artifacts, represent or symbolize broader, bigger-picture ideas—concepts. We conceptualize in order to transcend the local and particular of what we study to find possible applicability and transferability to more general settings and contexts. We also conceptualize to discover possible hidden meanings and deeper significance embedded in our everyday lives. If I observe kindergarten students lining up for lunch and recess in an elementary school classroom at precisely the same times and in exactly the same ways every day, I am watching actions suggesting the concept of *classroom management* at work, or witnessing a teacher who is conceptually, in the broader social scheme of things as a process, *regimenting young lives* or *instilling obedience.*

Concepts become essential building blocks for theory development. Once the concepts are labeled and defined to represent broader phenomena, they can be integrated into statements that suggest general applicability. For example, sociologist Joel M. Charon (2013) describes the concept of *destructive social conflict* as "governed by anger and hostility. . . . The other side is seen as the enemy, anger and a desire to hurt or destroy others are encouraged, and escalation to violence is common" (p. 323). *Constructive social conflict,* however, is characterized by negotiation and compromise for achievement and change: "People's interests are heard, and real problems are identified and dealt with" (p. 322). These two concepts are brought together to put forth the theory that *"destructive conflict partly arises when constructive conflict is discouraged or ignored and real differences and problems are neither faced nor resolved"* (p. 165, emphasis in original). Charon then explains and illustrates the dynamics of how these conceptual ideas are made manifest in humans, later noting that an important source of destructive conflict is another concept: *social inequality.*

A concept is somewhat comparable to a category's function. It is a label for an assemblage of comparable and patterned actions, reactions, and interactions. But whereas a category could consist of an observable process or something perceived (e.g., rejecting membership, hate speech), a concept—like social inequality—is broader in scope and intangible in sensory terms. Concepts are ideas that bring together and embody related realities.

For your mental Rolodex: As you progress through your fieldwork observations and data analyses, think of the bigger picture at work. Explore how you can conceptualize key artifacts and actions to transcend from the local to the general.

Thinking Abstractly

Most of us are familiar with the term *abstract* as a prefacing summary of a longer work, such as a paragraph-length abstract for a journal article or a one- to two-page abstract for a thesis or dissertation. Others might use the term for a work of modern art that presents an expressionistic interpretation of reality (see Figure 4.2). Still others use the term to refer to something that is not actual but instead a figurative representation (e.g., "I'm referring to *place* in the abstract."). What these different meanings seem to have in common is that an abstract is something apart yet derived from something else.

When you enter someone else's home for the first time, you'll naturally look around at the decor and might find one item in particular that stands out and strikes you as intriguing. It motivates you to ask the owner more about it. This knickknack or piece of art that caught your eye becomes a conversation piece—something that generates a series of questions and answers or a brief discussion about its unique qualities. Perhaps there's an intriguing history and story to its acquisition. Comparably, an abstract in qualitative research functions not just as a prefacing summary, but also as a conversation piece you present to the reader or listener. This conversation piece doesn't contain the entire story of your study, but it consists of one or more items that merit a brief discussion because they hold intriguing properties worth mentioning.

Thinking abstractly in qualitative research develops something separate from some component of your work, such as the field notes or the data analysis process or an idiosyncratic event of some kind. This separate item, be it a written summary, diagram, or narrative vignette, is a small piece that can stand on its own yet originates from the totality of your study. It doesn't necessarily have to summarize; it reveals a facet of the work that holds interest and has something to say. It is not a tangent—it is, for lack of better

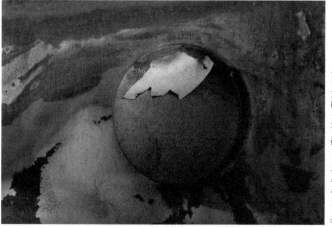

Source: Jupiterimages/Stockbyte/Thinkstock.

Figure 4.2. *Abstract* can refer to a style of visual art.

phrases, a significant footnote or an intriguing sidebar or boxed example with a small nugget of rich insight.

As an example, I adapted and dramatized for the stage the fieldwork of homeless youth conducted by Susan and Macklin Finley (1999; M. Finley, 2000) to create the ethnodrama *Street Rat* (Saldaña, Finley, & Finley, 2005). One of the main characters of the ethnography and the play was Roach, a young man with a "bad boy" edge who survived by his street smarts in pre-Katrina New Orleans. I remained faithful to Finley and Finley's data by adapting verbatim dialogue from their sources. Whatever became of the actual Roach was unknown, according to the researchers. But three years later when I taught an arts workshop in Baton Rouge, approximately 75 miles away from New Orleans, I struck up a conversation with the janitor of the complex that hosted the classes. He was in his late twenties or early thirties, appeared to have led a hard life, and had a slightly "badass" edge to him. As I spoke with him, it occurred to me that some of the phrases he used in our conversation ("The cops around here are fuckin' evil," "All's I gotta do is walk through it") were the *exact* same lines of dialogue documented almost a decade earlier by the Finleys in their ethnographic fieldwork and adapted into my ethnodrama. I was stunned by the realization that, serendipitously, I may have been talking with the real Roach.

That was an example of an abstract—a conversation piece that constitutes one small facet of the whole study but not the central part of it. These portraits in miniature are anecdotal, to some, yet can make an impact on the reader's memory because of their novelty and intrigue. Abstracts are brief yet meaningful moments of data that possess alluring properties. Sometimes a small detail, rather than a lengthy experience, captures our attention and stays with us.

For your mental Rolodex: When you complete your study, develop a traditional narrative abstract that summarizes the story of your research and its major findings. But as you progress through your fieldwork, look for interesting conversation pieces that derive from yet stand apart from the study and will make for potentially intriguing discussions.

Thinking Capsulely

A **capsule** contains something; it holds important contents necessary for other functions once the capsule is broken open—e.g., medication, seeds, historic artifacts. The capsule as container usually has its own label that identifies the contents (e.g., "Tamsulosin," "polysaccharide envelope," "1950 Time Capsule"). It is the labeling that is relevant here.

Newspaper headlines not only summarize the primary content of the article, but they also attempt to grab the reader's attention and interest her or him in reading the full story (e.g., "Homeless shelter faces closure"). Captions under pictures identify the individuals and the scene, yet sometimes they provide context to the photo and even subjective or ironic commentary (e.g., "Runaway teenager 'Gina' and her one-year-old child face an uncertain future on the streets"). In both cases, headlines and captions make summative statements about something larger. Selected newspapers quoted key phrases from U.S. President Barack Obama's 2009 and 2013 inaugural addresses as their headlines ("Hope Over Fear," "We Are Made for This Moment"), capsulizing the optimistic tone of the administration.

A title for a book, article, magazine, film, TV program, play, poem, song, or other work is an identifying, summarizing, and preferably evocative marker for the total piece. A book title can be as descriptive as *Learning About Spices for Cooking* or as fanciful as *Spice It Up in the Kitchen!* Each of these two books can contain exactly the same narratives and recipes, but each title suggests something different and evokes a particular feeling for what the reading experience may be like. Some titles and their works have become canonized or so popular that many people automatically know or know about the piece: *Romeo and Juliet, The Wizard of Oz, Fifty Shades of Grey.* In some cases, the font style and visual artwork for the title reinforce or support the contents. Men's fitness and bodybuilding magazines, for example, tend to display their titles in large, bold, and often capitalized and slanted letters that look hypermasculine, active, and aggressive to the eye. Black and red are prominent colors throughout these publications.

Thinking capsulely is reflecting on a significant portion of or all the content, meaning, or themes from the data or field experiences and labeling, headlining, captioning, or titling them. The label, headline, caption, or title captures a holistic impression of the larger body and symbolizes the essence of the contents. Sometimes these markers can derive from or serve as categories and themes developed from data analysis. A significant phrase or quote from a participant that seems to sum up the gist of the entire case or study can also function as a caption that works its way into the write-up as a heading or subheading, frontispiece, or subtitle.

For example, Bogdan and Biklen (2007) recommend giving each day's set of field notes a title that captures the spirit of the experience for the researcher or participants: "Orientation to the Field Site," "Power Plays," "The Day From Hell." Saldaña (2013) recommends that each analytic memo composed by a researcher also be assigned a subtitle that captures the content and general spirit of the analysis: "Patterns: Putting Out Fires," "Themes: New Guard vs. Old Guard." Kuckartz (2014) advises that each interview transcript be truncated into a short case summary— a simple bullet-pointed list of topics and content addressed by the participant—accompanied by a "motto," or a phrase that identifies the interview's overall tone or the participant's general persona, such as "A Rough Day at a Rough Job," "An Optimistic Outlook on Life," or a unique participant quote from the transcript that encapsulates a significant theme or idea ("When You Don't Believe in God, Luck Is the Next Best Thing").

Photos taken at the field site should not only be content-analyzed but evocatively captioned as part of the analysis. A daily blog or journal entry about the fieldwork might also be headlined as if it were a newsletter or newspaper story. Even the title for the entire study can evolve as it progresses and new findings emerge. In fact, *design* the cover page and title of your study as if it were a magazine or book cover's artwork. Create a home page for your study on the web with visual elements that capture the qualities of your field site and data analysis.

These capsule representations of the inquiry are not just isolated, arts-based exercises. They can be assembled and reviewed for any discernible patterns or themes. They can also be clustered into similar groupings so that noteworthy categories can be detected. Since everyone has her or his own story to tell, consider how different participants might label the same event differently, depending on their individual perspectives. An employee might see a token cost-of-living pay raise after years of dedicated effort as "an insult to my loyalty," while the employer might see the raise as "a fair and equitable reward" given to each member of the staff. Simple, descriptive summaries are fine as starters, but don't be afraid to extend your creativity by assigning attention-grabbing and provocative labels to the phenomena.

For your mental Rolodex: As you progress through your fieldwork, label, headline, caption, and title or subtitle larger chunks of data and experiences into capsules.

Thinking Metaphorically

A **metaphor** is traditionally a literary device, "comparing two things via their similarities and ignoring their differences. . . . Metaphors are thus a partial abstraction" (Miles, Huberman, & Saldaña, 2014, p. 281). For example, we might say that a faculty lounge creates an "oasis" for a teacher—a place where he can relax and refresh himself before returning to his classroom and students. The metaphor of a "maelstrom" may be used by an evaluator to suggest the workplace turbulence observed among employees in a large, dysfunctional organization. The home of a continually bickering couple might be called a "war zone" because it is a place of constant conflict and fighting. Even people can be assigned metaphors; perhaps you know someone whose personality reminds you of a "rock" or a "bear." Some might refer to a brave elementary classroom teacher as a "lioness" protecting her "cubs" (children) in her "den" (classroom). Lakoff and Johnson's (1980) classic text, *Metaphors We Live By,* is an indispensable reference for this topic.

Thinking metaphorically, primarily but not exclusively a right-brained skill, in qualitative research attunes you to how participants themselves use metaphors in their everyday interactions and in interviews to describe their experiences. In one of my qualitative survey studies about the lifelong impact of high school theatre on future adulthood (McCammon, Saldaña, Hines, & Omasta, 2012), several former students referred to *theatre as a parent* and *themselves as its developing children.* Survey respondents used phrases such as "born a theatre person" and "it's in your blood," describing how theatre "created me," "made me," "pushed me," "shaped me," "developed me," "made me blossom," or "opened me up." Metaphors can also be formulated by the researcher during fieldwork and analytic work to crystallize observations of phenomena—for example, a university may be perceived as a "business" or "factory machine" assembling student "products."

You may have noticed that some of the examples above were technically not metaphors but similes. We were taught in our literature courses that the literary device of simile uses *like* or *as* for its comparisons. Some of the more famous similes are "You're as cold as ice" and "You lived your life like a candle in the wind." Some may debate whether a metaphor or simile is the better device to use for writing, but they both serve the same purpose in the end: a comparison of something actual to an evocative referent. Either can work well for qualitative inquiry. Other comparable literary devices to consider and employ are *analogy* (in which two different things are noted to resemble or associate with each other), *synecdoche* (in which specific instances are linked to a larger concept), and *metonymy* (in which the whole is represented in terms of one or more of its parts).

Metaphors and similes might arise in your mind as you observe social life, your own personal memories and experiences are triggered, and similarities become apparent—that is, as something reminds you of something else. For example, a field site might look like a "prison" or feel like a "zoo." Metaphors and similes may also formulate in your mind as you're reviewing and analyzing data, particularly during classification tasks. The comparability of a certain cluster of codes (e.g., FAMILIARITY, FRIENDSHIP, SUPPORT, OPENNESS, INTIMACY) could stimulate a category label that is not just summative but metaphoric in nature: *family.* The literary devices also serve to represent the primary or central image of a study that captures the essence of the case or phenomenon. The classroom teacher as *juggler,* forced to keep many balls in the air simultaneously through expert, focused, and continuous action, is one example.

Metaphors and similes can enhance your readers' understanding by making the local and particular more generalizable, or at least comprehensible. The literary devices kick your study up a notch by venturing into the aesthetic realms of analysis. By comparing one thing with another, you engage in synthesis and creativity—two higher functions of cognitive processing. Your representation and presentation of metaphors and similes in your research demonstrate your ability to make connections within and among various domains of social life, so long as the connections and comparisons are logical, plausible, and evocative.

> **For your mental Rolodex:** As you collect data from your participants, make note of how they use metaphors and similes in everyday discourse or during interviews. Also explore how you as the researcher can construct metaphors and similes of the social phenomena you observe. Assign metaphors and similes to key participants.

Thinking Phenomenologically

A phenomenon actually represents something experienced by the senses, but the term has evolved in qualitative inquiry and in its subfield of study, **phenomenology**, to mean the description of lived experiences—the essences and essentials of experiential states, natures of being, and personally significant meanings of concepts such as *belonging, fatherhood, grief,* and *spirituality.* Generally, a form of "mean" can be included in the initiating research question to frame the inquiry: "What does it mean 'to belong'?" "What is the meaning of 'spirituality'?" Sometimes the inquiry can be descriptively driven: "What does 'grief' consist of?" The wording of questions should be considered carefully, for there are subtle differences between the inquiries, "What is a 'father'?" "What does it mean to be a 'father'?" and "What are the lived experiences of 'fatherhood'?" Notice that all of these questions begin with "what." Though not absolutely required, *what* questions seem to harmonize best with the goals of phenomenology. And asking "What is . . . /are . . . " questions takes us deeper into inquiries about states and natures of being.

Phenomenology asks you to set aside (or bracket) your own perceptions and experiences of the phenomenon you're studying and to see it from the participants' points of view. Thus, it calls upon your capacities to decenter your own values system and worldview, to listen to others carefully, and to empathize. It demands the ability to strategically and improvisationally construct finely tuned questions, for it is often difficult for people to articulate clearly what something is or means to them. It also requires your ability to review the database to detect similar experiences across a range of participants in order to construct patterns and, most importantly, the essences and essentials of the phenomenon—the "bottom line," "bare necessities," or "must-haves" that define it. Adams (2011), in his exemplary research of coming out for lesbians and gays, lists seven "conditions" that he constructed from autoethnographic reflections, interviews about others' experiences, and the research literature about the phenomenon of "the closet," or keeping one's nonheterosexuality hidden. One of these conditions summarizes the origins of such secrecy: "The closet begins to form when a person realizes that a marginal and devalued attraction or identity may encounter negative criticism from others *if discussed*" (p. 51, emphasis in original).

Though coding data is certainly one way to closely examine them, phenomenological analysis may be better served through the construction of themes—statements and theoretical constructs that provide a more narrative grounding to the story of lived experience (see *Thinking Thematically* in Chapter 2). Themes permit the articulation of meanings that a single word or short phrase may not be able to embody or evoke. For example, as I approach retirement and reflect on it with colleagues who are also retiring, one commonality to our experiences I've observed is "lasts." But without explication, the word alone does not advance anyone's understanding of what it means to approach retirement. Thus, a thematic statement, or the phrasing of the term as a theoretical construct, better serves the analysis:

- *Theme:* Impending retirement means noting "the last time" work-related tasks are being performed. [The accompanying narrative illustrates types of "lasts" and further describes the related mental and emotional interplay, such as "accomplishment closure" and "nostalgic regret."]
- *Theoretical construct:* Impending retirement as *calibrated finality.* [This construct is composed of the thematic statement above plus other related themes, such as counting the remaining days left to work, feeling unmotivated to work due to feelings of "senioritis," and avoiding commitment to long-term tasks.]

Thinking phenomenologically in qualitative research is not just for phenomenological studies. It is heightened attunement to the phenomena of what you're exploring. Peel away the complexity and unnecessary details to get at the core meanings of what you're investigating. Rather than composing a lengthy narrative, first bullet-point the essential constituent elements of the "thing" you're studying. What *must* be present for the phenomenon to exist? The phenomenon of *home* doesn't always require a physical dwelling—to some, home is a particular city; to others, it's being in the company of a specific cultural community of people. But what links or connects these various ideas is the central idea: *Home means feeling that you belong somewhere.* Madden (2010), reflecting on the meanings of home, conceptualized and assembled the following list: Home is familiar, parochial, discrete, habitual, permanent, birth, death, and ambivalence—the last referring to "a place I felt the need to leave, and to which I need to return" (pp. 45–46). See Brinkmann (2012); J. A. Smith, Flowers, and Larkin (2009); Van Manen (1990); and Wertz et al. (2011) for more on phenomenological analysis.

For your mental Rolodex: As you progress through your fieldwork, occasionally "press the pause button" on the action you're observing and reflect on the nature of your topic and the states of being and lived experiences of the participants. Think of what it means to be who they are and what they do in daily life. Summarize those meanings into as few bullet-pointed phrases or sentences as possible.

CLOSURE

Thinking symbolically condenses vast arrays of qualitative data about social life into more elegant forms of representation and presentation. As you progress through fieldwork, keep a sharp eye and ear out for details that seem to hold special significance for the participants or for you as a researcher. When appropriate, assign symbols, concepts, abstracts, capsules, metaphors/similes, and phenomenological interpretations that transcend your data yet remain firmly rooted in them.

Our information-laden world today bombards us with massive amounts of data that our brains cannot fully process. I recall a factoid that the average person encounters approximately 3,000 attempts each day to capture her or his attention through the barrage of print and media advertising, signage, people's voices, and so on. I may not have time to read an entire newspaper, but I can turn the pages quickly to scan its headlines. And I can't review every single article in the numerous journals to which I subscribe, but I'll take the time to read an issue's abstracts to assess whether an article's contents capture my interest and merit a full reading. These days, qualitative researchers must learn how to accompany their stories with economical and attention-arresting symbol systems to better guarantee the notice and readership or viewership of their work, and the retention of ideas in their audience's minds.

EXERCISES FOR THINKING SYMBOLICALLY

1. Brainstorm all the metaphors and similes you've heard about *life* (e.g., "Life is a dream," "Life is like a roller coaster ride," "Life is hell"). Unpack the connotations of each through writing or discussion—for example, what is inferred or suggested by the simile, "Life is like a box of chocolates" (aside from "You never know what you're going to get")?

2. Go through your immediate personal possessions (e.g., backpack, purse, wallet) or your living space, and select three and only three tangible items that you feel best symbolize your life at this particular point in time. Write or explain to another why you selected these three items and what these symbols represent or suggest about you and your values, attitudes, and beliefs. (If you are currently involved in fieldwork, ask your case study subject or a key participant to go through this exercise and interview her or him about the three choices, if appropriate.)

3. Visit a newsstand or bookstore and survey the titles in a section of books, magazines, or other print materials. What thoughts and feelings are evoked within you as you read just the titles? What do you infer that the content and tone of the publication will be like based on its cover art? Scan the publication after you've reflected on its title and cover and assess whether your assumptions and preconceptions may have been correct.

4. Do this next exercise with a partner. Each of you will develop a list of three simple, realistic actions or things that can be pantomimed for the other. One partner performs the action for the other, and an exchange of ideas is improvisationally given for transcending from the actual to the conceptual. The first conceptual idea offered should be a *gerund-based process* (an "-ing" word or phrase), and the second idea offered should be a *noun or noun phrase*. Here's an example:

Partner 1:   [pantomimes eating a slice of pizza]

Partner 2:   What are you doing?

Partner 1:   I'm eating pizza.

Partner 2:   No, you're not, you're fueling your body.

Partner 1:   That's right, this is sustenance.

*   *   *

Partner 2:   [pantomimes brushing her hair]

Partner 1:   What are you doing?

Partner 2:   I'm brushing my hair.

Partner 1:   No, you're not, you're grooming.

Partner 2:   That's right, this is impression management.

*   *   *

Partner 1:   [pantomimes throwing a ball in the air and hitting it with a tennis racket]

Partner 2:   What are you doing?

Partner 1:   I'm playing tennis.

Partner 2:   No, you're not, you're competing.

Partner 1:   That's right, this is a friendly challenge.

(Continue for three more exchanges.)

Thinking Ethically

LEARNING OBJECTIVES AND SUMMARY

- Your mind will reflect on your moral and emotional capacities for action and analysis.
- Your mind will acknowledge the desired interpersonal and intrapersonal qualities for social inquiry.

This chapter reflects on the introspective qualities of thought that deal with the ethical and moral landscape of human experience:

- Thinking Ethically
- Thinking Emotionally
- Thinking Empathetically
- Thinking Darkly
- Thinking Spiritually

The purpose of this chapter is to attune readers to the emotional dimensions of being human—the pervasive and necessary conditions for truly understanding how others and oneself think and feel.

Thinking Ethically

Ethics are a set of personal principles for intrapersonal action and interpersonal conduct, rooted in obligatory codes and the individual's value, attitude, and belief systems. These principles can be shaped by cultural upbringing and socialization, adherence and acquiescence to laws and regulations, and personal motives and goals for living. Gobo (2008) clarifies that "morals are concerned with a set of customs which orient our behavior in public and private places, while ethics concerns customs that regulate behavior in the professional sphere" (p. 136).

To many, ethics consist of "doing the right thing." But the right thing to one person may be the wrong thing to another; and the right thing in one particular circumstance may be the wrong thing in a different situation and context. Abortion to one person may be perceived as a woman's right to choose what she does privately with her own body. To another person, abortion may be perceived as an act of murder and a violation of his religious beliefs. The debate over this issue plays out in public rallies, demonstrations, and protests, with more official decision-making and resolution taking place in our courts. But legal one-upmanship over the issue also plays out in our legislative governance and voting booths. And the individual's or couple's choice to have an abortion is not completely black and white, for most women struggle with the emotional as well as physical impact of the procedure and the short- and long-term consequences of that decision.

The decisions we make to act or do the right thing are based on many factors, including our laws, religious or spiritual beliefs, personal integrity, fear of reprisal, guilt, sense of social justice or social activism, personal moral codes, role models and s/heroes, personal work ethics, personal values, compassion for others, instinctive need to help others in distress, and so on. A colloquial saying goes, "Things can be ethical without being legal, and things can be legal without being ethical." There may be laws in some municipalities that make it illegal for individuals standing on roadsides at traffic intersections to panhandle (ask for money) from drivers in cars stopped at red lights. But if I am emotionally moved to action by the panhandler's appearance and handwritten cardboard sign ("Please help, Homeless and hungry, Thank you, God bless"), I will support the lawbreaker by offering him or her whatever spare change I may have on me at the moment. Is it legal? Probably not. Is it ethical? To me, at that moment and under those particular circumstances, yes.

But researchers do not always have that much leeway. We are bound by our professional associations' codes of conduct for ethical research with human participants (e.g., those established by the American Educational Research Association, the American Anthropological Association, or the British Psychological Society). And if researchers are associated with an institution that receives federal funding (in the United States), they are also bound by regulations and procedures established by the government and its local overseeing bodies: institutional review boards (IRBs). IRBs ensure both the researcher's ethical and legal obligations for proper conduct with human participants. These agencies' application procedures require careful documentation of the details of the research design (e.g., number of participants needed, specific forms of data to be collected, interview questions to be asked) before a study can be approved:

An IRB application form . . . actually serves as an excellent template for a qualitative research design. The information that must be entered forces you to think through most of the methodological and logistical matters involved with a study. And its submission as one application packet brings everything together for committee review and, hopefully, constructive feedback for research design revision. (Saldaña, 2011b, p. 87)

It is not this book's goal to review these codes in detail or to describe application procedures to IRBs for conducting qualitative research studies, but to discuss some foundational principles for *thinking ethically.*

Remember that the root meaning of *datum* is something given, not something collected. Anything your participants give you in the form of interviews, observation opportunities, documents, and so on, should be seen not just as data but as gifts. They are giving the researcher, most often voluntarily, their time, knowledge, experiences, and insights. Participants sacrifice their privacy so that the researcher can learn *from* them, not "about" them. Respect and honor the people you study, for they are willingly vulnerable for you. Never coerce or intimidate them for your own needs or goals; maintain an equitable relationship that balances status and power. Consider participants your coresearchers by inviting them to review, assess, and comment on your analytic findings in progress—a form of corroboration often referred to as member checking. Honor their consent to participate, and honor their choice to withdraw from the study at any time for whatever reason.

Most qualitative researchers will not encounter extreme ethical conundrums during their fieldwork, but I have learned to expect the unexpected from my participants and field sites. Go into your studies ready to encounter the occasional problem, whether it be an illegal activity a case study participant confesses to you during an interview, a disturbing disciplinary action you see taken by a teacher toward a student, or a dysfunctional interpersonal relationship you observe between a husband and wife. There are no foolproof guidelines or hard-and-fast rules for if and when you should intervene in such matters. Everything has to be considered on a case-by-case basis, sometimes spontaneously and sometimes after a lot of private soul searching.

Research methods textbooks always describe the ethical responsibilities of the investigator, but virtually none of them advise the researcher to consider the morals or ethics of the participants themselves. Just as the qualitative fieldworker wrestles with moral questions, so do the people we observe. As we observe them in their daily interactions and listen as they reveal their values, attitudes, and beliefs during interviews, they too are wrestling with moral questions and ethical issues as part of daily living. Colin M. Turnbull's (1972) heart-wrenching ethnography of the African Ik in *The Mountain People* documents the atrocities of a people desperate for food. Robert B. Edgerton's (1992) *Sick Societies* dispels the myth that "simple" cultures are peaceful and serene; their peoples are often subject to malnutrition, severe illnesses, and cruel rituals. These are extreme examples, but they suggest that not all of our participants are flawless protagonists and model citizens. Yes, there are good people in the world, but there are also people of questionable character. Do researchers judge them? If we're being truthful and honest (i.e., ethical) with ourselves, then yes, we do judge them—in the privacy of our personal field notes or journal. As for what we choose to disclose about what we learned about them in our write-ups—well, that's an ethical issue for each individual writer to resolve. Thinking ethically is primarily an internal monologue and debate about open-ended moral issues, and decision-making over what course of action should be taken when disruptions to personal or social orders occur.

Thinking ethically is a necessary method of mind that serves several purposes:

- It better guarantees the welfare and protection of your research participants from risk and harm.
- It better ensures your compliance with legal requirements for the ethical conduct of research with human participants.
- It prepares you to anticipate unforeseen problems and to resolve ethical dilemmas in the field as you collect data.
- It creates stronger interpersonal and more equitable relationships between you and your participants.
- It develops more empathetic and humane insight into the public, personal, and private lives of participants.

The following methods of mind profile other modalities of ethical reflection for qualitative inquiry: *thinking emotionally, empathetically, darkly,* and *spiritually.*

For your mental Rolodex: As you investigate social life, follow prescribed codes of ethical conduct with your participants. Be prepared to encounter unanticipated ethical issues in the field.

Thinking Emotionally

Goleman (1995) defines an **emotion** as "a feeling and its distinctive thoughts, psychological and biological states, and range of propensities to act" (p. 289). Hundreds of words exist to describe emotions, and Kahneman (2011) offers a fascinating overview of how emotion and cognition interplay with each other to create broader psychological constructs and processes such as "loss aversion," "optimistic bias," and the "illusion of validity." *Thinking emotionally* means heightened attunement to and awareness of participants' feelings, and how those feelings stimulate action, affect self-concept, and emerge from memories. It is also heightened awareness of your own emotions during fieldwork and analysis, enabling you to empathize with those you study (discussed later) and to more deeply understand the human condition.

For too long, social scientists were advised to keep their emotions in check because this could skew or bias their collection and analysis of data. But emotions play a central role in our daily lives and constantly shift in various contexts of interaction and personal reflection: "One can't separate emotion from action; they are part of the same flow of events, one leading into the other" (Corbin & Strauss, 2008, p. 7). As a qualitative researcher engaged in fieldwork at various sites, I've felt anxious, scared, curious, bored, elated, disturbed, surprised, annoyed, amused, and even moved to tears on occasion. I'd like to think that these emotions brought me closer to understanding the social phenomena I was observing rather than invalidated my analyses and findings.

Emotions are not buried in some deeply recessed center of your brain, but rather processed in both hemispheres, with the right hemisphere processing more negative emotions and the left processing more positive ones (Wolfe, 2010, pp. 47–48). The structures responsible for deciding what gets stored in long-term memory are located in the brain's limbic (emotional) system, and the brain generally attends to information that first stimulates strong emotional arousal (Sousa, 2011, p. 20; Wolfe, 2010, p. 120). Emotions play a critical role in education; students need to feel safe and secure in their school environment before learning experiences can be meaningful and thus can be affixed in long-term memory. Unfortunately, many young people say that some subjects in school are "boring"; thus, the likelihood of information retention is minimized.

Stress, trauma, and illness, especially severe diseases

Source: Stockbyte/Digital Vision/Thinkstock.

Figure 5.1. Thinking emotionally means heightened attunement to and awareness of participants' feelings.

such as cancer, stimulate an ever-shifting array of strong emotions in clients, patients, and their family and friends, not to mention most health care providers. But even the daily, seemingly mundane work routines that many of us have can generate intense internal feelings and emotional states that remain suppressed rather than openly expressed among colleagues (Hochschild, 2003). Erving Goffman's (1959) landmark sociological study on the presentation of self reminds us that people frequently "perform" to convey to others a desired persona or set of attributes. Much may be masked behind a facade that an astute researcher can infer or empathize with. And our social intelligence (Goleman, 2006) refers to our ability and aptitude for nurturing constructive relationships, which requires such facilities as empathic accuracy, social cognition, concern for others, and ability to positively influence the outcome of interactions (p. 84), a form of brain-to-brain connection with neuroscientific rationale through what are called "mirror neurons." Participant observation can focus not just on the research topic of interest, but on whether and how the people we observe display social intelligence with each other.

The questions you ask during interviews can influence the types of responses you get from participants about their emotions. A participant may recall the facts of a past moment but not initially offer his or her accompanying feelings. If you follow up with, "What was going through your mind at the time?" the participant might answer with, "I was thinking that . . . ," which may not reveal the emotional dynamics of the story. But if you ask "What were you feeling when that happened?" the respondent may begin with "I was feeling that . . . " I have come to regard the often-used question, "How did that make you feel?" as an almost trite prompt that seems to generate superficial responses. But assuming that emotional memory is triggered as a participant recalls an emotion-laden story, more strategically phrased questions as probes for an interview might be

- "What are you feeling now?"
- "What kinds of emotions are you experiencing right now?"
- "You look like you're having a lot of emotions now. What are they? Can you name them for me?"

"I know exactly how you feel" may be a well-intentioned response on the researcher's part, intended to convey sympathy, but it could be interpreted by the participant as an insensitive or insincere comment. Relating to the action rather than the emotion may be a more affirming way to proceed. If I genuinely feel I can relate to the person and his or her feelings during an interview, especially when the participant has expressed something with honesty and vulnerability, I sometimes offer, "I've been in a similar situation," or I nod my head in agreement while saying, "Yeah. Been there, done that."

Researchers should feel free to document their own emotions during fieldwork in personal journals or field notes. It serves as a way to "blow off some steam" from the frustrations of researching humans, and potentially brings the investigator closer to the dynamics of the social world studied. The confessional tale of reporting (van Maanen, 2011) permits open disclosure of one's feelings throughout the study. Indeed, such writing humanizes the researcher with his or her audience. But be cautious of blending the confessional tale with the formal or analytic tale. There are times when I've read or heard autoethnographers and poetic and narrative inquirers present compelling stories about their own lives or the lives of those they've studied, but a moving passage of text is interrupted by a reference to the professional literature, or by a footnote explaining a conceptual framework or a related theory. I am jarred by this needless blending of the literary with the academic. I advise autoethnographic writers, "You don't need scholarship to validate and justify how you feel." Some fieldworkers wrestle continuously over whether their own emotions may be "contaminating" the study. Rest assured that if you want to understand what it means to be human, you have to think—and feel—like one. See Collins and Cooper (2014) for a thoughtful discussion of how emotional intelligence benefits the qualitative researcher during fieldwork and data analysis.

Source: George Doyle/Stockbyte/Thinkstock

Figure 5.2. **Many young people say that some subjects in school are "boring."**

For your mental Rolodex: As you investigate social life, inquire into the emotional worlds of your participants and your own emotions as you conduct the study.

Thinking Empathetically

If one of our goals is to understand the world of our participants and what it's like to live in it, then we need to empathize with them. *Thinking empathetically* is understanding and, preferably, feeling comparable to a participant's particular emotional state. Putting ourselves into our participants' shoes and seeing life through their eyes—perspective-taking—is the first step. The next step is to identify with "where they're coming from" and to connect deeply with their plight. To clarify, sympathy is feeling concerned or sorry for someone else's circumstances. Empathy is cognitive understanding and emotional reflection within us of what someone else is feeling.

Pink (2006, p. 172) asserts that women are generally better than men at empathetic response. I believe that a researcher's discipline, especially if it is one of the helping professions (e.g., education, health care, counseling) or if it involves the arts and humanities, religion, or the social sciences, can enable him or her to feel more deeply. But not all teachers are nurturing, not all pastors are caring, and not all psychologists are mentally well balanced, so it comes down to individual capacity. Empathic development begins in infancy and early childhood (Eisenberg & Strayer, 1990), with one of its most important skills being the ability to read the nonverbal cues in others' facial expressions and vocal tones. As an adult, empathy "builds on self-awareness; the more open we are to our own emotions, the more skilled we will be in reading feelings" (Goleman, 1995, p. 96). Recent neuroscience research on a special class of cells called mirror neurons scattered throughout the brain has observed that, in a way, emotions are "contagious," and mirror neurons "help us understand the motives and actions of others," suggesting that empathy and morality are rooted in our biology (Strauch, 2010, p. 188).

Participant observation as an active rather than peripheral member of the culture offers us more concrete experiences of their daily lives—a close-up angle for witnessing social action (Adler & Adler, 1987). It's one thing to sit in the back of a kindergarten classroom and watch a teacher work with 20 young children in the morning; it's another thing altogether to teach them yourself for four hours straight, five days a week, nine months a year. "Banana Time," a short but classic ethnography by Donald F. Roy (1959), describes the monotonous job of a machine operator, written from his own experience of working daily with the men:

> Standing all day in one spot beside three old codgers in a dingy room looking out through barred windows at the bare walls of a brick warehouse, leg movements largely restricted to the shifting of body weight from one foot to the other, hand and arm movements confined, for the most part, to a simple repetitive sequence of place the die,————punch the clicker,————place the die,————punch the clicker, and intellectual activity reduced to computing the hours to quitting time. . . . [T]here was the half hour for lunch, and occasional trips to the lavatory or the drinking fountain to break up the day into digestible parts. But after each momentary respite, hammer and die were moving again: click,————move die,————click,————move die. (p. 160)

Other ethnographies, by writers such as Ted Conover, chronicle the experiences of working as a taxi driver and corrections officer, living the life of a hobo, and walking the trails taken by illegal immigrants into the United States. These first-person accounts extend beyond peripheral observation and interviews of others to present a lived-experience perspective. The researcher's ability and willingness to take on the role of the people he or she studies and, most importantly, understand and emotionally empathize with them are critical for insight into the minds of others. For some, this awareness develops slowly yet often "clicks" in a moment of realization. Once that understanding occurs, the mind is then open to the emotional component of empathy.

Sometimes when we unobtrusively observe participant interactions, we become "armchair quarterbacks" who quickly assess the actions of others: "This is what I would have done instead." But a different take on social research as you're watching and listening to others is to ask yourself, "What is that person thinking and feeling right now?" and "How would I be feeling if that had just happened to me?" Writing in role (Booth & Neelands, 1998) is a technique of language arts practitioners in which students compose a text from a *character's* perspective. If adequate framing and improvisational experience have been provided beforehand, students are able to write with perceptive and poignant insight. Imagine if this same technique were applied to your field note writing. Occasionally document social life not from your researcher's perspective but from the participant's. Below is an example of my written narrative of a middle school student at her first competitive speech tournament:

> Beatriz, in her quiet and unassuming way, rose from her chair and scooted across her seated classmates as Elian shouted, "You go, Bea!" Nancy, her coach, smiled as she passed and gave her a "rah-rah" pep-rally gesture. Beatriz, dressed in a pale yellow dress, walked hesitantly toward the stage, obviously nervous, walking up each stair step to the platform with measured care so as not to trip as someone had done earlier. (Miles, Huberman, & Saldaña, 2014, p. 184)

Imagine if this same slice of social action had been composed by Beatriz herself. Written in role in the present tense instead of from the researcher's past-tense point of view, the field notes might follow stream-of-consciousness format:

> Oh God, I'm so nervous. I just want to go home. Teacher's smiling at me; I don't want to let her down. OK, don't trip, you can do this. God, there's so many people watching me. Why am I here? I really don't want to do this.

Thinking empathetically brings you deeper into the qualitative realm of research. It enables you to perceive the world through different lenses, filters, and angles. It reminds you that the study is not about you but about your participants. Empathy makes you more human and thus better able to grasp what it means to be human.

For your mental Rolodex: As you investigate social life, empathize with the people you study. Take their perspectives to understand their points of view and to emotionally connect with their daily lives.

Thinking Darkly

Fiction writers are taught to think of their characters as having three selves: a public self (what most others see in the person every day at work, on the streets, in social settings, etc.), a personal self (what only immediate family members, close friends, or intimate partners see, usually at home or in secluded spaces), and a private self (what no one but the individual sees, knows, and does in solitude—the actions, inner thoughts, feelings, and reflections of and about oneself). Good writers attempt to portray the major characters' three selves as a story unfolds for a more three-dimensional rendering of people in action. Horror writer Stephen King attempts to find the "monster" within his human characters that propels their aberrant behavior. Revealing the private self is tricky, however, and relies on literary and cinematic techniques such as inner monologue, voice-overs, stream of consciousness, and audience inference-making of nonverbal action to reveal or suggest what's going through a character's mind.

The personal and private selves are what most qualitative researchers hope to learn about through individual interviews and through reading the participant's personal writings. But not all participants are forthcoming or truthful about what they really think or do as their personal and private selves. Sometimes this information is completely irrelevant to the study at hand (why should you ask about someone's personal sex life when you're researching consumer behaviors in regard to breakfast cereals?). Sometimes people want to make a good presentation of self to a researcher (thus, couples will talk about their "wonderful" marriages, but may not reveal the actual number of arguments they've had with their spouses). And sometimes, it's simply none of the researcher's business what participants do behind closed doors or what skeletons hang in their closets.

The human mind is capable of concocting endless fantasies, and some people attempt to realize those fantasies with unfortunate and tragic consequences. I once heard on TV an interview with a Federal Bureau of Investigation (FBI) agent about the types of crimes and atrocities people commit. He said, "If the American public knew just half of what the FBI knows about what goes on in this country, they'd never leave their houses." Two of my friends are counselors in private practice who work with sex offenders, and I've heard some eyebrow-raising stories of the types of crimes their clients committed. One of my case study participants (Saldaña, 1998) was an adolescent male who, in public, appeared to be an upstanding and spiritual young man. But later interviews with him revealed a family recovering from alcohol and drug abuse and a personal history of bipolar disorder and suicide attempts.

Most of us have been conditioned to keep our deep, dark secrets to our private selves. We've been socialized to think that public disclosure of such secrets is inappropriate and

Figure 5.3. The private self possesses deep, dark secrets.

Source: Jupiterimages/Stockbyte/Thinkstock.

offensive to others. It also has great potential to damage our personal reputation, to be stigmatized as deviant, and to make us outcasts from social groups. Telling our secrets in what we assumed was a safe environment may result in awkward silence and embarrassment, then avoidance of future contact. Laud Humphreys (1970) and Harry F. Wolcott (2002) are two writers of "infamous" studies in qualitative inquiry that raised the eyebrows of their professional colleagues for their questionable research ethics involving sex. But each side has its own story to tell, and Humphreys and Wolcott presented convincing arguments for their actions (though not everyone in the research community was willing to listen and understand).

All of the above, however, can be negated in one fell swoop from the notoriety, publicity, and even greater success that comes from celebrity confessions or just getting caught. The "bad girl" and "bad boy" actions of actor Lindsay Lohan and singer Justin Bieber captured media attention and thus the public's consumption of their self-destructive stories. At the time of this writing, a few politicians who were plagued by sex scandals years ago while in U.S. public office have been reelected to serve by the majority of their constituents. Deep, dark secrets can break you or make you.

Media technology these days has taken away any concept of personal privacy. Our digital footprints can be followed by authorities and criminals to retrieve or reconstruct our most closely guarded information and personal communications sent wirelessly around the world. Accessible Internet pornography and the ability to disguise one's true identity have also made deeper, darker secrets a facet of some people's lives, even if they vehemently deny it (a respectable presentation of self, remember?). Television broadcasted in real time the court trials of Casey Anthony and Jodi Arias, revealing to the public lurid details about abuse, violence, sex, and murder. Some viewers were appalled and disgusted; others were riveted to the screen to learn more. Many people hunger for the scandalous story, perhaps enabling them to feel "holier than thou." But a litmus test to apply is this: If you were to die unexpectedly right now, what might those left behind find among your personal possessions or in your digital records that would have caused you shame had they been discovered by others while you were alive?

Thinking darkly reflects on the personal and private selves of those we study, particularly if the study focuses on some aspect of nonnormative social life. It acknowledges that deep, dark secrets are not a possibility but a given of being human. It acknowledges that some things about ourselves are deliberately covert, strategically hidden from others, or falsified for a reason. It acknowledges that the secrets we carry are internal scars, burdens, desires, or badges of honor, depending on the individual's perspective. You may not get the whole truth from those you interview, and your instincts may tell you as much. As a researcher, an important decision to make is whether to peel away at the pretense or to simply let it go. The latter option is not a bad thing, for it forces you to reflect on subtext (what's not being said) and why there may be a withholding of information.

But we also need to exercise caution in how far we can go with our imaginative thinking and probing or prying. It is very possible to make incorrect inferences, damaging assumptions, and inadvertent libelous statements. Cuzzort and King (2002) remind us that deviant activity is not always the product of a deviant personality (p. 59). We could not only ruin our credibility as researchers, but we could place our participants in jeopardy. Don't obsess or become paranoid about it, and remind yourself that, for the most part, other people's personal and private lives are none of your business. Some people are very uncomfortable talking about their private selves. Provide them with safe spaces and a supportive relationship, but don't push them if they're not ready, and don't open a door you can't close.

If there are those rare occasions when a participant divulges a deep, dark secret to you, listen without judgment, empathize with the teller, respect the participant's perspective, maintain your previously established agreements for confidentiality and anonymity, and feel honored that you were trusted enough to be told what someone else kept hidden. On the other hand, if that disclosure reveals an illegal act, you must then wrestle with the ethical dilemma of whether to contact authorities. If the act was an illegal offense of any kind by an adult toward a minor (e.g., physical or sexual abuse), you *must* report it to the authorities.

> ***For your mental Rolodex:*** As you investigate social life, consider what may be deliberately hidden from you as a researcher. Reflect on the deep, dark secrets that people sometimes carry and the possible influences and affects those secrets have on themselves and others.

Thinking Spiritually

In the Broadway musical *The Book of Mormon,* the main characters undergo a spiritual transformation of one kind or another by the end of the play, with the lead character Elder Kevin Price realizing after his own faith has been shaken, "You've got to believe in *something.*" One of the least explored facets of our case studies is what our participants believe in, whether that be a spiritual deity or a secular passion. *Thinking spiritually* is at most investigating, or at least reflecting on, the role of religion, if any, in our participants' daily lives, even if the research topic is not spirituality. To clarify, spirituality is the personal belief in a higher power and a commitment to leading a moral life; religion refers to membership in a socially developed organized faith (e.g., Protestant, Quaker, Buddhist).

Spirituality is a personal matter for many and something not generally discussed with people outside one's social circle (oral tradition advises us not to discuss politics or religion with friends lest we get into a heated argument). But some are quite comfortable discussing their religious beliefs; others prefer to keep their spiritual identity private; and some are agnostic and some are atheist. Some will simply identify their religious affiliation ("I'm Catholic") to acquaintances and let it go at that. Others will testify, even to strangers, how their faith has played a significant role in their personal outlook and how their place of worship is central to their lives. One of my case study participants, whom I observed for over 20 months as part of an educational ethnography, did not mention her religion or spirituality once in all the interview data I collected during that time. But a different case study participant, over the course of six months, spoke of his church and his relationship to God frequently, freely, and through his own initiative during interviews, even though education and career were the central concerns of my research.

But religion is a highly personal matter, and unless the core topic of investigation *is* religion or spirituality, the subject has no place in the researcher's protocol. My own way of working does not inquire about a participant's spiritual beliefs unless the participant himself or herself initiates it in our conversations. And even then, I do my best to assess whether it is something important to the participant's life that merits extended investigation, or whether it is best to simply listen to what the participant offers, and then move on to the primary topic at hand. Ethnographies of selected cultures will carefully document the religious practices of a people as part of the anthropological enterprise. The spiritual ethos of a larger community is somehow more acceptable to study than the intimate and personal beliefs of an individual.

In many societies and nations, religion influences not only an individual's values system and actions but political ideologies and their agendas. Several call the hot button issues in the United States—such as abortion, gay marriage, and health care—"social" issues. But they are, from my perspective, *religious* issues because the conflict originates from opponents objecting to advancement of these matters on personal religious (i.e., moral) grounds. One cannot research government and politics without reference to the role of religion in swaying legislation and public policy.

The majority of my own work did not explore religion and spirituality because my central foci were major disciplines such as education and the arts. Only one research study in over 20 years of inquiry projects contained a significant component of religion because the case study participant was dedicated to his church as an adolescent and later received a calling from God to enter the ministry (Saldaña, 1998, 2003). This unforeseen life direction meant that I needed to make the participant's faith, not his career, the through-line for my analyses. Young adult development was my original and consistent research lens, but as the study progressed it was covered with a Methodist spiritual filter.

Since a participant's religion or spirituality may be too sensitive a matter to initiate inquiry about, the researcher himself or herself could reflect on how personal beliefs might influence and affect his or her own worldview. For example, I've had former students who were Jewish, Buddhist, Catholic, LDS/Mormon, and Seventh-Day Adventist, and who set their research agendas and projects around the parameters of their respective faiths. They each made religion the central topic of their scholarly work through theses and dissertations and made substantive contributions to their fields. As chair of their master's and doctoral committees, I was not a member of any of those faiths, but I took the opportunity to learn from them about their religions and respected their open devotion to their spirituality.

My own spiritual journey has ranged from inconsequential indifference to total evangelical devotion to a complete loss of faith. I have reflected deeply on people's relationship with a deity and how religious beliefs have served as both a comforting and destructive force in the world. Some days I am righteously angered by the religious hypocrisy of selected groups toward their fellow citizens. Some days I am overwhelmed by the kindness I see demonstrated by one good Samaritan toward another in need. Some days I'm shouting obscene blasphemies, and some days I look upward to thank God for a positive outcome in my life. These varied experiences have not affected me as a research methodologist, but they have enabled me to better understand others for whom religion plays a central role in their lives.

For your mental Rolodex: As you investigate social life, explore the roles of religion and spirituality in your participants and in yourself. Reflect on matters of faith and how they play a role in personal development and social interaction.

CLOSURE

Writing about ethics, morals, emotions, spirituality, the private self, and the dark side of human nature takes courage but also requires caution. Some researchers use publication as a forum for exorcising their personal demons or grinding their personal axes. Writing can be a form of confession, therapy, and atonement but can also function as a self-indulgent act of revenge. An emotion-laden report may be a good literary narrative but might also be perceived as bad scholarship. Conversely, a report imbued with facts and theory alone makes for dispassionate and disengaged reading. The best writing is *revelatory*. It tells the reader facets about being human that were previously unknown to him or her. It describes personal motivations, entrenched beliefs, emotional reactions, and ways of living in the world that make us realize that other people do indeed act, think, and feel differently than we do.

You needn't deliberately put yourself in any dangerous settings for fieldwork, like Jennifer Toth (1993) did when she explored the underground culture of New York City's "mole people." Sometimes the most dangerous places to visit are inside other people's minds. It takes bravery to ask someone to tell you his or her life story, warts and all. And it takes even more bravery to listen with empathy and without judgment. Though it sounds harsh, I forewarn my ethnography students, "If you can't study the human condition in its entirety—from its triumphs to its atrocities—then you have no business being a qualitative researcher."

EXERCISES FOR THINKING ETHICALLY

1. Watch the film *Miss Evers' Boys* (HBO Home Video, 2002). Focus on the central protagonist, Nurse Eunice Evers, and her ethical dilemmas throughout the story. Discuss with others who have viewed the film the emotional conflicts faced by Nurse Evers, and the challenges the Tuskegee experiment posed to her professional practice and her personal value, attitude, and belief systems.

2. After securing any necessary permissions, conduct a 30- to 60-minute participant observation exercise at a site with a mix of adults and young people (e.g., public park, shopping mall, school lunchroom or playground). Focus solely on people's emotions by inferring how they feel based on documenting dialogue, vocal tones, facial expressions, body language, actions, reactions, interactions, and so on. Then, compare and analyze (both quantitatively and qualitatively) the differences between the young people's emotions and the adults' emotions exhibited in that particular social setting. Also reflect on your ability to read and infer others' emotions, plus your own emotional reactions to what you observed.

3. Write about or discuss with a peer when it would and would not be appropriate to compensate a research participant for his or her involvement in a study. If compensation is offered,

discuss the types possible (cash, gift card, services, etc.), appropriate amounts (hourly, per task, lump sum), for what kinds of participant contributions (interview time, written survey completion, etc.), and under what specific conditions (e.g., compensation only upon success-ful completion of participation, monetary compensation only for low-income participants, gift cards but not cash for adolescent participants). As an extension, discuss this ethical conundrum: Who "owns" the data?

4. Write a brief statement of faith that describes your religious or spiritual beliefs (if any), and explain how those beliefs may play a role in your daily routines. If you hold no personal religious or spiritual beliefs, write a statement of your core moral values. If possible and with permission, attend a worship service at a church, temple, mosque, or synagogue of a faith different from yours and observe the religious or spiritual beliefs promoted and practiced by members of that faith.

5. As a one-time, personal journal entry, preferably handwritten, list the deep, dark secrets in your own life that you keep to your private self. If you wish, use symbols or encrypt the writ-ing in some way to maintain confidentiality. Reflect on the contents and its meanings for you, then destroy the entry.

Thinking
Multidisciplinarily

6

LEARNING OBJECTIVES AND SUMMARY

- Your mind will acknowledge various disciplinary lenses, filters, and angles for social inquiry.
- Your mind will establish connections between and among various disciplinary knowledge bases.

This chapter explores the perception and examination of social life through various disciplinary lenses, filters, and angles. These methods of mind consist of

- Thinking Multidisciplinarily
- Thinking Historically
- Thinking Anthropologically
- Thinking Psychologically
- Thinking Developmentally
- Thinking Sociologically
- Thinking Communicatively
- Thinking Multiculturally
- Thinking Feministly

The purpose of this chapter is to expand your thinking beyond your central disciplinary interest or field of study, and to help you consider how other foci might alter your perceptions of social phenomena. Not all disciplines can be covered in just one chapter; I address certain ones below because they primarily (but not exclusively) relate to the social sciences. Each discipline can fill a library with relevant literature. Here, I offer only a few suggestions related to each topic.

Thinking Multidisciplinarily

Multidisciplinarily is an invented form of its core word, and there is even some interchanging of terms and disagreement about the word's proper prefix. Some use *inter-, cross-, trans-,* or *pan-* before *disciplinary* to describe what I mean here. Some also see a difference between a discipline and a field, yet some use the terms interchangeably or in combination to create a "disciplinary field." I can find no authoritative distinctions or definitions, so I will put forth my own, solely for clarification and consistency in this book.

A discipline is a major branch of academic study with related subject areas or fields. A discipline is like an umbrella that covers several fields underneath it. For example, education is a discipline but has fields of preschool education, elementary education, secondary education, special education, multicultural education, bilingual education, and so on. And, a field can have subfields, specialties, or programs, such as elementary education's programs in reading, gifted and talented, STEM (science, technology, engineering, math), and so on.

So now that a discipline is clarified as a major branch of academic study with related subject areas or fields, what's the *multi-* part of it, and how does that differ from *inter- cross- trans-* and *pan-?* Again, it depends on whom you talk to and what sources you read, but here's how I understand the differences. A review of the prefixes' root meanings are:

multi- = many

inter- = between, among

cross- = interchange, exchange

trans- = across, through

pan- = all

Whenever someone outside of academia asks me, "So, what *is* qualitative research?" I usually reply, "Well, it's a little bit of sociology and a little bit of psychology and a little bit of anthropology and a little bit of this and a little bit of that and a little bit of something else, too." As an educational researcher, my work is not just about what happens in a classroom. It's much more than that. It necessitates gathering information about and studying teacher education and professional development, state and national education policies, child development, educational psychology (with its current focus on neuroscience and brain-based learning), disabilities (like autism, ADHD, etc.), classroom management, curriculum studies, youth studies, gender studies, ethnic studies, cultural studies, critical pedagogy, education law, popular culture, media and technology, play and gaming theory, the sociology of education, the anthropology of education, and a host of other disciplines, fields, and subfields as the research study requires. In other words, there are many or multiple disciplines I have to consider in my research and initial thinking. And as I synthesize everything in my mind, there will certainly be some *multi- inter- cross- trans-* and *pan-* thinking and analysis involved. But to get me to those stages, I first need to take in **multidisciplinary** knowledge.

Anthropologist Clifford Geertz (1983) observed that the social sciences were becoming and utilizing "blurred genres" in practice and in writing. Disciplines like anthropology were no longer strictly anthropological. Its writers were delving into psychology, performance, the humanities, filmmaking, and other disciplines and fields to analyze and document their ethnographies. That same genre blurring continues today with "hybridity," "border crossing," "breaking boundaries," "multitasking," "multiplicity," "blending," "fluidity," "mash-ups," "mixed methods," and ever-evolving "versions" of previous work. A single handheld device serves as a phone, camera, audio and video recorder, television, movie screen, music player, Internet browser, instant messenger, GPS device, alarm clock, stopwatch, calculator, and other apps and functions. Qualitative research reports are no longer found strictly in books and journals; they appear on dedicated Internet sites, as documentary DVDs, as installations in art galleries, and on stage as live performances (see Chapter 7). Even scholarly publication content integrates various disciplines together via titles such as *The Sociology of Childhood* (Corsaro, 2011), *The Anthropology of the Performing Arts* (Royce, 2004), and *Medicine as Culture* (Lupton, 2012).

Many colleges and universities today include multidisciplinary units such as gender studies, cultural studies, and ethnic studies, which bring together faculty with varied backgrounds and specialties to create multidimensional curricula and programs of study. Several initiatives and grant programs encourage collaborative projects between and among researchers from different units to explore a topic from multiple perspectives; for example, health care and theatre units might collaborate to develop video documentary performances about metastatic breast cancer (Gray & Sinding, 2002) or women with HIV (Sandelowski, Trimble, Woodard, & Barroso, 2006). Such intersectionality initiates the mixing of knowledge bases and research methodologies, facilitating value-added outcomes for larger constituencies.

Thinking multidisciplinarily means that you don't have to know it all, but you do have to know a little bit about a lot of different things. The explosion of knowledge in our information and digital ages means that, with the right access, you can find out virtually anything you want to know quickly and almost effortlessly. But that instantaneous access does not guarantee that the information you read, hear, or watch is 100% accurate or credible. Critically assess the sources for your literature review, particularly if they are taken from disciplines outside your own. Trust a peer-reviewed journal article more than a stranger's Internet blog.

A large number of recently published books serve as primers for major disciplines and fields—series with titles like *Introducing _____, The Complete Idiot's Guide to _____,* and *_____ for Dummies.* These are not all to be dismissed as unscholarly works. Some, like Jay Gabler's (2011) *Sociology for Dummies,* are quite exceptionally well written and thorough. Read these for a quick introduction to disciplines you haven't had the opportunity to study in your academic career. But don't limit yourself to these popular trade books; do check out what a discipline considers its canon of essential works and most respected academic journals.

Also read some of the contemporary classics of qualitative inquiry and investigative journalism from multiple disciplines, such as Erving Goffman's *The Presentation of Self in Everyday Life* (1959) and *Stigma* (1963), Elliot Liebow's *Tally's Corner* (1967), Jonathan Kozol's *Savage Inequalities* (1991), Jennifer Toth's *The Mole People* (1993), Barbara Ehrenreich's *Nickel and Dimed* (2001), and Arlie Russell Hochschild's *The Managed Heart* (2003), as well as the more recent slate of best-selling psychology titles for general readers, such as Daniel Goleman's *Emotional Intelligence* (1995), Daniel Kahneman's *Thinking, Fast and Slow* (2011), and Charles Duhigg's *The Power of Habit* (2012). This is just a small sampling of recommended books. Consult your college or university supervisor for other titles. Know a little bit of something about a lot of different things. Abbott (2004) wisely notes, "Sometimes there's no faster way to come up with a new idea than to wonder how somebody from a different discipline would think about your issue" (p. 108).

Just as we benefit from knowledge of multiple disciplines, our brain stores information in different modalities or cortices—visual, auditory, and motor (Wolfe, 2010. p. 106). Your discipline of choice and related experiences have not only provided you with an information store of particular knowledge, but they have also influenced and affected the way you think about and perceive the world, including yourself. The memories you have, associations you make, and actions you take are shaped greatly by what you know, value, believe, and feel, and, of course, how you think about things. If your lens, filter, and angle cause you to see the world primarily as mathematical structures, formulaic algorithms, and statistical probabilities, then numbers may have greater meaning for you than words, and you may prefer an orderly, predictable lifestyle over a chaotic, uncertain one (like the character Sheldon Cooper in television's *The Big Bang Theory*).

But social life is made up of people with radically different interests, priorities, and agendas. To understand them, we need to know how *they* think. And to understand them better, we need to know what interests them and how to observe them multidisciplinarily. The colloquial advice to "think outside the box" means not just to think creatively for problem-solving but to think outside your own disciplinary experiences. "Boundary-crossers reject either/or choices and seek multiple options and blended solutions" (Pink, 2006, p. 136).

Thinking multidisciplinarily is a necessary method of mind that serves several purposes:

- It broadens your perspective, allowing you to perceive and analyze social life through different disciplinary lenses, filters, and angles.
- It enables you to cross disciplinary boundaries to find multiple connections between phenomena and explanations.
- It increases your knowledge base and cognitive resources for qualitative data analysis and interpretation.
- It enhances your ability to transfer findings from the local and particular to more generalizable settings and contexts.
- It advances communication and networking with colleagues from other disciplines.

The following methods of mind profile other modalities of multidisciplinary thought for qualitative inquiry: *thinking historically, anthropologically, psychologically, developmentally, sociologically, communicatively, multiculturally,* and *feministly* (an invented word). Again, not all disciplines that employ qualitative research (health care, business, education, technology, etc.) can be covered in this chapter.

> **For your mental Rolodex:** As you investigate social life, occasionally conduct fieldwork as if you were schooled in another discipline with its unique lenses, filters, and angles. Observe participants on one day as if your area of study were history; on the next day, psychology; on the next, communication; and so on. As you write up your research, consider how your work might inform colleagues from other disciplines and even the general public.

Thinking Historically

When a historian colleague of mine learned that I interviewed people for fieldwork, she quipped that she preferred to "study dead people because they can't talk back." Nevertheless, the living do have histories within them that are worth learning about, and history in general has shaped many ways of working and living today. *Thinking historically* investigates the pasts of your participants and the field site in order to place the present conditions into context. When necessary, it infers how those pasts may have significantly influenced and affected participants' current ways of thinking and acting. Thinking historically also examines the chronological development of your own research study, from conception through completion, to assess the progress of your cumulative analytic work. If your investigation is longitudinal, you have the opportunity to observe and parse any changes that may occur through historic patterns of action such as phases, stages, and cycles (Saldaña, 2003).

Though qualitative inquiry most often investigates the here and now of social conditions, qualitative researchers are historians by default. We review previously published work about our topic to assess the foundational knowledge that prepares our current study. Our interviews with participants might delve into their biographical backgrounds to gather significant facts, memories, and stories. We think retroductively when we attempt to reconstruct how their pasts may have shaped their present conditions. With enough data, we may be able to discern not just recurring themes but significant motifs, such as a fear of being alone, frequent job changes, or playing the peacekeeper role in the family as well as in the workplace. These thematic arrays have become a new way of plotting an individual's biography—not by traditional chronologies such as Chapter 1 Birth and Childhood, Chapter 2 Adolescence, Chapter 3 Young Adulthood, and so forth—but by salient themes that categorize the patterns and actions of one's life course— Chapter 1 Destined for Greatness, Chapter 2 Resistance, Chapter 3 Challenges and Triumphs, and so on.

Recalling one's past often evokes mental images and emotions about those memories. Asking participants to physically describe previous sites and artifacts from the time triggers more detailed responses during interviews. If it's comfortable for both you and the participant, ask about the feelings associated with or recalled by those memories. If appropriate to the study, conduct an interview centered around photographs from the participant's past that she or he may possess. Photos can prompt elaboration not just of their contents, but also their meanings and present-day significance to the participant.

Stilgoe's (1998) *Outside Lies Magic* presents a readable and insightful narrative about the evolution of social spaces, such as highways and town squares, and how their physical arrangements originated to serve particular functions. Your participant observation at a particular field site could also explore the current arrangement of architecture and interiors and devote some slices of time to the site's history and the rationale for its design. One elementary school I observed was built completely underground, with the flat rooftop of the facility at ground level doubling as its playground area. I later learned from veteran teachers who had been there when the school first opened that the design was intended to minimize airplane noise from arriving and departing flights, since a major airport was only 15 blocks away. But sunlight was a rare commodity in the building, since only a few rooms had glass windows. The facility appeared clean, modern, and well maintained, but the interior environment had the feel of a "bomb shelter"—an inescapable metaphor for this inner city school.

With a gatekeeper's permission, review any existing paper or electronic documents that chronicle the history of the field site. But remember that documents are "social products" that must be examined critically because they reflect the interests and perspectives of their authors (Hammersley & Atkinson, 2007, p. 130) and carry "values and ideologies, either intended or not" (Hitchcock & Hughes, 1995, p. 231). Just as an individual's memory can be faulty, so too can an organization's history be written in such a way as to present its past with partial or revised truth. The performed presentation of self, for the purpose of appearing in one's best light, is not just for people but for businesses, organizations, and social groups. Official documents in particular are "a site of claims to power, legitimacy, and reality" (Lindlof & Taylor, 2011, p. 232). Thus, rely not just on what's in print, but what long-term members of the organization recall about past ways of working and the evolution of the site through time.

Oral history (Janesick, 2010; Kelin, 2005; Leavy, 2011), a genre of qualitative research, collects extensive autobiographical narratives from an individual about her or his past through a series of open-ended interviews. Unlike the general national and cultural histories of a collected people, oral history offers a social "vehicle for the outsiders and the forgotten to tell their stories" through reminiscences of first-hand experiences (Janesick, 2010, pp. 1–2). Several archives and repositories of oral history collections are dedicated to particular groups or events, such as World War II Holocaust survivors; witnesses of the September 11, 2001, terrorist attacks in New York City; and survivors of Hurricane Katrina and its aftermath in the southern United States. The University of South Florida Libraries, for example, maintain a publicly accessible oral history collection of digital recordings with accompanying transcripts (http://guides.lib.usf.edu/content .php?pid=49131&sid=523867).

Oral history goes beyond the documentation of facts to elicit what I call "significant trivia" or rich details about past periods that few would remember or know about. Oral history also solicits the participant's feelings about those memories through personal testimony. In the excerpt below, a man in his mid-sixties recalls what it was like growing up as a teenager in the socially turbulent 1960s United States:

P: College students today study the Vietnam war, but they have a very hard time understanding the tone of the times. I tell them that the satire was very dark and very bitter in the 1960s and early 1970s. It was anger at the atrocities of what we were hearing on the news and reading in the [news]paper. It wasn't activist, it was radical. Everything seemed to converge at that time: hippies, drugs, anti-war, anti-establishment, political scandals, Nixon, um, Watergate, long hair, campus violence, Kent State, [Rev. Martin Luther] King's assassination. The country was falling apart socially, and it seemed like the older generation was at a loss for how to cope with the newer generation. Kids today have "Sixties Days" at high schools, and they think that all that means is dressing up in tie-dye T-shirts and bell bottom jeans and psychedelic colors. I tell them that at my high school in the sixties, girls were only allowed to wear dresses, and long hair on guys was seen as grounds for suspension. It was a crazy time of contradictions.

I: What's an example of a contradiction?

P: The principal of the school would get freaked out when girls started wearing mini-skirts, you know, they came high up the thigh, so they would get sent home to change into more appropriate clothes. Then another day a girl wore a granny dress that came all the way down to the floor, and *she* got sent home to change clothes! I mean, don't show your legs, but when they keep them completely covered, it was still wrong.

I: What else?

P: The draft card—that was a sign you became a man, when you had to go register for the draft. It was scary, because all we heard on the news was about all these guys dying and brought home in caskets from Vietnam. They would show the broadcast of draft number drawings on TV, birthdates, and I remember seeing photos in the paper the next day of young men reacting in tears because their number was called. A friend of mine in high school volunteered to join the army, and instead of thanking him like we might do today, we were all stunned and reacted like it was an automatic death sentence. He lived, thank God, but there were some vets who came back very bitter, very angry. . . .

I: So, how would you describe "the times"?

P: Scary, uncertain, questioning the things you were taught, a little horrified at the violence of the war on TV—and remember, this had never happened before. The fifties were called "the dull generation," so when the sixties' social radicalism exploded, you became very cynical at what people in charge were telling you was "right."

As qualitative researchers, we sometime get so involved with present needs and current conditions that the past seems irrelevant to our immediate investigative needs. We're often taught to ask ourselves, "What is happening here?" when we enter and stay in a field site—a mantra that keeps us rooted in the here and now. But the past holds a legacy and accumulated knowledge that has significantly shaped what exists today. Thus, we should also ask ourselves, "What happened before I got here?" Everything and everyone has a history, yet we needn't chronicle everything or everyone we observe. Charon (2013) describes history as patterns of social conflict, "the continuous struggle between tradition and revolution" (p. 199). Explore the history behind matters that seem especially troubling, conflict laden, or tension inducing, and think retroductively about how they may have emerged and why they're still unresolved.

 For your mental Rolodex: As you investigate social life, spend some time investigating your participants' and the site's histories. Reflect on how past conditions may have influenced and affected the current status.

Thinking Anthropologically

Culture is a slippery concept. Literally hundreds of definitions of and descriptions for the term exist, and there seems to be no real consensus, even among anthropologists, on a universally accepted meaning. Clifford Geertz (1973), one of the field's premiere anthropologists, offers that

> the culture concept . . . denotes an historically transmitted pattern of meanings embodied in symbols, a system of inherited conceptions expressed in symbolic forms by means of which [people] communicate, perpetuate, and develop their knowledge about and attitudes toward life. (p. 89)

McCurdy, Spradley, and Shandy (2005) state, "We define culture as: *knowledge* that is learned and shared and that people use to generate behavior and interpret experience. . . . [I]t is social knowledge, not knowledge unique to an individual" (pp. 5–6). Knowledge appears to be a recurring descriptor in many of the definitions of culture I've reviewed, and other ethnographers add that culture is not a thing but a malleable and ever-evolving abstraction:

> The observer knows of culture's presence not by looking, but only by conjecture, inference, and a great deal of faith. . . . A culture is expressed (or constituted) only by the actions and words of its members and must be interpreted by, not given to, a fieldworker. . . . Culture is not itself visible, but is made visible only through its representation. (van Maanen, 2011, p. 3)

Gobo (2008) clarifies that culture is not found in settings per se but through people's actions or "incidents" that take place in it: "Social conventions are not directly observable, but they assume material form in actors' rituals and ceremonies, in the social practices and routines that produce and reproduce the group or organization's culture" (p. 163). Other versions of culture include constructs ranging from "communities" to "systems" to "performances." This introductory collage of definitions simply emphasizes that culture exists by how you as the researcher define and operationalize it in your fieldwork and present it in your write-up.

Culture is not the only thing to examine when thinking anthropologically, but it is the central focus of this profile. *Thinking anthropologically* considers how culture, in its broadest sense, characterizes the participants' ways of working or living with others. As individuals we have multiple affiliations, whether voluntary or not, with different groups of people. Our types of belonging shape and are shaped by our social interactions with them. Researchers observe the particular forms of acting, reacting, and interacting that happen in particular settings in order to document in what ways these occur. The composite combination of unique interactions and the values, attitudes, and beliefs embedded within them help us identify and formulate what is "cultural" about the specific site and its members.

Local sites are more likely subcultures, microcultures, or even countercultures of larger cultural bodies, but that depends on how you perceive the field site and its participants. One particular doctor's clinic is not necessarily representative of an entire national health care system. But that microculture does contain constituent elements of the larger culture in addition to maintaining its own unique ways of working. That same local clinic can also be perceived as a microcosm of the national health care system—a symbolic product, if you will, of broader policies and practices created by its parent culture. When you study the local, you are studying a culture of some kind. What that culture consists of, though, is what you must investigate and document.

A few things start off my quest for understanding a people's culture. The first is the *argot,* or unique vocabulary of terms, used within the group. Many terms are uniquely local. For example, in my state university's teacher education program, "AIMS" (an acronym for a state standardized test), "TK20" (a database for student-teaching internship records), and "Level 1" (a top-status indicator for a fingerprint clearance card) are spoken and immediately understood by insiders but may be elusive terms to others. A culture's argot forces me as a participant observer to listen to and learn the idioms and slang around me—not just so that I can communicate competently with those I'm studying, but so that I can find patterns and themes in the ways they assign meanings to particular words and phrases and determine what those meanings suggest in the first place.

The second interesting aspect of culture is a contemporary look at the "mastery of sacred texts," valued as "acts of piety, discipline, personal transformation, and cultural preservation" (Moore, 2010, p. 212). Today's "sacred texts" can range anywhere from unwritten yet understood rules of the homeless surviving on the streets to a series of Internet web pages that promote a business. Sacred texts can also refer to what is committed to and embedded in memory, be they song lyrics and melody lines that obsess an adolescent, content knowledge learned by a working professional during her university years, or motherly advice and stern warnings given to a child for ways of interacting with others on a park playground. Sacred texts provide me insight into the "five r's" of people: routines, rules, rituals, roles, and relationships.

A third thing I look for is the traditions of the culture. Cultures are never static entities, and they continuously evolve through time. But at any given moment of observation, a body of established, assumed ways of working and living exist that have shaped the present condition and that continue to be practiced. Some of these traditions also take the form of the "five r's," but traditions have roots in the past and generally show constancy and consistency of *actions;* sacred texts are primarily *narratives.* Actions of tradition refer to what people do based on previous experience and knowledge—the "default conditions" of our cognitive software for operational existence (Erickson, 1997, p. 33). Walk into most social settings and the majority of people there know what to do; there are cultural scripts or schemata they follow. And if they are new to the site and its ways of working, then they navigate through the unknown, using heuristics to help them blend into the general action flow of others. All you need to do is recall your own first venture into a site such as a store or university campus or city, and remember your awkward, initial attempts to adjust and adapt to that culture's traditions (DeWalt & DeWalt, 2011; Winkelman, 1994).

A trend I've observed is how people assign the phrase "a culture of ____" to several concepts and phenomena: the culture of poverty, a culture of entitlement, a culture of fear, and so on. (Some have also used the phrase "the politics of ____," but that's another discipline and argument.) This may be loosely adapting the original meaning of the word, but there is something to be said for terming constructs as cultures, even though some may object to the term's misuse. Nevertheless, it is a good exercise to transform specific field sites, people's actions and values systems, and the artifacts they create and use into conceptual ideas for reflection that may transfer into theory. For example, I may conduct participant observation at a shopping mall and label it "mall culture," but conceptually it becomes a *culture of consumption.* I may observe youth playing Little League baseball in various outdoor fields, but after watching the emphasis that coaches and parents and even some young people place on winning, a *culture of competition* emerges as a salient construct.

Early anthropologists and their ethnographic studies were some of the first to study existing cultures systematically and qualitatively. They developed many of the methods we use today for participant observation, interviews, and document/artifact review. Framing your own study as an examination of a culture of some kind gives you a strong lens, filter, and angle for viewing social life. But be careful of pigeonholing a group of people too quickly with specific cultural, subcultural, microcultural, or countercultural attributes. Remember that culture is an abstraction, not a "thing." See how the unique, constituent elements of a group's argot, sacred texts, and traditions of action come together to give you an impression of its culture.

For your mental Rolodex: As you investigate social life, place culture as a central construct in your observations, interviews, and document/artifact reviews. Explore what is uniquely local within a particular social setting.

Thinking Psychologically

Eisner (1998) reminds us, "Brains are born, and minds are made" (p. 23). Science is still unraveling the mysteries of how the brain works, but each day seems to bring us new knowledge about its complex and intricate workings. *Thinking psychologically* focuses attention on the profiles of individual participants—their patterns of behavior in particular, for those reveal aspects such as personality, intelligence, needs, motivations, relationship dynamics, emotion management, environmental conditioning, life experiences, dysfunctions, trauma, and—most important—their thought processes. The researcher's lens and filter are positioned to observe the participant's whole-body language and zoom in close to the participant's facial expressions. The angle is one of attempting to get inside the participant's head to interpret the world as she or he perceives it and lives in it. We should always stay attuned to the actions of those we study, but this profile encourages particular emphasis on how an individual participant thinks and feels.

You don't have to be a trained psychologist or neuroscientist to think psychologically, but don't assume you can infer and interpret human behavior without an ethical compass. Unless you're trained in the discipline, you can make incorrect and even dangerous assumptions about someone based on scant evidence. But humans do it constantly. In everyday social interactions, especially when we meet someone for the first time, our minds infer a general personality profile of an individual, and we may even classify the person as a "type." We make assumptions about the individual based on physical appearance, dress, voice, and presentation of self (Goffman, 1959). We render quick judgments of the individual in terms of likability, sincerity, morality, outlook, physical attractiveness, and other domains of being human. But those first impressions can change for better or worse as we continue to interact with and learn more about the person.

Psychologists, like qualitative researchers, are trained to infer by looking carefully at people's facial expressions, body language, tone of voice, reactions, and particularly the content of their talk. Strategic questions are posed to elicit and reveal inner thoughts and feelings, which are then interpreted according to the psychologist's professional knowledge and experiences. But the parallels end there. For the psychologist, a recommended course of therapy follows diagnosis to help the client become a more functional human being. Positive and more constructive behavioral change is the goal. In a way, this does parallel the objectives of an action or community-based researcher, who also strives to create positive and more constructive change in a particular social setting. The difference is that the psychologist, as an expert in disorders, works with individuals (or couples, families, etc.) according to established disciplinary practices to help them meet their own or others' goals for their mental health, while the action researcher, serving purposely as a facilitator of change, collaborates with participants in a specific setting to encourage them to function as experts on the way they carry out their lives in that arena. If the study is more naturalistic, such as traditional ethnography, purposeful change agency on the researcher's part is usually not part of the methodology.

If we want to understand the case, we have to understand the human being we're studying. A psychological construct to discern is how the individual perceives her or his own **personal significance**—that is, her or his sense of self-worth and self-meaning through personal contributions, achievement, and deep relationships with significant others. Interviews with an individual can certainly address her or his biographical details as they relate to the topic of investigation. But if circumstances and mutual agreement permit, take some time to learn about the person. Converse with her or him, not as a research subject or participant but as a friend you'd like to get to know better and more deeply. The questions below are casual if not unremarkable, yet they are intended to reveal aspects of self that provide more dimension to who someone is:

- "How would you describe yourself?"
- "Which people or what things have been most influential in your life?"
- "Who are some of the people, or what are some of the things, that are most important to you now?"
- "What's your favorite _____ [movie, TV program, color, music, food, etc.]? Why?"
- "What makes you happy?"
- "What do you usually do when things go wrong?"
- "How do you feel about _____ [your work, your home, your social groups, what's happening now, etc.]?"
- "What are you most proud of about yourself or about something you've accomplished?"
- "What would you change about yourself if you could?"
- "What do you want out of life?"
- "What's your philosophy of or outlook on life?"

Some of these questions could be considered too personal and intrusive, depending on the topic of the study and the progress of your relationships with key participants. It's not necessary to know the answers to every one of these questions, but if you're able to talk about them outside of the formal interview setting, you may discover interesting facets of the lives of the people you're learning about and from. One of my own questions, based on a drama therapy exercise I facilitate with adult groups, asks the participant, "If you could have one and only one superpower, which one would it be?" I interpret her or his answer based on the premise that the chosen superpower reveals both the person's weaknesses and strengths. For example, if a person tells me his desired superpower is invisibility, I interpret the power through the weakness it suggests: If the person wants to be invisible, what is he trying to hide or hide from? What does he not want other people to see or notice about him? What secrets does he keep to himself? But I also interpret the power as a symbol of the person's strength. In other words, the person already possesses the superpower in one form or another. In this case, invisibility suggests to me a person who is intrapersonally intelligent, discreet, humble, a behind-the-scenes worker, and someone who does good things for others as their own reward. None of these readings are psychologically based; it would be irresponsible of me to assume they are valid. These are cultivated interpretations of mythic symbols and their suggested properties (Bettelheim, 1976) and of classic literary personas and the characteristics ascribed to them (Landy, 1993).

I keep my interpersonal relationships at a professional level with those I study, and cultivate collegial friendships with a few when it's appropriate as the study progresses. I admittedly ponder what issue(s) my key participant might discuss privately with a best friend, counselor, or therapist. But I don't go probing deliberately into people's minds to unpack their baggage. I tell myself, "My job is to learn what makes someone 'tick,' not what makes them 'tock.'" Unless you're trained in counseling, a researcher's job is not to serve as a participant's field therapist. But you should become a sympathetic and empathetic listener if any participant is in emotional distress and needs to talk through or work out a personal issue or concern. See Camic, Rhodes, and Yardley (2003); Forrester (2010); J. A. Smith (2008); and J. A. Smith, Flowers, and Larkin (2009) for discussions about psychology and qualitative research.

> **For your mental Rolodex:** As you investigate social life, compose personality profiles of key participants to render them as more dimensional beings. Examine the psychology behind people's actions, reactions, and interactions.

Thinking Developmentally

You may conduct a study that enrolls several adult participants who vary in age. Those who work with young people may have an easier time studying, say, a class of 30 children when most of them are within one to two years apart in age. But even then, there is a tremendous developmental difference between a child who is four years old and a child who is five. And there is also a significant developmental difference between an adult who is 30 and an adult who is 40.

Permit me to write about my personal experience: When I was 20, I was in the middle of pursuing my undergraduate degree, and life for me focused primarily on pursuing my vocational passion but included the occasional foray into young adult partying. When I was 40 and had been coupled for about 10 years, male midlife crisis set in and my physical appearance and dress underwent a tremendous change as I attempted to recapture my lost youth. As I approach age 60 and cope with arthritis and retirement paperwork, the reality of my mortality has sunk in and brief panic attacks of sorts occasionally enter my mind ("Aw, damn it; I'm not going to live forever."). Some things that excited me at age 20 are now offensive to me 40 years later. And some things I felt unable to do at age 20 are now carefree options for me at age 60.

Thinking developmentally acknowledges that participants' ages might influence and affect how they perceive the world and how they conceive of themselves. Certainly, age is a critical

Figure 6.1. A participant's age influences and affects how she or he perceives the world.

attribute if a study focuses exclusively on, for example, adolescents in a high school or elders in an assisted living facility. But there are times when the multiple participants of a project may vary greatly in their generational cohort. A group of medical professionals being studied at a hospital could comprise a pool of people ranging from their mid-twenties to their early seventies. Their personal life experiences as well as professional knowledge will create a broad spectrum of perspectives about matters such as wellness, illness, and death. And their respective ages shape not just what they know but how they think and feel about what they know.

The counselor who has worked for over 30 years possesses a body of therapeutic knowledge that the counselor with five years of experience can read about but must still learn on the job over the next few decades. Yet I have observed a few first-year classroom teachers demonstrate remarkable instructional skills with their students that rival those of the veteran educator of 10 years. And some professionals who have been working for over 30 years in their fields may be quite incompetent at their jobs due to burnout, an unwillingness to learn more and change, or arrogant assumptions of authority based on their presumed expertise. Age does not necessarily equate to wisdom, and years of work experience do not necessarily lead to flawless mastery.

If your study involves children, adolescents, or young adults, reference to and reviews of the literature on child development are mandatory, for knowledge of how young people grow and learn will provide insightful background context and corroboration with your own findings. There are also rich studies on adult career trajectories and professional development trends in several occupational fields. Explore how these observed patterns may harmonize with your own participants' levels of expertise. Remember that adults also have their own developmental life courses, but Giele and Elder (1998) note that recent life course study research has broken away from composing patterned models of general human development to acknowledge the unique character, unpredictable and diverse trajectories, and complex interrelationships of gendered individuals exercising agency within varying social contexts through particular eras of time. Life history extends beyond the sequential reporting of factual events, such as graduation from college, full-time employment, marriage, the birth of a first child, and so on, and now considers participant *transition* and *transformation* in such domains as worldview, life satisfaction, and personal values (Saldaña, 2013, pp. 237–238).

Sometimes our own age as researchers may help or hinder how we collect and even analyze data. Strauch (2010) asserts that the middle-aged mind is more adept at finding patterns and solving problems—not just from experience but from neural network development. You might feel confident assuming what participants younger than you may be experiencing, but you may not always correctly construct how older participants view their lives and the world. Nevertheless, if your goal is to understand people of different and varying ages, even if phases, stages, and cycles of the life course are not the focus of your study, consider how the participants' ages and cumulative experiences might influence and affect how they act and what they offer you during interviews. We are all human archives, and previous research has meticulously documented how people grow physically, cognitively, socially, and in other developmental domains, and how we study that growth through time (e.g., Belli, Stafford, & Alwin, 2009; Berk, 2009; Corsaro, 2011; Giele & Elder, 1998; Saldaña, 2003).

For your mental Rolodex: As you investigate social life, review some of the literature on life course development. Consider where your participants are on their personal life course trajectories and consider how that may influence and affect their perspectives and actions.

Thinking Sociologically

Thinking sociologically examines the social organization, structures, and ideologies of your participants in their cultural milieus, plus other research-relevant groups to which they belong such as families, congregations, neighborhoods, workplaces, and peer and recreational groups. This would also include attention to how demographic attributes such as gender, race, ethnicity, religious affiliation, political affiliation, economic class, generational cohort, nationality, and so on, influence and affect their ways of working and living among their social groups. Thinking sociologically reflects primarily on the various membership networks of your participants and their personal status within them as they interact with other people. What we are examining is the values-laden individual in her or his sociocultural contexts and conflicts: "Nearly any kind of individual problem has a sociological aspect as well. We are sociological as well as psychological beings" (Cuzzort & King, 2002, p. 435).

A sociological lens on natural life examines the social interaction dynamics of participants as they engage in the broader scheme of daily living. By studying the micro-level of social life, we might come to understand the meso- and macro-levels of a society. A conversational exchange between newlyweds is not just about a particular husband and wife, but an opportunity for commentary on gender roles and expectations, heteronormativity, and the married couple and their immediate families as a social unit. We also focus on the identities of individual participants, constructed in great part by and through socialization and social interaction. The newlywed husband, for example, has been socialized by his parents, peers, school, media, faith, and other influences to shape his perceptions and—most importantly—his values, attitudes, and beliefs about what it means to be a married man and the actions expected of him by his society at large. Sociologically, his relationship with his new wife, and, perhaps later, their children, can be understood in the context of the institutions of marriage and family.

Both anthropology and sociology closely examine the culture of a group of interest, though each discipline formulates different types of research questions and operates from different conceptual lenses. Kendell (2013) defines a society as "a large social grouping [of people] that occupies the same geographic territory and is subject to the same political authority and dominant cultural expectations" (p. 4), while Charon (2013) defines society as "a social organization of people who share a history, a culture, a structure, a set of social institutions, usually a language, and an identity" (p. 340). Thinking sociologically comes with multiple filters as social life is investigated. The study of the mundane is actually rife with examination of patterns of habit, conformity, control, obligation, compliance, duty, unquestioned routine (i.e., ritualism), and so forth—constructs of notable interest to those utilizing the work and theories

Source: Jupiterimages/Photos.com/Thinkstock.

Figure 6.2.   Sociological norms pervade public spaces.

of sociologist Harold Garfinkel. Erving Goffman's dramaturgical filter explores social life as performance, with its participants as actors creating desired presentations of self to others who serve as the audience. Max Weber's and Karl Marx's work examine macro-perspectives on power, economics, and the politics that rule us overtly and covertly in daily life. There is no one right way to think sociologically—there is a substantive body of literature and theory available, with certain writers being more appropriate than others for your particular study.

When I observe individual participants within a group in action, reaction, and interaction, or interview them about their lives, I reflect on a few questions of general sociological interest:

- In what ways, and by whom or what, has this participant been socialized to _____ [work, play, behave/act, believe, deal with a conflict, etc.]?
- What are the participant's perceptions of her or his role, status, and influence within the group or society studied?
- In what ways does the participant embody or reject the social norms of the group studied?
- What types of "social politics" is the participant involved with?
- What does this participant's personal values system suggest about the larger society to which she or he belongs?

There are specific governmental rules and laws for people to follow, culturally evolved and learned understandings among specific groups, and tacit knowledge about how people should behave in public and even private social settings. Deviance from those norms is generally perceived as a breach of the established social order among the majority of the social group. I am particularly attuned to the "breaches" participants enact with others or tell me about during interviews—their actions range on a continuum from conformity to nonconformity. This is only one facet of who they are, but it informs me greatly about their values, identities, and sense of place within various social landscapes. I observe crowd behavior in large outdoor settings such as state fairs and theme parks. Politeness and courtesy are generally expected from paid staff at these social spaces, but selected visitors are not above aggressive confrontations with other visitors if a breach has been perceived (e.g., cutting ahead in a long line, bumping into someone else, inappropriate behavior or language in the presence of children). How they handle these breaches—for example, with hostile threats, veiled remarks, sarcasm, dismissal of the concern, or apologies for misunderstandings—says much about their personal social intelligence (Goleman, 2006) and their personal understandings of justified social interactions with strangers in conflict. Delightfully ironic is how a social setting such as the Disneyland theme park, which advertises itself as "the happiest place on earth," is actually an assemblage of attendees experiencing continual micro-conflicts throughout their visit.

Sociology as a social science has a rich legacy of quantitative and mixed methods research in its literature. But the discipline's primary goal, studying social life, has also generated a substantive body of insightful and theory-rich qualitative work. For an excellent overview of key sociological theorists (e.g., Howard S. Becker, Robert K. Merton, Harold Garfinkel, Max Weber, Karl Marx) see Cuzzort and King (2002). For an accessible compendium of classic sociological principles and theories, see Charon (2013). And for a behind-the-scenes look at how selected contemporary sociologists think and work, read the interviews compiled in Fenstermaker and Jones (2011).

> **For your mental Rolodex:** As you investigate social life, focus on the individual participant's interactions within group memberships and assemblages, and the inferred meanings from the micro-level for the meso- and macro-levels of a society.

Thinking Communicatively

The discipline of human communication (and psychology, anthropology, etc.) has generated a number of methodologies and approaches to the analysis of talk and text (e.g., Agar, 1994; Drew, 2008; Gee, 2011; Gilligan, Spencer, Weinberg, & Bertsch, 2006; E. Jones, Gallois, Callan, & Barker, 1999; Rapley, 2007). These methods range from intricate systems for notation of transcripts for conversation analysis to open-ended, interpretive readings of texts for discourse analysis. There is also a canon of terms for dialogic interaction patterns such as turn-taking, adjacency pairs, response tokens, and so on. These sophisticated analytic methods encourage detailed, nuanced readings of intent, subtext, and the broader discourse of what people say and how they say it. *Thinking communicatively* is occasional, meticulous attention not just to the topics but to the substantive content of your participants' ways of speaking and writing—the messages they convey as you interpret them.

The data corpus of most qualitative studies is relatively vast, but not every datum needs extensive scrutiny. There are generally special "moments"—defined as significant passages of talk or text—that stand out as exemplars or anomalies that merit quality analytic time (Sullivan, 2012). These moments reveal salient participant characteristics, capture the essence and essentials of an issue, or demonstrate unique insight into some facet of the study. The passages can be monologic or dialogic, and they can be gathered from interview or focus group transcripts, field notes of participant conversations, or participant-generated documents such as journal entries or blogs.

As an example of a small moment, below is an excerpt from my field notes from when I observed an interaction between a female intern teacher and one of her male 10th-grade students. Notice how the italicized actions and emotions are included to document in print the nuances of what I saw and heard:

(A high school classroom; the teacher, Ms. James, is speaking to Kevin, a student, one-on-one as other students are engaged in small group work.)

MS. JAMES: Where's your paper?

KEVIN: I didn't finish it.

MS. JAMES: You didn't finish your assignment? *(marking in her grade book)* Sorry, Kevin, but I'm going to have to knock down your grade.

KEVIN: *(protesting)* God, Miss James, that is so unfair!

MS. JAMES: *(mildly surprised)* Kevin, what is "unfair" about you not doing your homework? *(Kevin is silent)*

The teenager's mild anger was quickly diffused when the teacher reminded him that he himself did not meet his responsibility as a student. Ms. James did not accept the blame for his reduced grade, but instead rationalized the consequence of Kevin's failure to complete his work. I selected this moment because, as an observer, I quickly thought of how I would have responded to the student's protest as soon as he uttered it. My first comeback to him would have been, "Well, life's unfair, Kevin," which in retrospect would probably have frustrated him even more and aggravated the encounter. I never would have thought to reply with Ms. James's tactful, "What is 'unfair' about you not doing your homework?" Her question was not condemnation of Kevin's failure but a logical argument that, as demonstrated by his silence, he could not refute. It was a moment of masterful teaching and gentle discipline that reinforced to the student that he, not the teacher, controlled his grade.

A conversational moment such as the one above could stimulate additional reflection and writing on teacher–student communication styles, the professional development of teachers, or the culture of high school. Goodall (2000) weaves human communication and culture together through his system of Verbal Exchange Coding. This approach serves as a precursor to evocative ethnographic writing, and the methods are most appropriate for initial analysis of conversations to determine first their general types (e.g., skilled conversation, personal narrative), and then their levels or practices (e.g., crisis, face-saving episode).

Researching how people communicate through talk and text is a complex endeavor. And since qualitative inquiry places great stock in words as data and presentation, we have rich opportunities for honing in on these micro-moments of speech or narrative that stand out and call for attention. I always search for the meaningful buried within the mundane. I place particular emphasis on the vocabulary and slang a participant uses (which suggests communicative competence), her or his verbal fluency (which reveals how her or his thought processes work—linearly or scattered), and voice dynamics and quality (volume, articulation, tone, variety, dialect, etc.), which reveals much about the individual's personality. Occasionally listening with your eyes closed during participant observation forces you to focus solely on the words and sounds of the environment. Most often, it is not what I read in a transcript or written field notes that grabs my ear—it is what I recall hearing my participants voice out loud in the field that stays with me as significant moments.

Virtually all of us can recall an occasional sentence or snippets of conversations that made an impact on our memory and replay silently in our minds. These moments are remembered for a reason, and their meanings are deeply personal. Fieldwork offers us opportunities to listen for these significant one-liners and dialogic interactions that hold and reveal significant themes for analysis. They are "quotable quotes" that merit inclusion in a report because the participant said it better than a researcher ever could. I am profoundly moved by steelworker Mike LeFevre, from Studs Terkel's (1972) *Working,* who offered the reason why laborers don't read in their spare time: "It isn't that the average working guy is dumb. He's tired, that's all" (p. xxxiv). I also treasure a line from one of my friends, an African American woman who gave me a positive perspective on diversity: "When I see all the different colors of all the races in this world, I see the creativity of God."

> ***For your mental Rolodex:*** As you investigate social life, listen attentively to the conversations of participants for moments of interaction that hold significance and meaning for the study. Attend to not just what participants say but how they say it.

Thinking Multiculturally

As population demographics shift across time, nations now wrestle with social changes and the varied colors of their citizenry. Major school districts in the United States enroll more children of color than White children, and the average classroom now consists of several young people who speak native languages other than English. Recent events, such as the elections of Barack Obama as the United States' first African American President, the trial of George Zimmerman for the murder of African American youth Treyvon Martin, the debate over U.S. immigration and border security with Mexico, and the legalization of gay marriage in an ever-growing number of states and countries, have brought issues of race, ethnicity, nationality, sexual orientation, and other classifications to the forefront of political debate and daily social life. Social media exhibit a range of opinions on these matters, from racism to homophobia, from nationalism to xenophobia, and from activism to compassion.

In some parts of the world, gay and lesbian couples can legally wed and are afforded the same rights and privileges as a married heterosexual couple. In other parts of the world, gays, lesbians, and the transgendered can be tortured and killed with impunity. Oftentimes homophobia and discriminatory actions stem from conservative religious or spiritual beliefs or learned patterns of thought about dichotomous, traditional, and "appropriate" gender roles. Discussing sexual orientation and even just sex itself can make some individuals very uncomfortable because it violates indoctrinated beliefs about modesty, decorum, and privacy. Research suggests that people who personally know a gay, lesbian, or transgendered individual in their social circle are less likely to possess homophobic attitudes (though parents often have a difficult time adjusting to and accepting their nonheterosexual child's orientation).

Thinking multiculturally is attuning yourself to how racial or ethnic identity, sexual orientation, and other cultural and community memberships may influence and affect your participants' identity, worldview, and daily interactions with others—the interwoven sociopolitical dynamics of power, privilege, and prestige (Charon, 2013, p. 78). Whatever your personal status or self-concept, consider that others may make their own demographic attributes highly central or merely peripheral to how they construct themselves and conduct their ways of thinking and living. Some of my White colleagues seem uncomfortable talking about race, and some gay friends have told me they abhor personal labels for their sexual orientation. Regardless of your own cultural identities, don't assume everyone holds conceptions similar to yours; and don't assume everyone within a particular cultural group shares the exact same values, attitudes, and beliefs.

Thinking multiculturally acknowledges your own positionality in a diverse world and within the field site you study. It reflects on how you can decenter your own values, attitudes, and beliefs and focus on the opinions, concerns, fears, and sometimes anger expressed by those

Source: Digital Vision/Digital Vision/Thinkstock.

Figure 6.3.   Thinking multiculturally is acknowledging your own positionality in a diverse world.

different from you. It is a willingness to talk with and listen to your participants about issues that may make you uncomfortable but that are important to them. It is not avoiding but inviting; not ignoring but attending; not denying but accepting.

An interesting task for fieldwork is to count the distribution and percentages of people of color at your field site. At restaurants, for example, compare the racial or ethnic proportions of people working in the kitchen, people waiting tables and serving food, and people eating as paying customers. Reflect on what these percentages suggest about the setting and its occupants. Also listen for assumptions of heteronormativity and whether any homophobic comments are made offhandedly. A worthwhile thought experiment is to consider how things might be different for key participants if they were of a different race or ethnicity. If possible, casually raise during informal conversation any current news items about race, nationality, or sexual orientation to hear your participants' perspectives about the issues. Some may perceive this suggestion as a covert and unethical tactic that might have nothing to do with the immediate research topic at hand. Plus, the participant may feel compelled to give a "politically correct" answer rather than an honest opinion. I offer it merely as an option for each researcher to consider. Besides, observing how people of different races and ethnicities interact informs me much more about their values, attitudes, and beliefs than what they say to me in small-talk conversation does.

Some research methodologists believe that interviewers do not need to share the same ethnicity as their participants to gather effective data, but people of comparable ethnicity (and age, gender, and sexual orientation) may be better able to establish an unspoken bond with the researcher and may be more willing to openly disclose perspectives on sensitive matters of culture. But regardless of your own attributes and those of whom you study, it is critical to have genuine respect for anyone you observe and interview, and to truly listen without judgment or challenge to people of different backgrounds, if you hope to understand your participants' worldviews.

This profile makes no secret of my own personal perspectives on these issues. As a Hispanic gay male, I have had my fair share of bullying, taunting, discrimination, exclusion, and stigmatizing throughout my lifetime. But I have also been fortunate to receive opportunity, invitation, equity, support, and inclusion by some wonderful allies. I assume that most readers of this book will be White—such is the nature of academia and research. So let me respectfully share the offense I've experienced the most and that I've learned other people of color and nonheterosexuals have also experienced: not being listened to and having our perspectives negated and dismissed. I'm not referring here to facts but to feelings. I take no issue with someone correcting me over errors I've made in regard to information. But when I express an opinion and that view is automatically countered as wrong or invalid, I feel as if the value of my thoughts has not been respected and that I have been given lesser status by someone who presumes authority (i.e., superiority). If someone of a different background offers you an opinion that you wish to immediately counter, rather than verbally reacting, stop and think about why that person holds that particular point of view, and think about why you wanted to react. Simply listen so that others can be heard. Oftentimes the best response is not a verbal challenge but a nonverbal affirmative nod of the head.

For your mental Rolodex: As you investigate social life, maintain heightened awareness of how your own and your participants' race and ethnicity, sexual orientation, and other cultural identities may influence and affect the data and their interpretation.

Thinking Feministly

Women in academia challenged the conventional positivist practices of social science inquiry in terms of its biased representation of subjects and researchers (i.e., they were predominantly men) and their limited scope of knowledge construction. Critical theory, epistemological theory, and qualitative inquiry by female scholars from the last third of the 20th century onward accelerated the feminist movement in research. Hacker (2013) states that "feminist theory focuses on the historical and cultural oppression of women and drives toward gender equality and empowerment" (p. 4). This empowerment, according to Hesse-Biber (2012, 2014), honors women's voices, issues, and lived experiences, and challenges "the encircling of knowledge claims by those who occupy privileged positions" (2012, p. 3). Hesse-Biber emphasizes that there is not one epistemological or methodological approach to feminist research but a multiplicity of perspectives, yet virtually all seem to share emancipation and social justice goals as a through-line. Just as there are different lenses, filters, and angles for qualitative inquiry, so too are there varying points of view on *thinking feministly.*

The feminist research process rejects the traditional power paradigms and disembodied relationship between the researcher and the researched in order to jointly construct a more equitable and collaborative venture among women. Participants are not viewed as objects of study but as coresearchers of the issue at hand to enhance ownership of and investment in the study. Ethical considerations and equitable treatment are prioritized. The interview replaces the question-answer model with a more dialogic and bidirectional exchange of perceptions. The analytic process is usually not conducted solely by the researcher but jointly with the participant-collaborators to further engage them in reflexive dialogue and enhanced awareness of the issues directly concerning them. Social change agendas for the betterment of women's lives are also common in feminist qualitative research fieldwork through action research or community-based projects.

Gender and *power* are two key filters for feminist inquiry. The theoretical writings of Judith Butler focus on gender as social construction and performance; and power—from its micro-dynamics in interpersonal relationships to the macro-dynamics of institutional and social control—is addressed by most feminist writers. During fieldwork, I consciously attune myself to many of the same tactics profiled above under "Thinking Multiculturally." I observe in particular how young women and men present themselves in terms of fashion and the enactment of their gender in same and mixed groups. I listen for subtle and overt interactions that reinforce or dispel gender stereotypes. In adult field settings, I inventory the proportion of men to women and assess who they perceive as those with leadership roles and authority. Most of my qualitative research fieldwork projects have taken place in elementary school settings with their predominantly female teaching and administrative staffs. Education is a fascinating discipline for observing how many women are "controlled by" various multilevel forces, and assume power through "controlling by" personal, subjective, and ethical decision-making processes (Flynn, 1991; Wales, 2009). I also attend to contradictory media representations of how women are portrayed and "audienced" in television and in print. At the time of this writing, I am observing how a national TV campaign to ban the word *bossy* as a descriptor of girls that could negatively influence and affect their potential development as future leaders, exists in the same empirical time and space as the *Sports Illustrated* 2014 Swimsuit Edition featuring three topless models in thongs on its cover.

Another filter and angle used in feminist research acknowledges that women are not one monolithic type; they include a diverse range of demographics and values—*standpoints*. Feminist writers of color such as Patricia Hill Collins and Gloria Anzaldúa brought to White female scholarship an awareness of how gender cannot be examined without attention to race, ethnicity, nationality, sexual orientation, and class. The educational writings of bell hooks (1994, 2003, 2010) elegantly address the connections between racism and sexism as well as give critiques on heterosexism and White academic privilege. It is important to note how hooks reinforces the premise that the social goals of feminism benefit not just women; they serve men through liberatory praxis and freedom from hegemonic constraint.

As a gay male, I mistakenly assumed that my nonheterosexual worldview softened my masculinist edge and would harmonize with the goals of feminism and feminist research. As a person of color, I mistakenly assumed that my experiences with ethnic discrimination paralleled the discriminatory practices faced by women, thus providing me with a more empathetic relationship with them. But I was still a man, raised in the 1960s, when the messages of female inferiority and male superiority taught to young adult men were being shattered by the emergent work of women such as Betty Friedan and Gloria Steinem.

Decades later, my gender role socialization has been modified through my experiences with liberatory education and social change projects. But I still observe how adolescent and young adult males are engaging in social performances of hypermasculine bravado; how adolescent girls are modeling their dress and behavior after female musical pop icons like Britney Spears and Miley Cyrus; how young adult females are obsessed with body image based on media representations of the "ideal" woman; and how middle-aged and senior (predominantly White) men are legislating restrictive policies affecting women's rights, health, and well-being. I look at the still alarmingly low numbers of women in influential corporate and government positions and the disparity of income between male and female workers, and realize that after almost 50 years of progress, much more work remains before we achieve gender equity. Qualitative inquiry can make a significant impact in reaching this goal. For more on this topic by a variety of chapter contributors, see the edited collections *Handbook of Feminist Research* (Hesse-Biber, 2012) and *Feminist Research Practice: A Primer* (Hesse-Biber, 2014).

> ***For your mental Rolodex:*** As you investigate social life, attune yourself to how the participants' genders play a role in their actions, reactions, and interactions. Adopt a feminist's lens to observe women's status in the field and critically assess whether equality and empowerment are present.

CLOSURE

I have grown significantly as a scholar by reading academic qualitative works outside my own field. Most surprising to me have been the connections I've constructed between seemingly disparate disciplines. Most of the time, that happened because I deliberately went into the reading experience with an open mind and with the goal of finding relevance. At other times, my reading serendipitously triggered a comparable personal memory that formed a new mental connection. If the writing was particularly evocative, I became emotionally engaged and discovered empathic bonds with the participants' stories. It wasn't that hard; humans are still human, regardless of their occupation, activity, or status. Though I may not be an athlete when I read about qualitative research in sport and exercise, I know what it feels like when your own body is no longer able to do the things it could in younger years. Though I am fortunate to never have been stricken with the cancer I read about in qualitative health journals, I know what it feels like to lose close friends to cancer and what it feels like to have no sense of control over your life. And when I read about the developmentally disabled from a sociological, anthropological, psychological, developmental, or educational perspective, I can resonate with the participants because I, too, have felt different, marginalized, and stigmatized from time to time. Multidisciplinary connections are your mind's constructions. Actively seek and make them happen.

The majority of the disciplines briefly addressed in this chapter are generally classified as social sciences, an area most appropriate for qualitative inquiry. Each discipline has generated its own vast amounts of methodological and research literature, and specialties and subspecialties within fields are quite common if not necessary for the intellectual advancement of the fields. Most qualitative researchers today wisely acknowledge that they cannot conduct their inquiries within isolated bins or narrow parameters of tightly categorized knowledge bases. Each individual we study consists of a complex combination of gendered, cultural, social, psychological, anthropological, developmental, historic, language-based, and other influential factors so tightly interwoven that it seems a nearly impossible task to disentangle them into distinct threads for comprehension and analysis.

The concept of strategically chosen lenses, filters, and angles for inquiry can provide researchers with a more reliable camera for the endeavor, but we may feel that our work is still incomplete if we have not addressed the suggested sociology, psychology, anthropology, and other "-ologies" of the investigated phenomenon. After a while, the report can become quite messy and unfocused if we attempt to capture and describe it all. Acknowledge that it's worthwhile to think about how your study and its topic might be perceived from various disciplinary lenses, but the actual written reportage of your findings requires clarity regarding the complex. Spend some quality time reflecting on the communication patterns, social dynamics, or individual psychology of a participant. This will give you a more three-dimensional understanding of the people you investigate. For the presentation of your research, tell readers what connections you've constructed or discovered between your primary discipline and others. C. J. Pascoe's (2007) *Dude, You're a Fag* examines heteronormativity and homophobia among adolescent males in a high school setting—suggesting an educational study—but the text also explores the developmental, sociological, multicultural, and feminist "intersections" suggested by her research. Carolyn Lunsford Mears's (2009) interviews with the parents of survivors of Columbine High School's 1999 shooting massacre profiled not only their responses to the tragedy, but the implications for parenting, child development, and social and governmental policies on school violence, media, and gun control.

EXERCISES FOR THINKING MULTIDISCIPLINARILY

1. Identify what you and someone of the opposite gender have in common. Identify the differences and similarities between you and someone else from a different ethnic group.

2. See Figure 6.4. Label each circle of the Venn diagram with a specific discipline of study (e.g., "Sociology," "Psychology," "Anthropology"). Include in each of the three circles a description of the relevant discipline. Bullet-point the characteristics and goals shared by each pair of overlapping disciplines (e.g., Sociology and Psychology; Psychology and Anthropology; Anthropology and Sociology). Then bullet-point the characteristics and goals shared by all three disciplines in the center. Employ the Venn diagram technique for two or three other kinds of items (e.g., historic periods, field sites, ethnic groups).

3. Find a top-tier, academic, qualitatively oriented journal whose core disciplinary focus is quite different from your own (e.g., if you're studying sociology, look at *Qualitative Health Research;* if you're studying anthropology, look at *International Journal of Qualitative Studies in Education*). Review an issue's titles and abstracts and select one or two articles to read, staying receptive to its contents and searching for connections between the article and your own disciplinary interests.

4. With instructor permission, visit and observe a one-hour college or university class whose core disciplinary focus is quite different from your own (e.g., if you're studying education, visit an engineering class; if you're studying business, visit a music class). Take participant observation field notes during class with a focus on the culture of the discipline—for example, its unique terms and vocabulary, its discipline-specific contents and knowledge base, the pedagogical (teaching and learning) methods that seem necessary for course instruction and student participation. Write a reflection afterward on the connections between the course's contents and your own field of study, and how those connections might contribute toward your own disciplinary interests or development as a qualitative researcher.

5. Contact a friend or family member who has chosen an occupation, vocation, or college major completely different from your own core interests. Interview the person about her or his job or disciplinary study and what types of skills and expertise are necessary for it. Perhaps frame the interview as if you are going to enter the other person's field and need to know what essentials are required for working effectively in it.

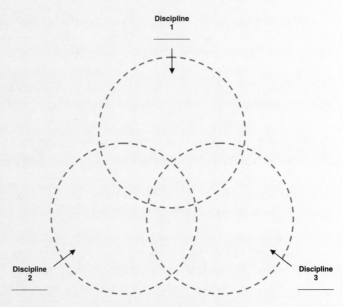

Figure 6.4.   Use this Venn diagram to complete Exercise 2.

6. With a partner, role-play a mock interview, with one partner playing a news reporter and the other an expert in a discipline totally different from your own (e.g., if you're a sociologist, role-play an art historian; if you're a political scientist, role-play a nurse). Have the "news reporter" prepare privately beforehand a set of five to seven general questions to ask the "expert" on the chosen disciplinary topic (e.g., major European artists, hospital emergency room procedures). The reporter will ask these questions one at a time, and the expert must spontaneously answer them with an air of authority and credibility. Afterward, both of you will drop out of role and discuss your respective abilities to ask and answer the questions by drawing on any previous knowledge about the topic (even though it will be minimal). Switch roles and repeat the exercise, choosing a different field of expertise.

Thinking Artistically

LEARNING OBJECTIVES AND SUMMARY

- Your mind will acknowledge artistic lenses, filters, and angles for social inquiry.
- Your mind will activate its creative processes through artistic epistemologies.

This chapter encourages "thinking like an artist" to view social life and its qualitative documentation and analysis through artistic modalities of representation and presentation. These methods of mind consist of

- Thinking Artistically
- Thinking Creatively
- Thinking Dancingly
- Thinking Visually
- Thinking Theatrically
- Thinking Cinematically
- Thinking Musically

The purpose of this chapter is to build on *Thinking Multidisciplinarily* with a focus on the major arts disciplines.

Thinking Artistically

"What is art?" is a seemingly straightforward yet deceptively complex question many artists struggle with. Philosopher and theorist Suzanne K. Langer (1977) defined art as *significant form symbolic of human feeling*. This conceptualization applies to all major arts disciplines, including dance, visual art, theatre, film, and music. (Poetry is also an art form to some but I consider it a narrative modality, discussed in Chapter 10.) And if we address the arts, we must also wrestle with the term *aesthetic*. Purely for simplicity's sake, let's assume that *aesthetic* means that which is arresting to the senses and which evokes a pleasing or powerful emotional response. "Beauty" or "beautiful" is often a traditional criterion for aesthetic, but more contemporary art theory proposes that the mundane and even that which is ugly possess aesthetics (or, underlying artistic principles) of their own.

Out of frustration with academics who attempted to write plays about their research as nothing more than dramatized, heavy-handed journal articles, I advised them to "stop thinking like a social scientist and start thinking like an artist." Here's what I mean: To think like an artist means to temporarily and occasionally abandon the constraining forces of traditional scholarly/academic research and reporting. To think like an artist means to acknowledge that the arts are epistemologies or ways of knowing the world (Barone & Eisner, 2012; Eisner, 1991). To think like an artist means to perceive social life not as idiosyncratic or random events but as happenings that have been deliberately and carefully arranged for aesthetic purposes. To think like an artist is to find the artist that may be hidden within you and let it come forth to explore the world you're investigating. And to think like an artist means to be willing to represent and present your findings not as a standard journal article but, when appropriate, as a dance, drawing, theatrical performance, short film, or musical composition.

The arts *in* qualitative inquiry provide insight into social life because they are symbolic and metaphoric extensions of human thought and feeling. The arts *as* qualitative inquiry also provide insight into social life because they utilize forms of expression that serve when words alone cannot adequately communicate our findings. Most of us have that one special song or favorite film that seems to capture the essence of who we are, what we believe, and what we enjoy most in life. Those cherished art products, even if we ourselves did not create them, are reflections of ourselves and of our values. If our participants could share with us as researchers their favorite genre of music or their top three films of all time and explain why their choices are meaningful to them, we might gain some unique insight into a facet of their worlds.

The arts *as* qualitative inquiry are a bit trickier, for not all researchers may feel comfortable or competent trying to compose an original portrait of a participant, for example. But asking a case study participant to assemble a collage out of magazine photos or other media that depicts a significant event or a state of being may reveal fascinating insights that we might never discover through interviews alone (Butler-Kisber, 2010). Transforming a participant's interview transcript of one hour in length into a five- to seven-minute monologue forces the researcher-as-artist to extract from the text the most salient passages, and to aesthetically rearrange the selected words into a coherent, self-standing piece for the stage that captures the essence of the participant-character.

The public exhibition or performance of an art form for an audience is a necessary condition for realizing the artist's creative vision. But performance as a conceptual process tends to get overused (and abused) in certain academic disciplines. A few researchers will write a prosaic article, read it aloud at a conference while seated behind a table, and preface their presentation by declaring that their work is not a paper but a "performance." The problem is that the aesthetic dimensions of good theatrical performance—such as well-paced delivery, articulate speech, meaningful oral interpretation, purposeful movement, and emotional engagement with the material—are very often missing. What these well-meaning but misguided scholars assume is that the text alone is performative. A performance is not ink on paper. A performance is an interactive live or mediated event between an artist's work and an audience—a work that has been crafted with careful consideration of its assembled aesthetic elements in order to create a quality artistic product. This criterion should not dissuade you from making art. I simply advise you to use the word *performance* in research endeavors cautiously and deliberately. In other words, if you're going to perform, you better mean it.

The arts enhance the growth of cognitive, emotional, and psychomotor pathways in the brain (Sousa, 2011, p. 217) and contribute to the development and even enhancement of critical neurobiological systems such as immune, circulatory, and perceptual (Jensen, 2001, p. 71). Our education since early childhood has provided virtually all of us with experiences in one or more traditional art forms. Before conducting an arts-based activity with non-arts-discipline adults, I often hear a hesitant, "Well, I'm not a dancer [artist, singer, actor, etc.] . . . " But you *are*. The arts are not reserved for a talented few or solely for leisure, and you should never feel self-conscious about expressing yourself through other modalities. The arts belong to everyone, whether as products that satisfy us aesthetically as audiences or as creative processes we engage in for personal fulfillment. But art strives for perfection, and so should we as its participants. If you make art, do the best you can.

Thinking artistically is a necessary method of mind that serves several purposes:

- It stimulates more creative approaches to fieldwork and data analysis for qualitative inquiry.
- It increases epistemological awareness through a range of methods and perspectives.
- It provides additional and sometimes more appropriate modalities for the representation and presentation of qualitative findings and social life.
- It offers personal satisfaction and aesthetic fulfillment through participation in the arts.
- It expands the field of qualitative inquiry through experimentation with progressive research forms and formats.

The following methods of mind profile other modalities of artistic representation and presentation for qualitative inquiry: *thinking creatively, dancingly* (an invented word), *visually, theatrically, cinematically,* and *musically.*

> ***For your mental Rolodex:*** As you investigate social life, view it through the lens and filter of an artist. Consider what arts form(s) might be appropriate for representing and presenting an exhibit or performance of your study and its findings.

Thinking Creatively

First, let's examine a critical component of artistry—creativity.

Creativity is not the sole province of the arts, but this thinking modality possesses valuable currency for artistic processes and products. And creativity is not exclusively for developing new artwork, for creativity is called into play whenever a problem needs to be solved (though musical composer John Cage attests that analysis and creation are two completely different processes). My university labels one of its faculty's job responsibilities as "research and creative activity." I have always had an aversion to this category name, for it suggests that research is not creative, and that creative activity—that is, the arts—is not research. The quantitative researcher employs creativity in the formulation of an original hypothesis, and the artist engages in research through the heuristics of new work development. Qualitative researchers exercise their creativity in all phases of a project, from the construction of a conceptual framework to determining the most appropriate form of qualitative data analysis. And our participants demonstrate their creativity every time they resolve their own unique conflicts.

At its most basic, creativity is the combination of two separate ideas to form a new, third idea. Crayons plus paper equals an original drawing. Paper plus folding equals intricate origami. Folding plus fabric equals a pleated skirt. Fabric plus earth colors equals camouflage. Earth colors plus wax equals crayons. And so on. Humans may have begun drawing with fingers etching into the dirt. But thanks to creative software developers, we can now take digital photographs and Photoshop them with fingers that manipulate a mouse.

Creativity is also subjective, for what is creative to one person may be mundane or unimaginative to another. Which film series is more creative to you: *Star Wars* or *Star Trek?* It depends on so many factors and variables, such as your previous television- and film-viewing experiences, your knowledge of film production and visual effects, your personal preferences for entertainment, your personal standards for quality, which characters appeal to you, which actors you find physically attractive, and even attributes such as your gender, ethnicity, and age.

To distinguish between terms: Imagination is what happens in the mind; creativity is what happens when an idea is realized by putting it into action or production. So why isn't this profile titled "Thinking Imaginatively"? Because imagination without creativity stays in your head. And your audiences aren't mind-readers; they need to see, hear, witness, and experience your work. Imagination is a question. Creativity is an answer. Imagination is "What if?" Creativity is "Here's how." Imagination precedes creativity, yes, yet both then work together synergistically to generate and actualize the new idea. Hahn (2011) divides the creative process into steps, which also seem to parallel the qualitative research and data analysis enterprises (not to mention the making of a child):

Step 1. The Spark (also the glint, the gleam, or that frisky feeling)

Step 2. Conception (you figure it out)

Step 3. Gestation (months of anticipation and nest building)

Step 4. Birth (painful but exciting) (p. 64)

The micro-level of creativity brings personal joy and satisfaction. Macro-levels of creativity suggest "innovations that become part of the culture, with the potential to change the way we perceive things or the way in which we live" (p. 100). Indeed, the millennium marked a noticeable cultural shift due to a combination of political, economic, technological, and social factors that gave rise to an emergent "creative class" of professions and lifestyles (Florida, 2002).

Thinking creatively in qualitative research is a "given." Investigators of social life even share many of the 18 characteristics of highly creative people—for example, observing things carefully, watching people, connecting the dots, empathizing, asking big questions (Gregoire, 2014). Virtually every new problem you solve during the enterprise involves creative action of one form or another. And since creativity involves action or production, that means strategic decision-making on your part. One of the most basic principles from design is this: For every choice, there is a sacrifice. In other words, if you make one particular choice to do something a certain way, you have sacrificed several other possible options. For *La Gioconda* (*The Mona Lisa*), Leonardo da Vinci chose to paint his subject with an enigmatic smile (see Figure 7.1). He sacrificed many other possible facial expressions, but his final choice seems to have paid off. It's quite possible that *La Gioconda* would not have the reputation it holds today as a masterwork if da Vinci had chosen to paint her with a stern, sad, or even neutral face.

Your choices during the initial research design stage are creative acts. You may be choosing one particular theory over another, one particular methodology over another, one particular site over another, and so on. But always think before you decide: "How might my study turn out differently if I choose that other _____ over this one?" (See Maxwell's *Qualitative Research Design* [2013] for a range of options.) Your fieldwork, data collection, data analysis, and write-up stages all contain multiple

Source: http://en.wikipedia.org/wiki/File:Mona_Lisa,_by_Leonardo_da_Vinci,_from_C2RMF_retouched.jpg.

Figure 7.1. Leonardo da Vinci's *La Gioconda* (*The Mona Lisa*) has an enigmatic smile.

decision-making options as well. But what makes one choice more creative than another? Since creativity is subjective, there's no set of standards to apply. But given a lack of clear benchmarks, here are a few guidelines.

The actions of creativity are what you do from start to finish for a research study. The products of creativity are perhaps what will matter most. Creativity in qualitative research is most often assessed by others based on their reading of your report (or exhibition, performance, etc.). You have discovered and constructed insights about social life that have not been noticed before, or you have revised current thought and practice by putting forth new considerations and visions. Your data analysis work and interpretations of meanings have assembled one idea plus another idea to form a completely new idea. That suggests a commingling and synthesis of aspects such as data collection, the data themselves, codes, categories, themes, processes, and so forth to generate an intriguing key assertion, new theory, or dynamic narrative. When you are able to make readers and audience members know or realize things they did not know before, or to enable them to vicariously experience what you and your participants experienced, *that* is a creative accomplishment.

Since imagination initiates creativity, you should role-play in your mind different scenarios of researcher decisions and the multiple pathways or domino effects they could set into motion. One of my play-directing colleagues first tried to see the ideal stage picture for his productions in his head by thinking to himself, "Wouldn't it be wonderful if . . . ?" Certainly, the limitations of time, budget, and human resources sometimes kept him from achieving his perfect dream in the theatre, but those realistic parameters then set into motion a revised set of ideal visions that further exercised his creative decision-making and final choices. He didn't settle for second-best; he created a new ideal that could accommodate the pragmatic realities around him.

And so it is with qualitative researchers. When our ideal site for fieldwork is rejected by its gatekeepers, then we renegotiate with them for access or look for a new site altogether. When you're stymied by a data analysis puzzle, imagine the ideal outcome in the form of categories, themes, narrative, theory, and so on. Think of all the possible and available ways to get there and choose the one(s)—and notice the plural—that may help in some way. Creativity is maximized when you consider many alternatives. That means you must first know the alternatives you have at your disposal. Qualitative data analysis seems to be the one thorn in most students' sides. Thus, the more you know about the data analysis options that are available to you, the better your imaginative envisioning, problem-solving options, and creative products. When people ask me, "What's the best book to read on qualitative data analysis?" I reply, "Read them *all. Know* them all. Because that way you'll be better informed when it comes time to figure out what's going on in your data."

Of all the profiles in this book, creativity is perhaps the one with the least amount of specific "how-to" offerings. I can't just encourage you to "think creatively"; that does neither you nor me any good. Reading all the profiles in this book is a start, though. It presents you with a range of options for lenses, filters, and angles for qualitative and thus creative thinking.

For your mental Rolodex: As you investigate social life, explore how your participants find creative solutions to their unique problems. Tap into your own creative energies by considering the many choices and alternatives available to you before selecting the final one.

Thinking Dancingly

To dance is to move one's body expressively and performatively. Dance does not need accompanying music or sound, but most dance utilizes them, while some performative forms of dance integrate speaking and singing. The action can take place anywhere from nightclubs to sidewalks to theatrical stages, ranging from spontaneous and improvisational to carefully choreographed movements.

Unless you're researching a performance program or company or a culture in which ritual is prominent, your ethnographic eye will not be attuned to dance in the traditional sense. But thinking artistically means processing what you see in different and multiple ways. Just as people speak in "organic poetry" through everyday discourse, according to verbatim theatre playwright and performer Anna Deavere Smith, your participants move in "organic dance" through their everyday actions in addition to carrying out the ritualistic and performative forms of dance you might observe on special occasions and events.

As qualitative researchers, we are often so focused on what our participants say that we neglect to pay periodic attention to how they move. As participant observers, we most likely pay more visual attention to a person's face than we do the rest of his or her entire body. I'm not advocating unseemly voyeurism or gazing, but a respectful focus on how we as a species maintain our own bodies, move through our environments, and make physical connections with others. We may not literally dance through our everyday routines, but we do move with purpose and, yes, style.

Thinking dancingly attends to our participants' gross and fine motor movements to observe how and how well they accomplish their tasks. It focuses on their nuanced gestures and body postures for inference-making and interpretations of their inner subtexts. It observes their physical bodies (weight, height, muscle tone, stature, etc.) and assesses how they might influence and affect their body image and thus their self-concept. It reenvisions everyday movement as dancelike motion with attention to dynamics such as rate and distance and qualities such as energy and fluidity. And it observes how much, what kinds of, and why physical contact with others is made in open or crowded spaces. All of these bodily actions and features are laden with inferable meaning.

On those occasions when you might observe more formal forms of dance (e.g., recitals, nightclub dancing, cultural ceremonies, street performers, flash mobs, TV competitions, organized children's activities), assess both the talent of the dancing participants and the audience members for their responses to and interplay with the performers. Observe the dance from an anthropological perspective as a ritualistic communal event. Reflect on why and for what purpose such actions are happening in the first place. Another interesting approach to arts-based data analysis is to listen to a significant passage from a participant's audio recording of an interview as you embody and dance the speaker's text. Explore how your aural interpretations of the data stimulate physical responses and movement through space, and how that kinesthetic experience informs your meaning-making of the participant's point of view.

Certain researchers place great value on the body as a site of meaning. You can tell from the frequent use of such variants as "body," "bodied," "bodying," "embodied," and "embodiment" in their writing that this becomes their primary way of perceiving and interpreting the world. Though I understand how and why this may be, I sometimes question their fixation on the body as scholarship. Granted, my body contains everything I am and it does what needs to be done. But from my readings of selected writers of qualitative inquiry, I find their focus on the body more of an obsession than a lens. I know there are those who will take offense at this opinion, but I offer that there are others who may interpret such heavy-handed, body-centric writing as, ironically, eyebrow raising.

But I will fiercely support the dancer within you. Regardless of your age, weight, stamina, or perceived physical limitations, dance is your legacy and your birthright. A classic folk saying for life goes, "Dance like nobody's watching"—meaning, never be ashamed to move expressively in private or in public. What you cannot put into words, try putting into movement, from the simplest gesture to the grandest motion. View John Bohannon's intriguing TED Talk on the power of dance to explain and understand complex concepts: http://www.ted.com/talks/john_bohannon_dance_vs_powerpoint_a_modest_proposal.html. And view choreographer Bill T. Jones's workshops with dance as a therapeutic modality for the ill: http://www.pbs.org/moyers/journal/archives/billtjones_stillhere_flash.html.

 For your mental Rolodex: As you investigate social life, spend some time focusing solely on how people move. Attend to participants' physical bodies and their implications for social action and interaction. Speculate on the performative and ritualistic contributions of formal and ceremonial dance.

Thinking Visually

Digital culture indoctrinates most of us who use the technology to perceive and think visually. The graphics of information and communication utilize images that can evoke instantaneous recognition and association. These days, words alone are sometimes inaccessible to audiences. Pictures and formatting often accompany texts to maintain our engagement with the content. Like young children, we often trust what we see more than what we hear. The eyes contain approximately 70 percent of the body's sensory receptors, sending millions of signals per second along optic nerves to the visual processing centers of the brain. The sighted take in more information visually than through any other of the senses (Wolfe, 2010, p. 183).

Observing social life as it unfolds is the stock-in-trade of the ethnographer. Fieldworkers carefully watch human action in given environments and document those actions as written field notes, photographs, and video recordings. But thinking visually is more than traditional participant observation. *Thinking visually* explores how the researcher renders visual interpretations—digitally or, preferably, by hand. The media available to us range from childhood utensils such as crayons and markers to more advanced media such as watercolors, oils, and Photoshop. Even simple pencil sketches and collages can articulate significant meanings when words alone are not enough.

Paul Mack (2012) interviewed public school art teachers about their experiences with job stress and career burnout. Mack, an art educator and artist himself plus a victim of teacher burnout, brought to the research his visual and artistic prowess. Not only did he profile his cases through evocative narratives, but he composed an original portrait of each case participant based on their biographies and the emotional content of their interview texts. Figure 7.2 shows a mixed media portrait he created of one of his participants, beleaguered teacher Bert Stabler. Mack describes his creative process:

Source: Mack, P. (2012). *Inside artist/teacher burnout*. Unpublished doctoral dissertation, Arizona State University, Tempe, Arizona. UMI Number: 3505797, ProQuest.

> For myself construction paper is associated with school. I personally refuse to use it because of that. I was surprised to see Bert working with it. Was this somehow related to his school experience? Cheap materials that are often discarded. When considering what medium to use in making Bert's portrait my usual materials would be paint, but somehow I felt it would not convey the depth of my colleague's struggles. I decided to use construction paper, a material which I despise. I hate the smell of it, its brittle texture and its pervasive association with schools. But why would I do this? Was it a symbolic gesture to take on some of Bert's burden? . . .

Figure 7.2.   Paul Mack's artistic interpretation of a participant, Bert Stabler, was an aggressive process (original in color).

> I matched the colored paper to the tones of Bert's skin, first cutting then layering, and gluing. Bert's face, in construction paper, began to emerge, but it was too clean. Teaching at Bowen [School] was raw and unpredictable. It wore you out. Took the life out of you. The edges of the paper needed to be torn. I started tearing the paper instead of cutting it. It was becoming an aggressive process of making art. The more I tore the angrier I got. How much of this is me? How much of this is Bert? . . .
>
> Considering the layers of cut and torn paper I started to pull pieces up. They would tear and leave fragments on the surface. It reminded me of peeling skin, a digging to see what was underneath. . . . I spray painted one [stencil] in pink and one in black framing the left and right side of Bert's face and then painted one over his hair as a symbolic gesture of what may have been on his mind everyday he went to work. . . . The black figure opposite the pink figure were intended to convey the complexity of working in a predominately Black school and being a Caucasian male and recognizing the inequities this reflects and perpetuates. (pp. 81–83)

You needn't be a gifted artist like Mack to think visually. Even text itself can be manipulated on a page and rendered in more suggestive ways. Figure 7.3 shows a diagram of a case study participant's concerns about personal finances during the recent shaky economic period (Saldaña, 2014). Each bin or node consists of a phrase from the interview transcript that the researcher interpreted as significant (such phrases are called *in vivo codes*), and the lines and arrows suggest how they connected or influenced and affected each other, based on the full interview text. Note that each bin holds the same font size and style, and the lines and arrows are of the same thickness. Now look at Figure 7.4 (Saldaña, 2014). Rather than rendering each quote in the same font style and size, the diagram utilizes rich text formatting, different font styles and sizes, and line variations to suggest the magnitude and status of each interacting phrase and yield a more dynamic product. Bin shapes are removed to suggest a more fluid and interactive illustration of the process.

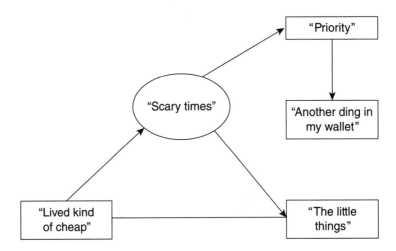

Figure 7.3. A standard diagram.

Figure 7.4. A dynamic diagram.
Source: Saldaña, 2014, p. 602.

As qualitative researchers, we rely on words to express our thoughts and findings. But an intriguing notion is to think about how your participants and the field site could be represented as a drawing, sculpture, or collage. If you feel reluctant to work by hand, use the medium of digital photography to capture the "significant trivia" of the setting—those small or inference-laden details that might escape the eye in real-time viewing. Imagine that all sounds and aural language were inaccessible at the site. How could you visually document your observations and analysis? Pablo Picasso reputedly said, "I never made a painting as a work of art; it's all research." For more on visual analysis, see Margolis and Pauwel's *The SAGE Handbook of Visual Research Methods* (2011). Also access the delightful and stunning website Thirteen Reasons Why Your Brain Craves Infographics at http://neomam.com/interactive/13reasons/.

> **For your mental Rolodex:** As you investigate social life, try drawing or photographing your observations rather than writing them down. Attempt to capture the essence of a participant through a portrait or another art form. Design and create a diagram that represents the totality of your study.

Thinking Theatrically

Qualitative research has utilized performance ethnography for several decades. This genre, which also goes by such terms as ethnodrama and **ethnotheatre** (Saldaña, 2005a, 2011a), employs the conventions of theatrical performance to stage for an audience a selected representation of fieldwork. Actors portray participants as characters voicing their stories and values systems through monologue and dialogue. Ethnodramas—the scripts—can be created from interview transcripts, adapted from existing research works, improvisationally developed from research with an acting company, or written as original yet authentic autoethnographic works by the researcher-as-playwright. Perhaps some of the best-known, most commercially successful ethnodramas today are Moisés Kaufman and the Tectonic Theater Project's *The Laramie Project* (2001) and Eve Ensler's (2001) *The Vagina Monologues* (2001). The Tony Award and Pulitzer Prize were awarded to *I Am My Own Wife,* Doug Wright's (2004) ethnodrama based on interviews with German transvestite celebrity Charlotte von Mahlsdorf.

Sometimes we feel the need to encompass the entire scope of the study as a play when only the most salient portions of the data corpus merit dramatization. A popular folk saying among theatre practitioners goes, "A play is life—with all the boring parts taken out." Thus, explore which portions of interview transcripts, field notes, and documents have potential interest for an audience. You may learn that only one 5- to 7-minute monologue may come out of it, but that in itself is noteworthy. Short monologues evoke character "portraits in miniature," and well-crafted pieces reveal much about the participant's values, attitudes, and beliefs in under 10 minutes of well-performed text, as in this adaptation of a veteran high school teacher's anecdote of a problem student (note the use of stage directions for the depiction of setting and action):

(DIANE speaks to the audience as she cleans up her classroom after a long day)

DIANE: Why are freshmen so unruly and disrespectful? One of my students today rolled his eyes at me—*again*. I stopped him and said, *(as if talking to the student)* "When you roll your eyes at me, you are basically saying 'fuck you' to the person you're talking to. And that is disrespectful and not acceptable in my room."

(to the audience)

I don't take crap from anybody. At this school, *respect* is the number one issue. I enforce that and I teach that every day by being *honest*. Now, some kids get freaked out by that, but they eventually get used to my style and appreciate it. They always come back to me and say,

(as if portraying a dense student)

"Wow, I never looked at it that way."

(as herself, shakes her head, laughs)

Isn't that weird? (Saldaña, 2010, p. 64)

Thinking theatrically asks you to assume the lenses, filters, and angles of all major production company members: the playwright, actor, designer, and director. It is not just creating a written script out of your research but imagining it realized as a performance. Be aware that a play is not a journal article. By choosing the artistic medium of theatre, you give up the conventions of academic writing (explaining your conceptual framework, references to the literature, etc.) and let your participants speak for themselves. Envision them on stage in carefully selected clothing (costumes) with just the right lighting to support the mood of their pieces, speaking directly to an audience about who they are and what's important to them.

Good actors immerse themselves in their characters by committing their texts to memory and discovering meaning through repetition of lines during rehearsals and performances. Too often when we construct and review interview transcripts, we keep the participant's words on the monitor screen, on paper, or in our minds. Both cognitive and embodied ownership and richer understanding of a participant's perspectives may emerge if we actually voice their texts out loud. Assuming the role of the person you interviewed takes you deeper into his or her mind when you replicate that person's speech verbatim and nonstop. You needn't perform in front of anyone; simply speak their texts aloud in private—at a moderate pace and while thinking about every single word you say.

Even if your research doesn't venture into formal performance, think theatrically by looking at the performative in your participants. In what ways do they exhibit impression management and their presentation of self to others, including you? If their occupations or life roles require that they interact with others in certain ways, how do they perform those actions—literally and figuratively? If all the world's a stage, when are your participants onstage and off? And are they protagonists, antagonists, a supporting role, a chorus member, or an extra? The performative can also be found through improvisational on-your-feet exploration of ideas with team collaborators and even the participants themselves in a research studio. Norris (2009; http://www.joenorrisplaybuilding.ca/) provides expert guidance on how nonverbal images and dialogic role-play can assist the exploration of social issues and writing.

Quality live performance potentially brings its spectators closer to the worlds of the participants portrayed on stage. But research on stage is effective only if the medium is the most credible, vivid, and persuasive way of presenting the thoughts and stories of those you interviewed. Like all art forms, theatre must be done well for its audiences or it doesn't make its case.

> *For your mental Rolodex:* As you investigate social life, explore how participants' interview transcripts can be reassembled into monologues for the stage. Discover which fieldwork scenes you observed can be replicated as performance. Observe how people perform in everyday life.

Thinking Cinematically

Television, video, and film are chemical, digital, and electronic forms of live theatre. The media present crafted constructions of entertainment and education, most often featuring humans as central characters in conflict and action. Some have termed us a "cinematic society" due to the pervasiveness of film and its impact on popular culture (Denzin, 1995). The almost instantaneous access to thousands of film titles, and the transformation over the past decade of box-shaped television sets into flat screen models with film screen dimensions, are indicators of how homes have become virtual movie theatres—or of how the film industry has ubiquitously implanted itself in nontheatrical spaces.

Thinking cinematically brings a documentary lens to your research endeavors, but also an artistic lens to you as a director with an imaginary handheld camera. It envisions the sphere of focus around your participant, and whether it would be appropriate to capture him or her in a close-up, medium shot, or wide shot, and from what angle (plus it entails writing your field notes as if words could capture the details of close-ups and the scope of panoramic scenes). Thinking cinematically selects the top 60 to 90 minutes of "footage" from your data corpus—field notes of real-time action, key portions of interview transcripts, significant researcher journal entries, and so on—as material that could be edited together for a feature-length documentary film with you as the narrator. Consider what its title and tagline could be (e.g., for *Fargo:* "A lot can happen in the middle of nowhere"; for *Super Size Me:* "A film of epic portions"). If you do have film production expertise, consider whether a filmic representation of your research study is at all possible. Qualitative researcher and visual artist Kip Jones interviewed gay elders in England reflecting on rural life in the 1950s, and codeveloped a fictional yet fact-based film by compositing their stories (see http://www.rufusstonemovie.com/).

Even a written screenplay could serve as a viable representational and presentational form for ethnographic fieldwork. Berbary (2011, 2012) researched sorority culture in the southern U.S. and transformed her observations into constructed dialogue between young women and richly descriptive camera shots of action:

> *The camera leaves the front room to focus on a girl entering the house as she opens the door, says hello to other passing Zeta Chis, waves to an older White woman (the house mother who lives in an adjacent apartment), and picks up a cookie from a plate left for the girls by the house cook, Miss Althea. The camera follows the sophomore Zeta Chi as she devours Miss Althea's famous chocolate chip cookie and moves up the flight of carpeted stairs leading to the second floor bedrooms where sophomore members and sorority officers (mostly juniors and seniors) dorm. While there are strict rules for living in the house, such as no boys or alcohol, most sopho-mores hope their GPA's are high enough to earn them a place in the house so that they can build stronger friendships with the other girls in Zeta Chi.* (Berbary, 2012, p. 608)

Also see Park (2009) for an intriguing autoethnographic bilingual screenplay with subtitles, and search through YouTube for short ethnographic films.

A fascinating exercise I experienced during a drama therapy demonstration session reinforced the power of cinema: If you could have been cast to portray any character from any film, which one would it have been? Your role choice may suggest a deep personal need if you reflect carefully on the character and his or her actions in the film. For example, Dr. Hannibal Lecter from *Silence of the Lambs* is my personal choice—but not because I want to be a psychopathic murderer! Dr. Lecter has keen analytic insight, a "high-powered perception" of others. Growing up, I was frequently called "stupid" by my mother, and my subsequent education was driven by a personal need to achieve high grades and other scholastic accomplishments to prove her wrong. Dr. Lecter's level of analytic brilliance, albeit shrouded in criminal notoriety, is what I myself strive for in my own qualitative data inquiry (Saldaña, 2009, p. 260). It would be fascinating to ask our key participants this same question and to discuss their responses: If you could have been cast to portray any character from any film, which one would it have been?

For your mental Rolodex: As you investigate social life, envision it as preparatory research for a documentary or even a "based on a true story" film. Condense the data corpus into the most intriguing 60 to 90 minutes of "footage" that would serve as material for the screenwriter and digital video editor to reassemble into a finished film.

Thinking Musically

Music is perhaps the most ubiquitous art form in everyday human life. Whether it's a country-western ballad we hear on our car radio, a rap song we've downloaded to our iPhone, an orchestrated soundtrack playing on a television program, or a pop tune coming through a restaurant's speaker system, music is all around us. And if we regard soundscapes as music, a fieldwork environment contains a fascinating array of human and mechanical sounds orchestrated to create a sense of place and values. Unforgettable melody lines and lyrics become hardwired in our brains, as if they have been recorded in us for automatic playback in our minds and for singing out loud. Music may be incidental or critical to each person's life, but it's an art form virtually everyone shares from infancy onward.

Music plays a powerful role in generating mood. Composers know that a carefully chosen and sequenced series of chords and notes may generate certain responses from their listeners. I play strategically selected music (e.g., Enya, Abba, Broadway musicals) before my classes to energize sleepy students and to establish a more welcoming and upbeat classroom. Classical forms of music are also powerfully evocative. Samuel Barber's Adagio for Strings, Op. 11, one of the best-known examples of music, captures a sense of melancholy. You hear this selection often in film and television soundtracks over somber or tragic imagery. Many of us can also imagine real-life settings and their accompanying actions in which Barber's Adagio would be appropriate as a background score (e.g., somber processions, funerals, hospital rooms, military combat, news footage of natural disasters).

Music in (and as) qualitative research has several applications. In composition, Steve Reich's innovative work *Different Trains* (1989) integrates excerpts from interviews with selected participants about trains in America and Europe before, during, and after World War II. He includes and arranges some of the interviewees' texts into vocal rhythmic and inflection patterns as melody lines throughout the piece ("From Chicago to New York," "And he said 'Don't breathe,'" "Black crows invaded our country"). Documentary and music come together in this masterwork to capture the spirit of a train's cross-country motion and the horrors of transport to concentration camps.

Thinking musically heightens your attunement to the aural aspects of your field site and the creative attribution of possible musical forms to your research experiences. Like visual art and dance, music expresses that which we may not be able to communicate through words alone. A popular saying goes, "Life should come with a soundtrack." What song or type of score would you select for your field site? What music would be appropriate for a participant's entrance into the space or as background or underscore as he or she speaks during an interview? A professional ethnotheatrical

Source: Hemera Technologies/Photos.com/Thinkstock.

Figure 7.5.   Music is perhaps the most ubiquitous art form in everyday human life.

production company, The Civilians, occasionally integrates actual participant texts into song lyrics for their musical plays. How intriguing it would be if selected excerpts from an interviewee's transcripts inspired an original song or even a short aria.

A participant's preferences for and tastes in music say much about the values system and lifestyle of the individual. Though it may not be a standard or expected interview question, ask the participant what his or her favorite music, singer, or composer is, and why. Music educators have employed narrative inquiry to present stories of young musicians and their teachers engaged in the art form. This creative nonfictional form of qualitative inquiry seems to lend itself readily to vignettes about people's relationships with music, as do more standard approaches such as case studies and ethnography.

See Bresler (2005) for the intricate connections and parallels between musicianship and qualitative research. See also Manovski's (2012) award-winning autoethnography utilizing evocative narratives, poetry, sheet music, and photography as an example of identity work, describing his development as a singer and gay man.

 For your mental Rolodex: As you investigate social life, listen to a setting's soundscapes and the forms of music that are naturally played in the environment. Reflect on the possible accompaniments and soundtracks that might be played to represent the participants in action or during monologic reflection.

CLOSURE

People who dismiss the combination of traditional social research with the arts are closed-minded—literally. By rejecting the possibilities of creative integration for insightful discovery, they have narrowed their options for understanding the human condition. Their brains lose opportunities for new synaptic connections and development through artistic experiences. Imagination and creativity are processes transferable to any task. Liora Bresler (2013), one of arts education's most noteworthy scholars and advocates, testifies that prolonged engagement through ethnographic study of artwork itself deepens one's personal capacity for empathy—a critical attribute for the qualitative researcher. I myself declare that being an artist has made me a better researcher, and being a researcher has made me a better artist.

Remember that the arts are a way of knowing. They are not clever add-ons to qualitative reports but legitimate epistemologies that may provide us deeper understanding of participants' experiences and meanings. The arts as inquiry enable researchers to tap into the emotional and aesthetic realms of who we are, which is what it means to be human.

EXERCISES FOR THINKING ARTISTICALLY

1. Read selections from arts-based research methods collections (e.g., Knowles and Cole's *Handbook of the Arts in Qualitative Research* [2008], Leavy's *Method Meets Art* [2009]). Speculate how a standard, traditionally written qualitative research study in your discipline might utilize arts-based methods for data representation and presentation of its findings.

2. Take a verbatim interview transcript and transform the data into a written monologue for a five- to seven-minute stage performance. Not everything in the full-length transcript must be used, only those portions that seem noteworthy. Edit, rearrange, and revise the interview text as needed for a more coherent and self-standing performance piece. Include stage directions for suggested actor movement, plus any necessary set pieces and hand properties for the one-person vignette. Voice out loud what you wrote to test the monologue's potential. See Saldaña's (2011a) *Ethnotheatre: Research from Page to Stage* for playwriting guidance.

3. Watch a 10- to 15-minute video clip in which a moderate number of participants engage in naturalistic social action (if this is not available, watch a TV program with a moderate number of characters). Turn the sound off and take field notes with an exclusive focus on the participants' bodies and their movement through the environment. Notate not just whole-body movements but gestures and facial expressions as well. Also record aspects such as touch, proxemics, eye contact, physical fitness, and rate and range of motion. Analyze the

field notes and reflect on your methods of describing and documenting bodies and physical movement.

4. Write about or discuss with a peer one or more of these short yet complex questions: Why do we dance? Why do humans create visual art works? Why do we create live theatre? Why are movies/films so popular? Why do we sing and play musical instruments?

5. Speculate and discuss with a peer why the performing arts professions seem to have a large number of awards ceremonies and why their television broadcasts generally draw large viewerships.

Thinking Summarily

LEARNING OBJECTIVES AND SUMMARY

- Your mind will reflect on how to condense and synthesize the essential attributes of a qualitative data corpus.
- Your mind will employ various processes of deductive reasoning toward summative thought.

This chapter explores ways researchers can think about summarizing their observations and qualitative data analyses through statements and visual representations and presentations that put forth major constructions—that is, findings. These methods of mind consist of

- Thinking Summarily
- Thinking Assertionally
- Thinking Propositionally
- Thinking Hypothetically
- Thinking Theoretically
- Thinking Diagrammatically
- Thinking Conclusively

The purpose of this chapter is to review ways of summarizing a vast database and extensive analytic work so that the reader or audience can grasp the core meanings of a research study. Several of the principles profiled in Chapter 4 ("Thinking Symbolically") are also relevant to this discussion.

Thinking Summarily

Summarizing condenses a larger work into a much briefer one. Note that I did not use the verb *reduce*. I purposefully use the verb *condense* because that suggests a richer outcome of summative efforts. *Reduce* suggests that something has been taken away or lost; *condense* implies that core content has been retained. Technically, a summary does both of these things, but it's the conceptual idea and process of condensing that adds value to the final product.

Many of Campbell's brand soups are condensed. The can contains the thick essence of a food; all we need to do is add water, milk, or broth to double its contents. I jokingly tell my students, "Qualitative inquiry is making cans of Campbell's soup." We condense (i.e., summarize) a vast amount of related literature into a preparatory literature review and conceptual framework. We condense our field observations and experiences into field notes, transcripts, and other documents. We condense our raw data into codes, categories, and themes. We condense our data analyses into matrices, diagrams, and assertions. And we condense our final reports into key words, abstracts, and major findings.

Thinking summarily is the continuous act of condensing massive amounts of qualitative data into briefer accumulations of meaning. Though a computer and software can store large amounts of information, as human analysts we can process only a portion of that information at a time. Periodic and cumulative summation enables us to take stock of where the journey has taken us. Summary is our brain's way of detecting critical attributes (Sousa, 2011, pp. 163–165). Imagine taking a one-week vacation: Your documented record when you return home is not a 24/7 video of absolutely everything that happened. It's more likely a set of photographs, perhaps a few video clips, and some carefully chosen souvenirs and artifacts. Those records don't just represent but summarize your holiday adventure. When you share those items with your friends, accompanied by your narrative highlights of the trip, they can get a general idea of your experiences without having to sit through over 150 clock hours of continuously streaming video. A qualitative study and write-up are like that: a brief account of memorable moments and highlights from your research journey.

We value our own writing and have great investment in what we've composed, especially after working so hard to create it. But our readers have limited time and often prioritize other tasks. The information age provides so much intriguing textual and visual material to consume that we cannot possibly read it all. We serve our readers both by writing the primary narrative elegantly and by summarizing our work succinctly. Wolcott (2009) wisely notes,

> The major problem in writing up descriptively oriented research is not to *get* but to *get rid of* data! With writing comes the always painful task of winnowing material to a manageable

length, communicating an essence rather than compiling a bulky catalog that would provide further evidence of one's painstaking thoroughness. . . . The lengthier a study, the more costly to produce it, and, correspondingly, the greater the risk if it does not attract a wide readership. (p. 16)

Chapter 4 ("Thinking Symbolically") contains other summative strategies such as abstracts, capsules, and metaphors that relate to this discussion. I could continue with other principles about thinking summarily, but that would contradict my purpose, so I'll conclude the section here. (As Forrest Gump states, "That's about all I got to say about that.")

Thinking summarily is a necessary method of mind that serves several purposes:

- It forces you to condense vast amounts of qualitative data into more manageable units for analysis.
- It encourages you to reflect on and extract the essential meanings of your work.
- It motivates you to produce more focused and clearer writing.
- It provides streamlined accounts of your fieldwork and analysis for your readers' ease.

The following methods of mind profile other modalities of summative representation for qualitative inquiry: *thinking assertionally* (an invented word), *propositionally, hypothetically, theoretically, diagrammatically,* and *conclusively.*

> **For your mental Rolodex:** As you investigate and document social life, analyze your data, and write up your report, condense the volumes of text and other representations into briefer forms.

Thinking Assertionally

I use the invented word *assertionally* rather than *assertively* because the latter refers to something else altogether. An assertion is an interpretive "read" or "take" that synthesizes a larger portion of data. Assertions are summative statements the researcher puts forth that can be supported by evidence. If any disconfirming evidence appears that does not substantiate the statement, the assertion is revised. It is a holistic yet systematic way of reviewing the data corpus and composing claims about what the researcher interprets to be true.

Thinking assertionally incorporates the heuristics of Frederick Erickson's (1986) landmark chapter on qualitative research in education. Figure 8.1 illustrates that the central argument or all-encompassing interpretive claim about the fieldwork observations is labeled the *key assertion.* This statement derives from, is supported by, and is linked to its related *assertions,* which are in turn further supported by their constituent *subassertions.* Though you may be reading the model from the top down, the subassertions and assertions provide the evidentiary warrant on which the key assertion is built. The key assertion and assertions themselves should also interrelate with each other through *key linkages* or statements of connection.

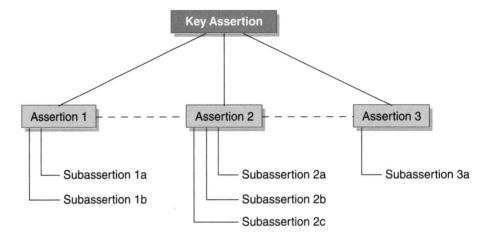

Figure 8.1.   Thinking assertionally outlines the interrelationships between and among a key assertion, assertions, and subassertions.

Source: Based on Erickson, 1986.

As a brief example, below is an excerpt from a verbatim transcript of an interview with a man in his thirties, during which he recalls one of his most recent attempts at dealing with his digestive difficulties:

> My, my chiropractor sent me to a doctor because she's like, "I can't prescribe medication but I really think, to kick this out of your system, we want to prescribe this," and she told me that, what she wanted. So she sends me to a person I know and a person that she knows and this doctor was just, she was a medical doctor but a quack. I'm just like, "You don't know anything." And, I'm like, she was testing, which is fine, testing me for all these, testing my blood, testing my liver and all this. And, she's like, "Well, I don't know what to do." I'm like, "What about that medication, you know, Doctor—she suggested?" "Well, I could put you on that and I think that's the best thing, but I just don't know what's going on with you." And, I'm like, it's all like going back to the medieval days for me. It's like, I'm like, I spent time with my doctor and we've been treating this and we want results to just kick it. But, she's all—doctors have that ego, like, "I'm God, I know better than anyone."

One goal of assertion development is to summarize the content or implications of a passage into one sentence. It is a holistic, interpretive act, since each person will read and extract something different from a story. Low-level inferences address and summarize what is happening within the particulars of the case or field site—the "micro." High-level inferences extend beyond the particulars to speculate on what the story means in the more general social scheme of things—the "meso" or "macro." A reasonable low-level assertion about the participant's story above might read:

The patient experiences frustration with inconclusive diagnoses.

Another person examining the same data might put forth a differently worded low-level assertion:

The patient perceives the doctor as incompetent when an inconclusive diagnosis is provided.

A high-level inference extends beyond the case, yet derives from it to posit a synoptic generalization (a view of the whole) about the data's suggested broader meanings. Thus, one high-level inference might read:

Patients desire specific and definitive answers about their medical conditions from physicians.

A different high-level inference to propose as an assertion might be:

The medical sciences do not always provide the need for certainty that patients seek.

Chapter 1 reinforced that all propositions are assertions, but not all assertions are propositions. Propositions put forth a conditional event (if/then, when/then, since/that's why, etc.). Thus, "The patient perceives the doctor as incompetent when an inconclusive diagnosis is provided" is both an assertion and proposition (more on this is discussed in the next section).

Erickson promotes analytic induction—**constructivist** exploration of and inferences about the data—based on a careful and thorough examination of the data and an accumulation of knowledge with each reading. The goal is not to look for "proof" to support the assertions, but for the plausibility of inference-laden observations about the local and particular social world under investigation. If our research study had included another patient—a former nurse—who found inconclusive diagnostics an inescapable reality of health care based on her own professional knowledge, this discrepant case would have provided disconfirming evidence of our original assertion (i.e., "The patient perceives the doctor as incompetent when an inconclusive diagnosis is provided"). We would therefore have had to revise that assertion to accommodate both the first and second case, perhaps as follows:

An inconclusive diagnosis generates a range of patient responses, dependent on their background knowledge of medical practices.

Assertion heuristics are ways of summarizing human actions as you interpret them. As you compose these summative statements, it is necessary not just to think about but also to store and recall the data corpus in your mind. Certainly, a review of the database can jog your memory and reveal any discrepant cases as disconfirming evidence for your initial claims. The collection of statements serves as material that can be outlined into related assertions and subassertions for an organizational array of the analysis (see Figure 8.1). You compose the key assertion after reflecting on the totality of assertions. This narrative approach to condensing a data corpus keeps you grounded in the particulars of the data while transcending them to suggest more general applications. See Erickson (1986) for a full description of his methods, or Saldaña (2011b) for an extended overview. Also see Adams (2011, pp. 85–108) for the use of 12 interrelated "premises" (statements comparable to assertions) that build on and connectively flow from each other to describe the general *process* of coming out of the closet for lesbians and gays.

 For your mental Rolodex: As you investigate social life, condense the data corpus by composing summative assertions and subassertions about the actions you observe, and revise them as any disconfirming evidence appears. Make inferences about both the particulars of the field site (low level) and their broader, general applications (high level).

Thinking Propositionally

Chapter 1 introduced the idea that a proposition functions as an evidence-based statement that puts forth a conditional event (if/then, when/then, since/that's why, etc.). It is somewhat comparable to an assertion, but explanation or causation is purposefully embedded in it. An example of a low-level inference from the profile above is, "The patient perceives the doctor as incompetent when an inconclusive diagnosis is provided." If that assertion about a specific case were transformed into an "if/then" proposition with broader applicability, it might read:

Inconclusive diagnostic results may lead some patients to believe that their health care professionals are incompetent.

Thinking propositionally establishes evidence-based reasons and rationale for what, how, or why things happen when certain antecedent conditions are present. It composes statements that put forth logical arguments in short storylines that are then fleshed out through extended narratives. The proposition above tells the reader that *if* or *when* a certain action occurs, something (or *what*) may *then* happen:

- *if* or *when*: inconclusive diagnostic results are given, and
- *what* or *then*: a patient may believe that health care professionals are incompetent.

The extended narrative then explains the details or conditions behind that claim, such as the severity of the illness, the temperament of the patient, the type of health care professional, the nature of the patient–doctor relationship, and so on. Recommendations might also be provided to those concerned, such as advice to health care professionals on how to better inform patients of inconclusive test results to lessen frustration and anxiety, and medical protocols to follow when certain types of tests reveal ambiguous outcomes.

Propositions have a predictive element to them that could transfer to other settings, contexts, and times. But notice how much conditional language is often woven into these types of statements: "may," "might," "likely to," "it is possible that," "sometimes," and so forth. Certainty is uncertain. Thus, we need to couch our claims with a tinge of likelihood rather than bold absolutism. Even quantitative researchers present statistical "fudge factors" to account for possible errors.

The best propositions are pattern-derived and pattern-driven. When you observe certain antecedent conditions, mediating variables, and consequential actions or outcomes happening frequently, this provides more substantive evidence for your propositional claims. You are summarizing patterns of influences and affects (i.e., cause and effect) that provide a little bit of order to what we sometimes perceive as random or chaotic in life. Your propositions need to be asserted with firm confidence after a rigorous examination of evidence. You are telling readers "if/then," "when/then," and "since/that's why." If they adopt your claims into their practice, you carry some responsibility for not only your own observed outcomes but for *their* outcomes as well. Think before you propose.

> ***For your mental Rolodex:*** As you investigate social life, observe patterns of antecedent conditions, mediating variables, and consequential actions or outcomes to compose propositional statements of explanation or causation.

Thinking Hypothetically

A hypothesis, used primarily in empirical research, is a deductive and predictive statement, somewhat comparable to a proposition, which is field-tested or put through field experimentation to assess its reliability and validity. Hypotheses may be formulated by qualitative researchers after initial observations to test the credibility and trustworthiness of their assertions, propositions, and theories in progress. O'Dwyer and Bernauer (2014) specify that a research hypothesis is "a tentative statement that predicts the specific relationships, similarities or differences, or causal mechanisms that the researcher expects to observe among the attributes being investigated" (p. 54).

Thinking hypothetically means asking yourself, "I wonder what would happen if . . . " or "If these particular things are present, will this other particular thing happen?" Just as an assertion can be transformed into a proposition, a proposition can serve as the basis for a hypothesis. One of the original assertions about the health care case described above was, "The patient perceives the doctor as incompetent when an inconclusive diagnosis is provided." By massaging or tweaking that statement into something that can be observed, inferred, or assessed, we can reword it into a hypothesis for field testing:

> When a patient receives inconclusive diagnostic results, she or he will attribute them to the doctor's incompetence.

But another patient we spoke with, the nurse, understood that inconclusive test results were not (always) the fault of the doctor but possibly of the test itself or the unusual medical condition of the patient. Thus, the hypothesis might be rewritten to better accommodate the more diverse range of responses possible:

When a patient receives inconclusive diagnostic results, she or he will assign blame to someone or something else as a form of denial.

We would then find ways to determine how patients who get incomplete, ambiguous, or uncertain results from medical tests react, and interpret whether their responses are some type of denial through blaming—and if so, of whom or what. As data come forth, we may find several "it depends" conditions at work; for example, reactions may depend on the severity of the illness, the patient's ability to emotionally cope with uncertainty, and the physician's tact and compassion with patients. These conditions are disconfirming evidence of sorts that force a revision of the initial hypothesis into one that better includes the "it depends" factors.

Hypotheses are forms of predictive thinking and assessment. As when formulating propositions, you are investigating and establishing reasons and rationale for what, how, or why things happen when certain antecedent conditions are present. In other words, you are predicting what particular reactions and interactions will occur when certain actions are initiated. No one can predict the future with 100 % accuracy, but our minds are hardwired to make predictions to gain some sense of control over our lives.

We may not always construct hypotheses as a formal heuristic for qualitative inquiry—the method is actually more the domain of the quantitative paradigm. But qualitative researchers are still human, and in our minds we will occasionally speculate now and then on how things we observe may turn out. This informal hypothesizing originates from our brain's primal survival instincts, by which we assess whether danger might be present in the conditions surrounding us and attempt to determine what may or will happen so that we can protect ourselves. We carry this impulse into our everyday lives today, trying to make sense of the conditions around us in order to stay safe. Hypothesizing is natural, and as qualitative researchers observe what's happening now they will have fleeting thoughts about what might happen later.

An interesting thought experiment might be to speculate on what might, could, or should happen in the field site six months to one year after you leave, or to imagine what a key participant's life might, could, or should be like three to five years after the study ends. Both of these experiments can be field-tested through follow-up investigation, if possible. But I have lived long enough to testify to the cliché "You never know what the future holds," even though I have also lived long enough to advocate that "The future is what you make of it." Individual agency notwithstanding, we must always reconcile with uncertainty, the unforeseen, and the unpredictable when we predict.

For your mental Rolodex: As you investigate social life, construct selected hypotheses based on initial, observed patterns, and field-test them for assessment and revision.

Thinking Theoretically

Chapter 1 described a *theory* (as it is traditionally conceived in research) as a generalizable statement with an accompanying explanatory narrative that:

- predicts and controls action through an if/then logic,
- explains how and/or why something happens by stating its cause(s), and
- provides insights and guidance for improving social life.

Gobo (2008) proposes that a theory consists of a series of hypotheses that have been tested by the researcher (p. 242), but assertions and propositions can also serve as preparatory groundwork for theory development. Several methodologists offer that a theory should weave together the interaction effects between two or more variables, which the first two criteria above acknowledge. But the improvement-of-social life criterion is Gibson and Brown's (2009) primary recommendation, and I feel it is wise advice for promoting a theory's functional efficacy.

Thinking theoretically summarizes the totality of your research experiences into a single sentence about social life that holds transferable applications to other settings, contexts, and possibly time periods. It is, for lack of a better phrase, a foreseeable "truth" you posit based on your observations of repeated patterns of specific actions, reactions, and interactions. Your theory claims that, given a particular set of circumstances and conditions, something specific will most likely happen. And, good theories are elegant and have practical value. They don't just coldly demarcate their if/then variables, but weave them together to suggest intricate interrelationships. Theories are insightful predictions and commentaries about social life that help us to plan ahead, be forewarned, and make our lives better.

For example, Kelling and Wilson (1982) popularized the well-known literal and metaphoric "broken windows" theory in their article on police and neighborhood safety. This one-sentence theory has been italicized in the excerpted passage below, and the narrative before and after it unpacks its meanings. Notice the suggestions of prediction throughout the excerpt, which meet the if/then criterion for a theory; the explanations of what and why certain things will happen, which meet the second criterion; and the recommendations for how to make social life—namely, public safety—better, meeting the third criterion:

> Social psychologists and police officers tend to agree that if a window in a building is broken and is left unrepaired, all the rest of the windows will soon be broken. . . . Untended property becomes fair game for people out for fun or plunder and even for people who ordinarily would

Source: Hemera Technologies/Photos.com/Thinkstock.

Figure 8.2. The "broken windows" theory has achieved staying power and almost canonical status.

not dream of doing such things and who probably consider themselves law-abiding. . . . [V]andalism can occur anywhere once communal barriers—the sense of mutual regard and the obligations of civility—are lowered by actions that seem to signal that "no one cares." . . . [This is] a bit of folk wisdom that happens to be a correct generalization—namely, that *serious street crime flourishes in areas in which disorderly behavior goes unchecked* [emphasis added]. . . . Just as physicians now recognize the importance of fostering health rather than simply treating illness, so the police—and the rest of us—ought to recognize the importance of maintaining intact communities without broken windows.

Several law enforcement agencies adopted this theory into their policies for crime prevention, monitoring, and arrests. Later research and reportage after the 1980s, however, clarified that the initial theory had never been substantiated by empirical evidence. The coauthors themselves called it "folk wisdom" in the passage above. Social researchers and criminologists have attempted to either prove or disprove the broken windows theory and expand on its nuances, but the idea has achieved staying power and almost canonical status (Kirchner, 2014).

Each discipline will maintain its own body of theories for professional practice. For example, education puts forth for teachers the theory that *the more students are engaged with the content of a lesson, the less management and discipline problems may occur in the classroom*. This suggests that educators should employ pedagogical methods with their students that will focus young people's attention on the subject matter. Engagement-enhancement methods might include such strategies as explaining relevancy and applicability, media presentations, manipulatives, participatory involvement, and humor. Without such engagement, teachers will most likely face a number of bored students who will soon be off task and exhibit disruptive actions.

Some researchers and methodologists place a lot of stock in theory development as an essential outcome of qualitative inquiry. As for me, if it happens, great; if it doesn't, it's not the end of the world. I would rather read a well-formulated set of assertions about the local and particular contexts of a site and its participants than a weakly constructed and ambiguous theory with little utility or transferability. And if I do read a theory, I need it stated in one sentence—bolded, italicized, or underlined—with an accompanying narrative that explains the details of it. Some people may protest this directive, insisting that theories cannot be reduced to a single statement and that detailed explanations need time and space to unfold. But I counter with an if/then statement: "If you can't state your theory in one sentence, then you haven't thought it through carefully enough."

Thinking theoretically is not just constructing theory but thinking *with* theory. Jackson and Mazzei (2012) profile various noted theorists (e.g., Derrida, Foucault, Butler) and illustrate how their ideas can serve as conceptual and analytic frameworks for your own study. Alvesson and Kärreman (2011) approach theory development as a matter of problematizing the data and resolving "breakdowns" in emergent patterns and fieldwork observations for stronger theory construction. Chapter 10's "Thinking Proverbially" profile will introduce you to proverbs as theories and additional summative statements about your research.

> **For your mental Rolodex:** As you investigate social life, use assertions, propositions, and hypotheses as heuristics to construct one or more theories based on your observations of patterned actions, reactions, and interactions.

Thinking Diagrammatically

Umoquit, Tso, Varga-Atkins, O'Brien, and Wheeldon (2013) examine the nuanced differences between such terms as *diagram*, *map*, *figure*, *chart*, *table*, *drawing*, and *illustration*. Miles, Huberman, and Saldaña (2014) refer to any form of qualitative matrix and network, in general, as a data "display." In fact, one of their mantras is "You know what you display" (p. 13), meaning that your construction of a visual representation is a synthesis of your analytic work and findings. For simplicity's sake, I use diagram in this profile as a global term to refer to any summative visual representation and presentation of qualitative data and analysis.

Thinking diagrammatically creates visual forms of information and knowledge transfer. You represent your data and present your findings in graphic ways to both summarize and communicate the essential elements of your work. These diagrams can range from simple, conventional, boxed matrices with text in their cells (see Figure 8.3) to networks showing various connections and flows among key variables or constructs (see Figure 8.4).

Diagrams symbolize your data and analyses. They serve the researcher by condensing the data corpus into at-a-glance references for reflection, and they serve the report's readers by enabling an at-a-glance cognitive grasp of the study's core findings. Diagrams are visual storytelling of the major plot points of your research tale. They show rather than tell your readers on one page or on one unscrolled monitor screen of the salient turning points that occurred as your participants' stories unfolded through time.

INITIATING SMOKING CESSATION PATTERNS	MONTH 1	MONTH 6
NEGATIVE EMOTIONS	Anxious, nervous, angry, aggressive	Occasionally anxious
PHYSICAL CHANGES	Gained 5 pounds, felt "burning" sensation in throat and lungs	On weight loss program after gaining 20 pounds, heightened sense of smell
RESTLESS JOURNEY	Wandering and habitual movements	Habitual movements
REGRETFUL LOSS	"Felt like crying," hyper-conscious of cessation	Nostalgic for smoking, "hangs around" smokers

Figure 8.3.   A matrix of smoking cessation patterns.

Source: Miles, Huberman, & Saldaña, 2014, p. 92.

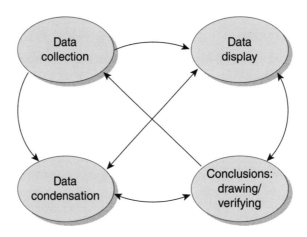

Figure 8.4.   A network of data analytic components.

Source: Miles, Huberman, & Saldaña, 2014, p. 14.

Constructing a diagram is not just a matter of creating a product intended for publication but part of the analytic process. The brain doesn't outline information—it organizes it in networks and maps (Wolfe, 2010, p. 190). Dey (1993) offers that diagrams are heuristics, for they "help us disentangle the threads of our analysis and present results in a coherent and intelligible form"

(p. 192). Friese (2012) adds that diagrams display not only our analytic variables and categories but also the answers to our research questions (p. 214). Working with pencil and paper for initial diagrams may seem "old school," yet this method permits you to transfer the visual images in your mind somewhat quickly into tangible albeit rough-draft form. If your study and analysis are variable-, category-, or process-oriented, place each label on its own separate index card or sticky note for easier layout and rearrangement on a flat surface. Continue "noodling around," yet remain firmly rooted in the data from which your key concepts originated to explore plausible interrelationships among them.

The lines and arrows linking each bin are not just linear connections; they are active and varied relationships. Urquhart (2013) reminds us that identification of relationships is needed in order to develop assertions, propositions, hypotheses, and theories. Instead of using merely lines and arrows as connectors, imagine that a word or phrase were placed in between two separate category bins. Thus, "Category 1 → Category 2" might be phrased as "Category 1 *accelerates* Category 2" or "Category 1 *depends on the types of* Category 2" or "Category 1 *increases the difficulty of* Category 2." Spradley's (1979) semantic attribute relationships also connect the categories: Category 1 *is a way to do* Category 2; Category 1 *is a cause of* Category 2; Category 1 *is a reason for doing* Category 2, and so on. Give equal attention to the lines and arrows as well as the bins in your diagram to illustrate their action, reaction, and interaction.

Chapter 7's "Thinking Visually" profile and Figure 7.4 encourage you to think outside the box when it comes to using rich text features and lines of varying styles for diagramming. Digital photographs of fieldwork and participants are one of the most easily collected forms of display for a report, assuming proper clearance from human subjects has been obtained for publication and dissemination. Computer software for graphics has advanced and become accessible to most users so that sophisticated visual models can be assembled somewhat easily on a monitor. Figure 8.5 illustrates Thompson, Windschitl, and Braaten's (2013) model of "novice teachers' developmental trajectories of ambitious practices [as they negotiate] conflicting contextual discourses" (p. 608).

This study examined how 26 beginning secondary school science teachers developed their instructional practice as they participated in two types of communities: one infused with discourses and tools supportive of ambitious teaching (usually learned at their university teacher education programs), and another that reinforced traditional practices (usually reinforced by the staff at the secondary schools where they taught). But rather than lumping all 26 teachers' experiences together into one composite flow diagram, the researchers observed among the participants three particular trajectories of practice—each with "distinctive signatures" for how the novices engaged students intellectually. The authors' accompanying diagram illustrates those three different trajectories with a note that explains, "Novice teachers differentially affiliated with communities in the university and school contexts (large arrows), developed different types of critical pedagogical discourses, and differentially used tools and routines within and across communities (processes indicated by smaller arrows or broken arrows)" (p. 608). The findings detailing the diagram's meanings are a necessary read for understanding the stories of the three different trajectories—a point that reinforces how diagrams emerge *from* analytic narrative

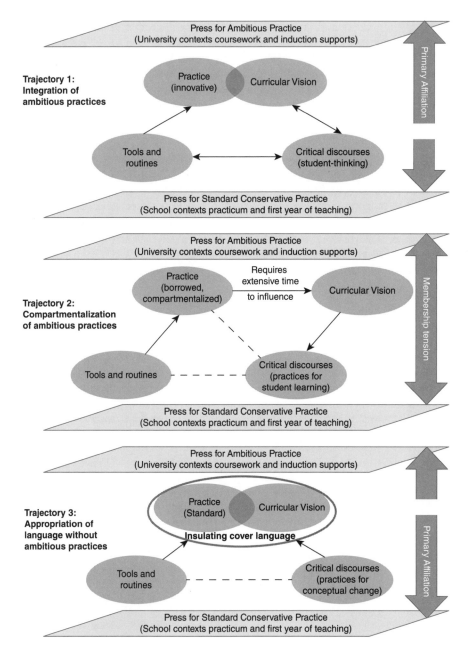

Figure 8.5.   Novice teachers' developmental trajectories of ambitious practices when negotiating conflicting contextual discourses.

Source: Thompson, Windschitl, & Braaten, 2013, p. 608.

work, and that diagrams do not speak for themselves. But the purpose here is to illustrate how subtle changes in bin labels, line styles, arrow directions, or the placement of any of these can completely change the storyline of a diagram.

Thinking diagrammatically asks that you first visualize a graphic template in your mind and then transfer those thoughts onto paper or onto a monitor screen. And since every design choice means a sacrifice of other possible choices, consider what would happen if the line you drew was dashed instead of solid; if the bin shape you chose was square rather than oval; if the arrow pointed left instead of right; if the text was italicized rather than bolded; and so on. Diagrams, like text, are infinite in their composition possibilities. Yet the principle of elegance advises that we select our visual elements strategically to communicate our message in as few graphic symbols as possible.

For more guidance on diagramming your qualitative data analysis work, see Knowlton and Phillips (2013); Miles et al. (2014); Rosenbaum (2011); Wheeldon and Åhlberg (2012); and the user manuals of CAQDAS programs. Access "A Periodic Table of Visualization Methods" for a fascinating online overview of representing data in various visual forms (http://www.visual-literacy.org/periodic_table/periodic_table.html), and explore free downloadable software for constructing concept maps from CmapTools (http://cmap.ihmc.us/download/). Also, don't discount the elementary-school-level concept maps many of us were taught to draw (McKnight, 2010, 2013). Basic yet classic template structures such as Venn diagrams, story maps, pyramid charts, fishbone models, webs, chains, and networks have strong applicability for diagramming qualitative analyses.

> **For your mental Rolodex:** As you investigate social life, transform the narrative findings of your research into visual representations. Explore the multiple formats and design choices available to you as you construct and assemble a diagram's elements.

Thinking Conclusively

My succinct advice for *thinking conclusively* is: You can't; so don't.

Let me explain what I mean. I do not like the heading "Conclusions" toward the end of a research report. Conclusions are a traditional scientific formality that require the researcher to synthesize the discussion thus far into take-aways for the reader. They often summarize the major or key findings of the study into a brief review. I do find summaries quite helpful as "remember this" passages of text that reiterate the essential features of the report. But if they are summaries, then call them "Summaries." "Conclusions" has an arrogant ring about it, as if the certainty of what you have "concluded" is unquestionable, its longevity timeless, and its transfer foolproof. Certainty is uncertain (which, paradoxically, I seem to state with some degree of certainty).

I prefer open-ended, tentative completion, for all research is work in progress. There will most likely be future studies about the same social issues you're addressing presently. Those works may build and elaborate on what you produce today, or they may reproduce the exact same topic for inquiry, not knowing that you've already done comparable investigations. But times change, people change, and qualitative research changes right along with them. If constructs such as fluidity, hybridity, and emergence are some of the primary operating principles of today's world, then "Conclusions" seem incompatible with rapidly evolving social dynamics. Clarke (2005) reinforces that "life on the planet is changing too quickly to claim permanence" (p. 293).

The final portions of various research reports go by different names aside from "Conclusions": "Results," "Findings," "Implications," "Discussion," "Suggestions for Future Research," "Coda," and so on; and the profiles in this chapter and in the next two are recommended ways to reach those conclusions. Yet I myself prefer "Closure" as an appropriate final heading, because it suggests a door shut but not locked. Perhaps we can employ different phrases for our final summative passages, such as "Heuristic Discoveries," "Analytic Synthesis," "Key Learnings," "Major Revelations," or even something as informal as "Answers to the Research Questions" or "The Bottom Line." I do not object to researcher-developed conclusions themselves, just the artificial labeling of them in a report. A researcher's job is to condense a vast qualitative database and to formulate from rigorous analysis and thoughtful reflection both answers and their essential meanings from the study. Telling me, "This is what I found out [or formulated, constructed, devised, etc.]" leads to enhanced reader awareness. But following up with, "And this is why it's significant or important that others know what I found out" has more transferable impact.

I ponder how some of the smallest cultural traditions have maintained themselves for generations, and I marvel at the thought that people who lived thousands of years before us experienced the same emotions we experience today—happiness, sadness, jealously, fear, love. Many things endure, yet it feels somewhat wrong to conclude. If I do make a conclusion from qualitative inquiry, I had better be 100% confident about my claim, for all it will take is just one outlier, one anomaly, one exception to the rule, or one "it depends" to knock the house I've built down to the ground. Thus, I prefer temporary closure for a qualitative study, not fixed conclusions.

For your mental Rolodex: As you investigate social life, maintain an open-ended perspective as you reach the end of your fieldwork and write-up stages. Acknowledge that conclusions are generally incompatible with qualitative research paradigms, and that closure is a preferred means of labeling study completion.

CLOSURE

Gordon (2014) reports contested findings by citation analysts that approximately 50% of all published academic papers are not read by anyone other than the author, journal editor, and reviewers; and approximately 90% of all academic journal articles are not cited by other authors. Summaries of our long hours of research are necessary for maintaining a cumulative cognitive grasp of our own work and for essentializing it for our readers. The overload of information available to each of us can overwhelm us. Time does not always permit us to take leisurely reads of lengthy research materials. We need to formulate and communicate our methods and findings as "quick looks" for accessibility and transfer. We need to make statements that get to the point and draw diagrams that represent the major highlights of the research story.

See Belcher (2009) for her detailed article-writing advice, which strongly reinforces the necessity of a central "argument" to propel the project. And, as Wolcott (2009) advises for "concluding" your write-up, "When you come to the end, stop" (p. 6).

EXERCISES FOR THINKING SUMMARILY

1. Write out the major findings of your study (or a published journal article from your discipline) on one 3- by 5-inch index card. (Note that journal article abstracts do not always include the researcher's key findings. Read the entire article to extract and synthesize them.)

2. Compose, then voice out loud, at a normal conversational rate, a description of your study (or a published journal article from your discipline) and its major findings in three minutes or less.

3. Harry F. Wolcott (2009) asked his students to write periodic, one-page progress reports of their individual fieldwork and post-fieldwork writing stages. Some of his former students testified how difficult the assignment was, but also how it forced them to think economically with words. Maintain this weekly assignment during one of your own research studies as a form of cumulative summation.

4. Select a particular social setting or event (e.g., hotel lobby, fourth-grade classroom, professional baseball game, amusement or theme park). If needed, secure permission to observe and document in writing and/or photographs your observations at the site for at least one hour. Construct assertions, propositions, hypotheses, and theories about the environment and the social actions, reactions, and interactions you observed.

5. Find a qualitative research journal article without any accompanying diagrams. Construct a diagram (e.g., matrix or network) of its key findings. Show the visual model to a peer and ask her or him to describe what the illustration suggests about the research study you selected.

Thinking Interpretively

LEARNING OBJECTIVES AND SUMMARY

- Your mind will integrate various ideas for reconceptualizing initial analyses.
- Your mind will reflect on the transfer of investigative experiences to other contexts.

This chapter explores how higher and deeper levels of analytic thought may be developed through reflection on essence, intricacy, and transfer. These methods of mind consist of

- Thinking Interpretively
- Thinking Elegantly
- Thinking Connectively
- Thinking Complexly
- Thinking Transcendently

The purpose of this chapter is to profile realms of analytic thought that extend beyond the descriptive in qualitative inquiry.

Thinking Interpretively

First, is an advanced realm of analytic thought going higher or deeper? *Higher* suggests rising above the surface of data, while *deeper* suggests mining for treasure beneath their surface. I offer that as researchers we metaphorically do both, and thus I put forth the compound word high-deep to represent this broader realm.

Interpretation, as it applies to qualitative inquiry, is a somewhat slippery concept to explain, for it relies on you to interpret what interpretation means. And using the word itself to define its meaning contradicts the purpose of, well, interpretation. So if I were to offer a synonymous explanation, interpretation is not necessarily a methodological approach as much as it is a *high-deep level of understanding.* Wolcott's (1994) definition of qualitative interpretation reaches beyond the particular study to find highdeep application, meaning, and sense-making dimensions that address the question, "What is to be made of it all?" Interpretation proposes to readers the big ideas about the nature of what you've investigated (Saldaña, 2011b, pp. 153–154). Interpretation is your reply to the infamous "So what?" question that ruthlessly functions as a criterion for the purpose and relevance of your research for your audiences. Interpretation informally begins with you stating, "OK, bottom line, here's what it all means: . . . " Your interpretation of the meaning of your study hopefully makes your readers think, "Ah, *now* I understand."

Part of *thinking interpretively* is looking at the local and particular of your unique field site and reflecting on the possible transferable meanings suggested by that synoptic (affording a view of the whole) microcosm of social life for the population at large. Those meanings can be applied to other sites, times, and contexts. You may be observing 20 fourth-grade children on a playground in a middle-class suburban school, but your attention to which young people get included and excluded from games says something about how humans learn early in life to *stigmatize* the other—an action that continues throughout adulthood in various overt and covert forms (Goffman, 1963; Saldaña, 2005b). You may have observed the staff of a local veterinary clinic over the course of a month interacting with each other and with clients and their pets. The process of not just providing pet care but *dispensing compassion* strikes you as a key phenomenon in this specific setting. Your discussion examines the merits of this practice and reflects on why dispensing compassion is not seen as much outside the helping professions, and how the social world might be better off if its citizens exercised this action with each other more often.

Thinking interpretively also asks you to extend beyond the tangible and real of your study into the conceptual and abstract (see Chapter 4). Those fourth-grade children stigmatizing others raise the broader construct of *power;* and the playground they're including and excluding on becomes a metaphor for *life.* The process of dispensing compassion at a veterinary clinic is an action that involves *emotional labor* (Hochschild, 2003); and pets are not aspects of "animal ownership" but of *intimate relationship.* These extensions beyond the particulars of your study begin the theory development stage of your research. This involves highdeep thinking beyond the case or site into the more general applicability of the phenomena.

A media representative in charge of news promotion at my Arizona university always asked the faculty she interviewed a particular question that forced us to think about the contributions and significance of our work to the general public: "Why should my 80-year-old grandmother in New Jersey care about the work you're doing here?" Our answer to the media representative gave her an angle that could potentially sell the story to local, regional, and national news outlets. It was also a humbling challenge for ivory tower faculty to truly think about how their research had applicability beyond the university campus or peer-reviewed journal. Though it seems a bit ludicrous, the question is nonetheless a legitimate one for you to ponder and answer as a litmus test of your ability to interpret the significance of your study and its transferability, not to mention its utility: Why should an 80-year-old grandmother in New Jersey care about the findings from your research?

Thinking interpretively is a necessary method of mind that serves several purposes:

- It develops highdeep levels of reflection and highdeep forms of writing.
- It prods you into extending beyond your particular research study toward more general applications.
- It motivates thinking toward conceptual, abstract, and theoretical domains.
- It challenges you to consider the practical and utilitarian value of your work to others.

The following methods of mind profile other modalities of interpretation for qualitative inquiry: *thinking elegantly, connectively, complexly,* and *transcendently.*

> **For your mental Rolodex:** As you investigate social life, "highdeep" the data and reflect on how the local and particular of your field site and participants might transfer to the more general and abstract.

Thinking Elegantly

Elegance does not mean "fancy" or "elaborate," as some people think. **Elegance** means *simplicity.* To think elegantly is to perceive and find core purposes or meanings, and to put into as few words as possible what something "is." This sounds comparable to thinking phenomenologically (see Chapter 4), but thinking elegantly is different. Thinking phenomenologically takes something complex and finds its essences and essentials that make it what it "is." Thinking elegantly is thinking with simplicity from the very beginning. And this does not suggest thinking simplistically but thinking *with simplicity.* Hahn (2011) proposes that simplicity is not a sign of weakness or naïveté but of strength: "In a complex and detail-laden world, simplicity is a very powerful thing. Life is noisy and complex. Simplicity is a strong and compelling counterforce. A blank page in a cluttered magazine has power. A silence in a symphony has power" (p. 190).

Elegance, sometimes known as *parsimony* in selected genres of research, is the guiding force of Occam's razor, a famous principle of logic positing that, among competing hypotheses, the hypothesis with the fewest assumptions should be selected. As an anecdote, I was noticing in my older age that small objects like keys, plastic forks, and pencils kept slipping through my fingers. I thought I was grasping things sufficiently to hold on to them, but my arthritic hands and aging mind seemed out of sync. I told my doctor about this issue, thinking that a program of physical therapy might alleviate the problem, or perhaps some type of medication over time might lessen my arthritis and strengthen my hand muscles and joints. Her solution to my dilemma was unexpectedly elegant. If things were slipping through my fingers, she advised me, I should simply "grip harder."

Our minds think elegantly on the immediate task at hand. "The brain is sometimes referred to as a sponge that soaks up information. A better metaphor might be a sieve; by some estimates, 99 percent of all sensory information is discarded almost immediately upon entering the brain" (Wolfe, 2010, p. 112). Though it would be unwise to discard 99% of our total data collected from fieldwork, we should nevertheless consider carefully what is absolutely necessary for us to analyze and to write about. In the classic film *Silence of the Lambs,* the brilliant but criminal Hannibal Lecter teaches FBI agent Clarice Starling the principle of simplicity: "Of each particular thing ask: 'What is it in itself? What is its nature?'" Lecter prods Clarice to speculate on the motivations of the murderer she seeks: "What is the first and principal thing he does? What *needs* does he serve by killing?" Agent Starling attempts to guess by putting forth static nouns such as "anger," "social acceptance," and "sexual frustration," but Lecter proposes an active verb: "He covets! *That* is his nature." That one verb elegantly captures the murderer's drive for his heinous crimes and holds a hidden clue for Agent Starling to pursue.

Thinking elegantly is a necessary process for grounded theory's search for a core category, an action that helps lead toward the theory itself. Kathy Charmaz (2009) studied how serious chronic illness affects the body and self-identity. A core category or mode of living with physical impairment that she identified from her interviews was *adapting.* This gerund elegantly captures the primary process at work:

> By adapting, I mean altering life and self to accommodate to physical losses and to reunify the body and self accordingly. Adapting implies that the individual acknowledges impairment and alters life and self in socially and personally acceptable ways. Bodily limits and social circumstances often force adapting to loss. Adapting shades into acceptance. Thus, ill people adapt when they try to accommodate and flow with the experience of illness. (p. 155)

A good researcher acknowledges the complexity of social life, but an excellent researcher elegantly describes that complexity in the simplest of terms. Elegance is the ability to streamline a long story into a short one, to focus in on the key issues or participants, to filter out what is unnecessary to understanding the phenomenon, and to explain in clear terms how or why something is as it is. I once received a journal article manuscript to peer-review. The writer attempted to include everything about a three-year research project, from its conception to its conclusion. The manuscript was far too long, and I became lost as a reader wading through the excessive description and extraneous details. I advised the writer—not to edit and condense the article to simply make it shorter—but to select the one most interesting facet about the study and to focus on that angle for a revision. That one facet could be a unique stage of the project, a key participant as a case study, or a central theme or issue suggested by the data. I could understand the researcher's enthusiasm for wanting audiences to know everything about the project, but I advised the writer that readers would most likely retain only a small percentage—10 % at most, according to learning lore—of what was included. I posed to the writer: "What's the top 10 % of this study about? Write about that, and only that, instead."

Elegance is a feature of visual design and minimalism, its famous principle being "Less is more." Thinking elegantly does not "reduce," but sees things in economical forms and terms. However, qualitative significance is subjective: The top 10 % of a study for me is a different top 10 % of the study for you. You can't write about everything, but you must write about something. And that something should be what readers will most likely remember after finishing your write-up.

> **For your mental Rolodex:** As you investigate social life, focus your lens, filter out what is unnecessary, and choose an angle that elegantly captures the significant aspects of your research study.

Thinking Connectively

Humans construct various types of connections between things, and these connections go by different names: *correlation, association, interaction, interplay, relationship, interrelationship, reverberation, link, jointure, network, web, synergy, unity, blending, weaving, integration, intermingling, intermixing,* and so on. Our brains are hardwired to find connections between things because our brains themselves operate through intricate synaptic connectivity. Our brains as sense-making organs attempt to create order from chaos, and part of that sense-making consists of **connecting** disparate pieces of information into a coherent and more unified scheme. We tacitly operate with preprogrammed cognitive scripts driving us to deduce that "*this* goes with *that*." Most of us wouldn't put a refrigerator next to a toilet in a bathroom but keep the appliance in the kitchen where it seems to best belong. The act of categorizing connects various things, like codes, that seem to go together. Categorizing the categories further connects the still-separated items into an even more tightly knit assemblage. And a theory connects two separate things as an if/then statement.

Quantitative research posits that statistical procedures for correlation (such as Pearson's r) imply relationship, not causation. And it is *relational connection* discussed here, not causation (discussed in Chapter 2). A classic example of correlation is the relationship between your aptitude as a high school student and your potential success as a college student. In other words, if you earned good grades in high school, you should earn good grades in college. But we know that some exceptions to that connection exist, for some high schoolers who did only satisfactory work at the secondary level can excel at higher education, while a few outstanding achievers in high school might encounter personal difficulties during their college years that prevent them from graduating. Connections are not always perfect; they are our best attempts to discover what seem to be plausible, most likely relationships.

We've all been taught to avoid the spurious correlation—the falsely applied relationship. This may happen from hastily drawn deductions, but it also may occur as a result of poorly informed beliefs and stereotyping. In the United States, the 2012 death of Black 17-year-old Trayvon Martin and 2013 trial of George Zimmerman for his murder heightened the stigma attributed to young African American men based on the assumption that a teenage African American male wearing a hoodie does not belong in a predominantly White neighborhood at night and that Martin must have been engaged in some type of criminal activity. A spurious correlation—that is, false connection—may have been made by Zimmerman, leading him to conclude that Martin was a "thug" based solely on his physical appearance and his particular location in space and time. The consequences were the unfortunate loss of Martin's life and a trial verdict of not guilty for Zimmerman that polarized the nation. Ironically, the story and its outcome also seemed to connect the populace around the nature of race relationships. Even when there was heated disagreement, there was still connection to the issue.

There is also an opposite perspective whereby some philosophies or theologies suggest that *everything* connects in one way or another—that all humans throughout time are tied to each other genealogically and genetically, that our species is "part of the earth" or "one with the universe." *Thinking connectively* is a matter of relativity. You can either perceive yourself as feeling terribly alone, or you can perceive that you and approximately 7 billion other people share a planet at the same time. Emotional connections between individuals can range from passing acquaintance to the intimacy shared by life partners. And some posit that electronically mediated technology (e.g., Facebook, Twitter, Skype, and other online chat programs) does not distance them from human relationships but actually strengthens their sense of connection with others. Connections do not "exist" in the social world; we construct them. Connectivity is subjective.

Thinking connectively is reflecting on how the various pieces of your research puzzle fit together, or how they simulate a connect-the-dots challenge, to reveal a bigger picture at work. Qualitative connections should never be forced, but sometimes they can be actively and inductively explored for plausible relationships. The **codeweaving** technique purposely integrates the codes and categories created from data analysis into narratives such as analytic memos and even the final report itself (Saldaña, 2013). For example, a series of codes and their assigned category from Chapter 2's "Thinking Categorically" section were:

Category 2: Spending Strategically

Codes:

PICKING UP THE TAB

BUYING BARGAINS

STOCKING UP

Rather than keeping these phrases as isolated units, the analyst can codeweave or connect the phrases into sentences:

Spending Strategically consists partly of money saving tactics when shopping, such as keeping an eye out for bargains and stocking up on "good deals." But these strategies can be waylaid when unforeseen expenses, such as dental insurance deductibles, mean "picking up the tab." (Saldaña, 2014, pp. 587–588)

Qualitative matrices assemble data units into rows and columns to discern relationships between and among cells. Diagrams that connect key variables or concepts through lines and arrows establish empirically based relationships between isolated, self-standing units (Miles, Huberman, & Saldaña, 2014). Figure 9.1 illustrates the phases and stages of the successful, collaborative creative process, as configured by student artists. Serendipitously, I learned that this process paralleled the collaborative dynamics of small-group work for a research project. The vertical and horizontal processes tell the story of how something novel to be accomplished must go through a collaborative venture with others. The struggle people encounter as they exchange ideas and collaborate eventually leads to cohesion. If the quality of the product exceeds the expectations of the original goal, the audience validates the artist's (or team researcher's) work, giving that individual a sense of pride in his or her accomplishments.

Connections unify the individual elements of our research work. They weave together the individual threads of our inquiry into a rich tapestry. When you are at a loss to explain how the separate and disconnected components of your analysis fit together, purposely but logically assemble a few of them at a time and explain how and/or why they seem to connect.

> **For your mental Rolodex:** As you investigate social life, establish connections between and among the elements of your analytic work. Construct a plausible rationale for how and/ or why you made those connections.

Thinking Complexly

Our minds are designed to work efficiently, and that efficiency seeks elegance in its processing of information and formulation of ideas. We don't really multitask cognitively—we *task-switch.* The adult brain can work with up to five to seven "chunks" of information at a time, but we cannot work with them simultaneously; instead, we rapidly switch from one chunk to another (Sousa, 2011, pp. 31–33). Yet, our brains are not genetically predisposed to limitations; we learn from an interaction of nature *and* nurture (Dubinsky, Roehrig, & Varma, 2013, p. 319). We do have the capacity to challenge our own patterned, linear thinking by pondering alternatives—an internal prompting through statements that begin with "What if," "Yes, but," or "Instead of _____, why not _____?" *Thinking complexly* acknowledges that—sometimes—there are no easy answers. It also acknowledges the intricate details and messiness of an issue.

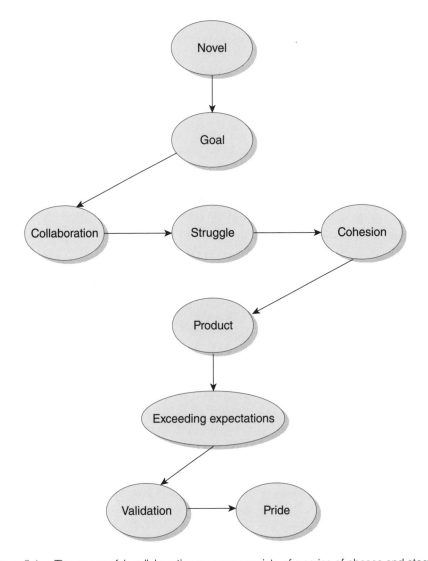

Figure 9.1.   The successful, collaborative process consists of a series of phases and stages.

Source: Developed by Enza Giannone Hosig, Teresa Minarsich, Kathleen Arcovio Pennyway, Ebony Tucker, and Brianna Stapleton Welch.

Some scholars find value in problematizing their inquiry. This generally means unpacking or contesting what may be generally accepted, taken for granted, or unquestioned as a norm or standard. Problematizing or refracting (see Chapter 1) involves examining the **complexity** and multifaceted nature of a phenomenon to gain a broader understanding of it. For example, *community* is a term used frequently to describe a group, and each person reading that word may have an initial definition of the term based on his or her own personal memories, associations, and experiences. But does community include only people, or does it also include geography and ideology? For a group to be a community, must a sense of cohesive unity exist among its members? And does one belong to a community by mere presence, voluntary choice, forced choice, assignment, or attribution, or just conceptually in one's mind (Hacker, 2013)? It will behoove you as a researcher to think through and carefully define key constructs of a study, lest there be unquestioned assumptions about what selected terms mean.

Another way of thinking complexly is to acknowledge the intricacy of a phenomenon and to challenge oneself to consider the many possible variables at work within it. Figure 9.2 illustrates the complex process of the "lifelong impact" of theatre and speech programming on adolescents as they move into adulthood (McCammon, Saldaña, Hines, & Omasta, 2012). Each bin represents a major variable or factor extracted from written survey responses from 234 participants. The lines and arrows connecting the bins represent the connections directly indicated or suggested by respondents' narratives. The figure displays an intricate web of relationships, conditions, processes, and causation that came from careful documentation and mapping of participant testimony. The diagram itself, originally drawn with the CAQDAS program NVivo, needs an accompanying descriptive outline to reveal the storyline and explain the interplay of the variables. But by itself the illustration demonstrates the detailed analytic work that went into its construction. To simply say that participating in speech and theatre activities in high school generates a lifelong personal sense of confidence is an elegant assertion. Yet the detailed description of how and why that outcome occurs provides the complex yet necessary explanation. The lesson is this: Rather than assuming the linearity or circularity of human processes, consider intricate and complex *networking* of those processes.

A classic saying goes, "Things can be complex without being complicated." Grounded theorists, for example, generally work toward finding a core category from their data, such as *balancing, adapting,* or *personal preservation while dying.* The related theory and its accompanying narrative explain such aspects as the conditions and consequences of participant action in order to explicate the nuances and complexities at work in the social process. But Clarke (2005) advocates acknowledging the messiness of social life from the very beginning of a study and working toward mapping the complexities of the issue rather than disentangling and reducing them to a single category or grand theory.

> ***For your mental Rolodex:*** As you investigate social life, acknowledge that the complexity of social life cannot always be reduced, distilled, or condensed into one word or a single phrase. Explore the complex connections and interplay of phenomena.

Thinking Transcendently

Harry F. Wolcott (1994) labeled three stages of qualitative data transformation as *description, analysis,* and *interpretation.* But the key word here is *transformation,* which Wolcott later stated also includes transcending the data. This suggests rising above your initial analyses to reach

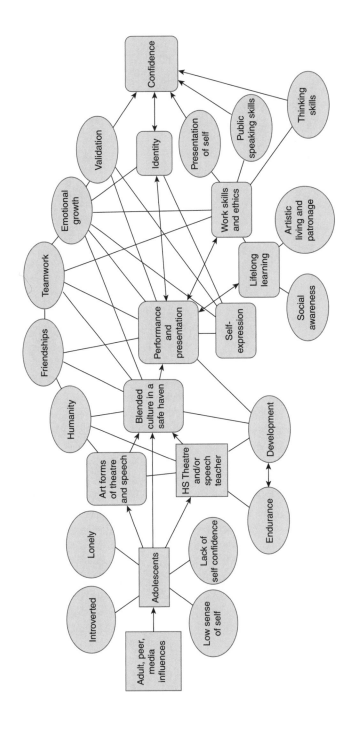

Figure 9.2. This model of lifelong student and teacher impact from high school theatre and/or speech programming illustrates a complex network of interrelationships.

Source: McCammon, Saldaña, Hines, & Omasta, 2012, p. 14.

higher (or highdeep) levels of meaning. How a researcher does this is not necessarily by formulaic method but by the heuristics of reflecting on the ideas of his or her work.

Thinking transcendently progresses from the particular and local of your study toward the more universal aspects suggested by your case. Note that the goal is not necessarily to achieve understandings about the abstract, conceptual, or theoretical from your analysis, but the possible universal applications of them.

Some researchers propose that the universal does not exist, since we all perceive, construct, and interpret life differently inside our brains' more than 1 billion neurons and more than 1 quadrillion possible synaptic connections (Dubinsky et al., 2013, p. 319). No two minds can ever be exactly comparable in memory, association, and thought. But nitpicking aside, there are a few universal concepts we possess and share as a human species: We are all born and we will all die. We must eat food of some sort, drink water, and breathe to survive. We all have bodies with specific anatomical features and biological functions, such as blood coursing through our veins. With the exception of rare cases, we all experience thoughts and emotions, feel physical pain, touch, taste, and smell. Though some cannot hear or see, we all experience things as we live, regardless of sensory proficiency. We are all, as humans, living on one planet with land and water, animals and weather patterns, lit by a moon, orbiting the sun, surrounded by other planets and stars.

There are things that most but not all of us will experience that are put forth as virtually universal. All humans grow up and age, but we will experience different childhoods, adolescent periods, and adulthoods due to different social, cultural, and geographic environments. Even the stages I just mentioned—childhood, adolescence, and adulthood—are social constructions rather than universal facts. Most of us will feel the need to bond, to love, and to reproduce, but the landscape of varying sexual orientations influences and affects our affectional actions and identities. We are all capable of killing other people, but most do not. Not everyone is religious or spiritual, yet many believe in a supreme or higher entity. Universals seem conditional to some extent, for there may always be exceptions to what we offer as something everyone shares. But we can feel confident putting forth what many if not most others might experience as a common phenomenon.

James P. Spradley (1979, 1980) devised six levels of ethnographic writing as a heuristic for thinking transcendently. He begins with the universal and proceeds to the particular, but I reverse that order to illustrate how we might not only write but think about **transcendence**. The first level describes *specific incident statements* of participant action. As an example, I once saw at an airport boarding area a male in his late twenties or early thirties standing with whom I inferred was his three- or four-year-old daughter. The young girl, clothed in a dress, held a stuffed doll, frowned, shook her arm, and whined, "No, I don't wanna!" The father took her hand and told her straightforwardly with a hint of pleading, "Come on, be a good little girl for Daddy."

The second level that transcends above this is *specific statements about a cultural domain*. This level works with classes or categories of events, objects, or activities labeled by participants. Their terms, organized by the researcher into taxonomies, become the basis for progressing from the first level's *example* to a second level *type*. If I had had the chance to interview the father in the airport about *parenting* his child, I might have learned that he identified some of his child's behaviors as "fussy" and that he had a specific repertoire of strategies to respond to that, with one type being "reason with her."

Spradley's third level transcends up to *general statements about a specific cultural scene.* These are descriptive, low-level abstractions that suggest general themes about a culture. Notice that the writing now shifts away from the participant's verbatim terms and employs the researcher's. If my case study of the father and daughter was about the culture of parenting in public spaces, I might offer a statement asserting, "In public settings, most parents quickly quash their children's disruptive behavior." The fourth level consists of *general statements about a society or cultural group.* I now transcend parenting in public spaces and focus on parenting, or the culture of the family, in general. Perhaps my general statement based on level one's father–daughter interaction at the airport might read, "Part of parenting is the regulation of children's behavior."

Spradley's level five expands thinking beyond general cultural statements to develop *cross-cultural descriptive statements* about two or more societies. This contrasting technique generates broader and hopefully richer statements about the culture under investigation. It expands the researcher's thinking to place ideas in context, allowing him or her to ruminate on highdeep cultural meanings. My example thus far has been about a father's response to his preschool daughter. But how might a mother react in a comparable situation with a young girl? I've observed mothers saying such things as "Quiet!" and "Hush, baby, please." What if the gender roles had been reversed and it was a mother talking to her young son? What if the father had been talking to a boy instead? What if that father was an older adult responding to an older adolescent daughter? I've overheard interactions in which the male parent tells the teenage girl sternly, "Stop whining about it!" One of my male African American students told me his beloved grandmother would discipline him as a child with the warning, "Boy, I'm gonna beat the black outta you!" In my reflections on gender at that airport scene, I was struck by the idea of an older male controlling a young female's behavior with the statement, "Be a good little girl for Daddy." In one sentence, the girl was told to be a compliant subject for the male. The power dynamics and disparity between different ages and genders were made manifest in this one interaction at the airport. My cross-cultural statement might eventually be formulated into: "Oppressive gender roles and expectations are formed during early childhood."

The sixth and final level of Spradley's ethnographic writing consists of *universal statements,* the heart of transcendence. These "statements about human beings, their behavior, culture, or environmental situation . . . are all-encompassing" assertions (1979, p. 207). Spradley acknowledges how difficult these are to compose but notes that many ethnographies contain them. Based on the particular airport incident I observed between father and daughter, I could make the inferential leap to "Males assume a dominant role over females." I could also offer, "Children are under the control of adults." But Spradley encourages a narrative about the universal that transcends cultural categories and speaks to the human condition in general.

Thus, a possible universal to propose is, "As early as childhood, humans are judged and regulated to conform to acceptable social norms by those in power." (Notice that this universal simulates a theory.)

Thinking transcendently helps you extend beyond the case incident and transform general implications into broader applications that can be used in a wide variety of contexts. Harry F. Wolcott's classic response to those who challenged his preference for case study research with "What can you learn by studying just one of anything?" was "All you can!" My own response to those who ask me the same thing is, "A lot more than you think."

> ***For your mental Rolodex:*** As you investigate social life, reflect on the possible universals in your unique study. Transcend the local and particular of your case to address its broader interpretations and meanings.

CLOSURE

Remember that interpretation is not so much a method of analysis as it is a highdeep level of thinking. Interpretation examines elegant ideas and the complex connections embedded within them. Interpretation transcends the descriptive and obvious to reach, as much as possible, the more universal meanings suggested by the study. Our goal as qualitative researchers is to put forth ideas and understandings about social life that most others have not yet considered or formulated. To achieve this, we must position our researcher lenses, filters, and angles in new settings to reflect and refract on our data.

EXERCISES FOR THINKING INTERPRETIVELY

1. Discuss with a peer or write a short essay on the differences between "the purpose of life" and "the meaning of life."

2. In as few words or sentences as possible, elegantly define one of these concepts: *identity, culture, God.*

3. Think of a vivid yet positive childhood memory (e.g., a favorite toy, best friend, beloved teacher, favorite television program). Think connectively about how that childhood memory may relate to or hold significance for you in your adulthood. For example, if your childhood best friend had certain personality traits, does a friend in your adulthood possess similar traits? If your favorite television program as a child was a comedy, are your favorite television programs as an adult also comedies?

4. Some of the most controversial social debates in the United States today surround gun control, abortion, gay marriage, and health care. Choose one of these issues and think complexly about the variables, factors, concepts, policies, laws, ideologies, people, organizations, and so on that drive the conflicts and tensions. Diagram the interplay of this issue as a network with bins, lines, and arrows.

5. Find a significant "moment" in a set of participant observation field notes or an interview transcript and analyze it using Spradley's six levels of ethnographic writing (see "Thinking Transcendently").

Thinking Narratively 10

LEARNING OBJECTIVES AND SUMMARY

- Your mind will reflect on different narrative approaches to qualitative research presentation.
- Your mind will explore a variety of literary representations for social inquiry.

This chapter explores how the writing of qualitative research studies can be enhanced through different ways of thinking about presentations aside from traditional scholarly article prose and formats. These methods of mind consist of

- Thinking Narratively
- Thinking Monologically
- Thinking Dialogically
- Thinking Poetically
- Thinking Proverbially

The purpose of this chapter is to acquaint you with various prosaic and poetic forms of thinking and writing for evocative qualitative research representation and presentation. (Dramatic writing is another literary genre, but that modality is addressed in Chapter 7's "Thinking Theatrically" and in several of this chapter's sections).

Thinking Narratively

A narrative is a storied account of events, a symbolic representation of knowledge and experiences. It documents, in written, visual, or oral form, participant actions and emotions, yet does so in such a way as to grab the reader's or listener's attention and engagement with the tale. A *literary* narrative adds stylistic dimensions to the telling, providing a potentially evocative and aesthetic experience. Read this descriptive field note passage:

> At the outdoor social, a man sits on a brick ledge looking at other people standing in front of him and talking to each other.

The composition of this note jotted in the field serves its purpose in documenting the action the researcher observed. But notice how, with a few carefully selected words and different syntax, yet remaining firmly rooted in the original observation, a different picture of life is created:

> Howard sat by himself on the hard brick ledge as sunset approached, feeling so alone as he gazed at the crowd drinking and noisily socializing around him.

If my intended effects as a writer have been successful, I have accomplished several things. First, I have assigned a pseudonym to the participant ("Howard"), but in doing so I have transformed him from an anonymous person into a central character. I have portrayed a sense of time and place ("sunset," "hard brick ledge") and established a problem, conflict, or tension, interwoven with an emotion ("feeling so alone"). Lastly, I have chosen the omniscient observer as a point of view that can reveal the internal thoughts and feelings of people. Much has been accomplished in just one sentence, and the next steps are to set these initial prompts into motion in my narrative describing the phenomenon of *social isolation*. I could just as easily have begun my account with a more objective and general assertion, such as:

> Individuals experiencing social isolation often initiate their own physical separation from other people.

But by reporting a mere fact, I have potentially distanced my reader from the essential *feeling* of the phenomenon—a key facet of understanding the nature of social isolation. What if the research story were to begin like this:

> Alone and lonely. No one but you, even in a crowd. Afraid to make contact. Fear of rejection. Keep to yourself. Safer that way.

Thinking narratively considers the stylistic writing choices available for conveying to readers the journey and destination of the research. It is heightened attunement to various storied forms of social experience—the construction of vignettes, short tales, chronicles, poems, life lessons, life trajectories, and especially the characterization of our participants as we document their lives. Our minds retain information longer when a narrative string connects the memories. And if that narrative possesses an aesthetic dimension that carries emotional impact, we can cement the memory more firmly in our readers' brains.

Fictional and nonfictional literature tends to get classified according to its *genres*, *elements*, and *styles*. Genres or forms are literary types, such as short story, biography, poetry, and drama. Elements refer primarily to literary devices incorporated throughout a work, such as protagonist, antagonist, symbolism, foreshadowing, and alliteration. A style suggests the overall tone of the work: for example, tragedy, comedy, satire, romance, or fantasy.

Qualitative research also has genres, elements, and styles (Saldaña, 2011b). The genres or forms range from methodologies such as grounded theory to phenomenology to ethnography. The elements of inquiry are not just literary but functional: participant observation field notes, interview transcripts, literature review, and so on. The styles of qualitative research refer to its write-ups and the various approaches to tale-telling: realistically, confessionally, critically, analytically, interpretively, and so on (van Maanen, 2011; Wolcott, 1994). It is these styles of writing that primarily determine a study's narrative texture.

A classic design saying goes, "For every choice, there is a sacrifice," meaning that if you choose to summarize in your own words what a participant said, rather than quoting her or him verbatim in your report, that choice sacrifices direct evidence for researcher interpretation. If you choose to present your study's write-up in the straightforward, descriptive manner typical of most traditional reports, you sacrifice the possibilities of critical, poetic, dramatic, and other representational and presentational genres and styles. And if you choose to document your ethnographic fieldwork and findings as a scripted, performed work for the stage, some readers may find the choice bold and innovative while others may find the play artistically self-indulgent and lacking in rigor and credibility. The precision of quantitative research rests in its statistical accuracy. In qualitative research, precision rests in your word choices.

If someone were to ask you, "So, what's your research about?" your answer would generally be the plot (or, overall structure) of your research story. When you develop the purpose statement of your study, you are formally composing its plot. A statement for a project might read:

The purpose of this study is to explore how doctoral candidates perceive their college/university coursework as preparation for their independent research projects.

The characters of a qualitative study are its participants. Their actions, recalled through interviews or observed in the field, generate various storylines within the plot. Monologues may emerge from individual interviews with the participants, while dialogues may be documented as you observe participants in seminars with a professor and peers. As for the life lessons learned by the participant-characters as their action storylines progress through the research plot, those might consist of a key assertion, a core category, a set of themes, or a theory you construct from your data analysis.

The parallels between a research study and literature can extend further when you consider how diverse literary styles such as romances, mysteries, and tragedies can inspire more creative nonfictional writing for your reports (Gibbs, 2007). An interesting question I once heard at a qualitative research conference presentation by Daryl Ward was, "What classical or contemporary piece of literature does your research remind you of?" A project exploring stigma or shame might evoke recollections of Nathaniel Hawthorne's novel *The Scarlet Letter*; participants feeling trapped in unfulfilled lives are reminiscent of multiple characters from the plays of Anton Chekhov. A return to literary masterworks can provide a researcher additional insights on the human phenomena under investigation. Just because a work is considered fiction doesn't mean it isn't truthful in some ways.

Creative nonfiction employs the devices and conventions of exemplary literary writing for the reportage of rigorous, systematic investigation. The work is not "based on a true story," as is often claimed when media producers take creative license in their dramatization of the facts. Creative nonfiction simply tells the research story in an engaging way for its readership. Social scientist Brené Brown muses, "Maybe stories are just data with a soul." **Narrative inquiry** has made great strides in this field, and this methodology has much to offer more traditional qualitative researchers in terms of the representation and presentation of their work (see Clandinin & Connelly, 2000; Coulter & Smith, 2009; Gutkind, 2008; Holstein & Gubrium, 2012; Murray, 2003; Riessman, 2008). For an amusing and intricately designed online reference to narrative elements, see The Periodic Table of Storytelling (http://designthroughstorytelling.net/periodic/index.html).

Thinking narratively is a necessary method of mind that serves several purposes:

- It stimulates the search for stories in the data and thus the character and processes of participants.
- It encourages you to document your own and your participants' perceptions in written forms and formats that best represent their intended meanings.
- It offers a variety of choices for literary genres, elements, and styles to consider as you compose the account.
- It stimulates creative ways of rendering the qualitative report through more progressive forms of writing for enhanced reader engagement.
- It forces meticulous attention to language as a powerful medium for communicating human insights.

The following methods of mind profile other modalities of narrative representation and presentation for qualitative inquiry: *thinking monologically*, *dialogically*, *poetically*, and *proverbially*.

For your mental Rolodex: As you conduct fieldwork, stay attuned to the storylines of action within the social settings you observe. In interviews, actively prompt and solicit self-standing stories from participants. Consider how your own written account of the study might take on literary dimensions for the representation and presentation of fieldwork experiences.

Thinking Monologically

A **monologue** is an extended, one-person account told in the first person. It most often appears as a performance convention of plays, teleplays, screenplays, and stand-up comedy, but monologic accounts can also be found in standard research articles as longer, indented passages of an interviewee's transcribed text. Monologues are also solo narratives of varying length, such as individual blogs, vlogs, Facebook postings, and even the occasional tweet on Twitter. In fact, the single-authored narrative about the study itself functions as a monologic account.

When we think to ourselves, our minds experience stream-of-consciousness monologues. These internal, solo narratives are rapid and complex thoughts to and for ourselves that reason, reflect, panic, problem-solve, and carry out other processes that we enact most often when we speak aloud to others in everyday life. Psychology's thinking-aloud protocol (Ericsson & Simon, 1993) attempts to record what a person is thinking and feeling as she or he voices uncensored the thoughts going through her or his mind while working on a task like solving a math problem, reading, or watching a film. One of its purposes is to construct a cognitive map of mental processes through a detailed microanalysis of thought sequences and patterns. Writing monologically for qualitative inquiry more coherently documents one person as she or he thinks out loud, preferably with the same uncensored complexity one would use when thinking to oneself.

Some perceive the monologue as a one-sided, even oppressive concept because the opportunity for dialogic exchange and meaning-sharing is missing. But monologues should be treasured as opportunities to read or listen to a person's valued perspective, uninterrupted. Monologues provide not just forums for one's voice; they are participant portraits in miniature. These solo works offer windows into the person's private mind—her or his values, attitudes, beliefs, emotions, and experiences. Monologues give our participants an "open mike" to address an audience with vulnerability and honesty.

Thinking monologically finds passages in your database where participants say things that you cannot possibly "top" through your own words. These are moments when gripping stories are told, when poignant moments are expressed, when the little things seem important, when strong emotions prevail, and when profound insights are made. But they must also add value to the monologic account by revealing something about a participant's personality and character.

Alan Peshkin's (1986) *God's Choice: The Total World of a Fundamentalist Christian School* includes several monologic passages from key teachers and students in the setting. Chapter 1 consists primarily of an extended monologic narrative from Pastor William Muller, headmaster of the school, expressing his personal religious beliefs, the philosophy and approach of the school, and the way he perceives the world today. An excerpt from that monologue reads:

> There is no way of getting in to heaven except through Jesus Christ. Fewer and fewer people believe in the fact that Jesus was God. You're extreme if you do, and I point out in this speech that we are extreme in our belief of the Virgin Birth. We are extreme in believing that Jesus is coming again, we are extreme in believing in salvation by faith, and we are extreme in witnessing to others.

What I'm saying is that Christians are extremist in the eyes of the world. I don't look at myself as a conservative. I can see kooky people to the right of me, but if somebody else looks at me from their perspective, and if they're outside the fold of Christ, they'd look at me as a conservative. I see myself as obeying the Bible. Our belief has got to affect our behavior; if we're Christians, our behavior is going to be conservative politically.

We look around us and see Satan. He's prince and power of this age and he has stronger involvement with this world than Christians do. (p. 6)

Seidman (2013) advocates three separate interviews with the same participant for qualitative case study research. One of the analytic approaches he prescribes is the creation of a "profile," a monologic assemblage of the richest passages from transcripts—approximately one-third of the total corpus. The researcher cuts and pastes transcript excerpts on a monitor screen to create a more organized narrative in terms of chronology, storyline, climactic build, and so on. In the resulting self-standing account, the participant tells her or his own story for the researcher to analyze further, or for a reader to learn about from a first-person perspective. Remember that there are times when the participant herself or himself can take center stage in the study without researcher intervention.

I myself prefer to document for my readers verbatim accounts by participants, including all original grammatical constructions, erratic flows of speech, and extraneous utterances like "um" and "uh." Some label this verbal debris, but I consider it part of an authentic *voiceprint*, as it's called in theatre parlance. I do not attempt to spell out phonetically any cultural dialects, nor do I include "sic" whenever an error (as I perceive it) appears in the transcribed text. The monologue must showcase and honor the participant's unique voice.

But don't forget that you, too, have a researcher's voice. Your thoughts and feelings, especially when they venture toward the confessional and impressionist or the critical and advocacy tales of writing (van Maanen, 2011), can engage your readers with their up-front starkness. I once wrote a conference presentation about one of the most frustrating students with whom I've ever worked, a young man whose intellectual stubbornness brought out the anger in me, and labeled it not a case study but a "case rant." My 15-minute diatribe was an experiment in autoethnographic storytelling that set aside the conventions of academic decorum and focused on the "messy truth" of what sometimes runs through a teacher's mind. Autoethnography (Chang, 2008; S. H. Jones, Adams, & Ellis, 2013; Poulos, 2009; Spry, 2011), a methodology of qualitative inquiry, situates the researcher's personal lived experiences front and center in the writing. In fact, I recommend that all researchers do some soul-searching and undergo the examination of themselves in a report. Doing so will heighten your awareness of what you're asking your participants to do for you. As I advocate in my workshops, "You can't learn how to tell someone else's story until you first learn how to tell your own."

For your mental Rolodex: As you investigate social life, construct monologic work from your participants or yourself that offers insight about human experiences.

Thinking Dialogically

A form not seen too often in academic writing is dialogic exchange. Most qualitative research projects collect data through one-on-one interviews, so documentation of interaction between participants is sparse. There is abundant methods literature on conversation analysis, but studies from that genre tend to parse the narratives extensively through their analytic detail, interrupting the flow of dialogue on the page.

Thinking dialogically finds passages of text from your data that reveal participants engaged in **dialogue**—that is, significant conversational action, reaction, and interaction. It reflects carefully on how the power and nuances of language don't just communicate but influence and affect things into motion. Thinking dialogically examines how the conversationalists themselves perceive the verbal exchange, and how you as the researcher retrospectively interpret what was spoken between them. Some interviews contain dialogic exchanges between the researcher and participant, but most of these tend to consist of question/answer turn-taking. Focus group transcripts however, particularly during tension-laden passages, contain rich sources for dialogic encounters. Chapter 6's "Thinking Communicatively" offered several considerations for conversation analysis, such as Goodall's (2000) Verbal Exchange Coding and the microanalysis of dialogic "moments." This section focuses on the documentation and writing up of those conversations for your readership.

The formatting of conversation generates different effects on readers. When dialogue is woven into a prosaic rendering, the narrator has the opportunity to add supplemental description and commentary. Below is an excerpt from Finley and Finley's (1999) narrative inquiry account of homeless youth in pre-Katrina New Orleans. Two young men, nicknamed Tigger and Roach, plan their strategies to "sp'ange" (ask passersby for spare change):

> Tigger has several years of practice and a high school diploma to separate himself from the rank and file gutter-punk. He was even in the military, for a short while, but couldn't get through the boot camp thing. Often times, he's the voice that gets things moving along.
>
> "We better make quick work of the schwillies, man," Tigger says in a quick aside to Roach, then addresses the entire group. "We gotta sp'ange enough for all weekend today; it's gonna rain tomorrow."
>
> "How do you know that?" Roach feels comfortable challenging Tigger. It's always done in a friendly tone, and his challenges often let Tigger explain his rationale, swaying the whole group to his point of view. Roach takes a long swig of whiskey in his turn. "Are you a weather man now?"
>
> Tigger rolls his eyes. "I read it in the paper. Town is gonna be packed and we can make bank. The Clover has a sign welcoming some conference, so there's plenty of green around. We just gotta get it while the weather holds." (p. 327)

Now examine the same dialogic exchange, adapted and formatted as an ethnodramatic script:

TIGGER: We better make quick work of the schwillies, man. We gotta sp'ange enough for all weekend today; it's gonna rain tomorrow.

ROACH: How do you know that? Are you a weather man now? *(he takes a long swig of whiskey)*

TIGGER: I read it in the paper. Town is gonna be packed and we can make bank. The Clover has a sign welcoming some conference, so there's plenty of green around. We just gotta get it while the weather holds. (adapted from Saldaña, 2005a, p. 147)

Both formats are available to qualitative researchers, and each offers its unique advantages as a rendering of social life. Prosaic formats permit more nuanced descriptions reminiscent of field notes and an omniscient point of view. Dramatic formats provide an economic sense of action happening "here and now" and ask the reader to make more inferences and interpretations of the dialogic exchanges. Your format choice for a written report should be strategically selected to render the account in its most powerful manner.

One of the more fascinating methodological genres of qualitative inquiry to evolve recently is duoethnography (Norris, Sawyer, & Lund, 2012; Sawyer & Norris, 2013). **Duoethnography** is a collaborative research methodology in which two (or more) researchers juxtapose their life histories to provide multiple understandings of a social phenomenon. Duoethnography compensates for the potentially limited vision of a one-person autoethnography, and the potentially diffuse findings from large-team research, by establishing a two-person project.

Each writer provides both individual contributions and commentary on the other researcher's reflections, usually but not exclusively through e-mail exchanges. Individual positions can be supplemented, enhanced, supported, challenged, and revised through dialogic response. Awareness becomes further heightened when two individuals from different backgrounds collaborate as duoethnographers (e.g., when gender issues are discussed between a man and a woman or sexual orientation and identity politics are discussed between a straight man and a gay man). The premise of the genre is based on the simple adage, "Stories beget stories," meaning that one person's shared personal experiences stimulate and generate additional narratives from another. Both researchers play the roles of storyteller *and* listener in this new methodology. Perhaps the most refreshing quality of duoethnography is its honesty. The methodology, and thus the writing, permits collegial and unpretentious exchanges of thoughts and insights. However, contributors do not sacrifice rigor for their straightforwardness. They cite the professional literature when necessary and propose new theories as ideas accumulate—not as intellectual "talking heads" but as collegial interactants reflecting on the issue. Duoethnography is scholarly conversation at its best. Topics vary from the small details of everyday living to the grand and important meanings of life. Feelings are just as valid as facts, and insights deepen from the opportunity to exchange and build upon another's perspectives.

Even a researcher and a key participant can dialogue (in real time or electronically) as duo-ethnographers, so long as the time and effort do not tax the respondent. I have conducted many interviews with participants who contributed profound insights on the topics I investigated, but I have not had many opportunities to "talk shop" with them about the nature of the study itself and its data analysis. When those exchanges did occur, a few of them offered me intriguing factors to consider and even some "Aha!" revelations. As time permits, dialogue with your participants about the research process itself—not just as a means of conducting member checks to confirm accurate data documentation and reportage, but to gain their perspectives on how to go about understanding the very phenomenon you're attempting to study.

> ***For your mental Rolodex:*** As you investigate social life, listen for and extract significant conversational moments between your participants. Understand that dialogue is not just communication but inquiry in its broadest sense.

Thinking Poetically

Poetic inquiry (Prendergast, Leggo, & Sameshima, 2009) is a methodological approach to qualitative research that utilizes the conventions of poetry as representational and presentational modalities. The poetry can originate from the researcher's own reflections about her or his experiences, or it can be adapted from the qualitative data collected (most often from interview transcripts) and constructed as "found poetry." As an example, the following poem (Miles, Huberman, & Saldaña, 2014, p. 187) represents an elementary fine arts magnet school's philosophy and curriculum goals according to its principal. The words were extracted from a portion of a one-hour interview and arranged by the researcher to capture essential content and, hopefully, to stimulate an aesthetic experience for its readers. The mission of this arts-centered school is to

Teach attitudes

    create whole people

    lifetime learners

Learn attitudes

    a love of problem solving

    elegance of expression

Teach and learn

    respectfully

    supportively

    joyfully

Performance artist Anna Deavere Smith (2000) asserts that people speak in "organic poetry" through their everyday discourse. She takes the most intriguing portions of their verbatim interview transcript texts and arranges them in free poetic verse formats for monologic presentation. An example of this technique is taken from an interview with a second-year doctoral student regarding his university program of study:

I'm 27 years old and I've got over $50,000 in student loans that I have to pay off and that scares the hell out of me. I've got to finish my dissertation next year because I can't afford to keep going to school. I've got to get a job and start working. (Saldaña, 2013, p. 18)

If this excerpt were arranged into poetic form, it might read thus:

I'm 27 years old

and I've got

    over $50,000 in student loans   that I have to pay off

and that scares

the hell

    out of me.

I've got to finish my dissertation next year because

    I can't afford to   keep going to school.

I've got to get a job

    and start

       working. . . .

The parsing (i.e., each phrase on one line) and selected indents are strategies for emphasizing the constituent thoughts and erratic emotional journey of the doctoral student, which may get lost in an unbroken prosaic quotation. All the words in the poem are exactly the same as in the original quote, but the reformatting highlights each specific struggle and heightens the tension of the participant's dilemmas. Such exercises attune the analyst to each and every word of the text and force the careful search for nuances of meaning. See Mears (2009) for powerful examples of how organic poetic transcription and found poetry assist analysis.

Another approach to poetic inquiry is the researcher as self-reflective poet, composing original work synthesized from field experiences, methodological or analytic musings, or autoethnographic memories. As I composed this paragraph, I thought poetically about how to best express an example. What emerged (after five drafts) was the following poem about my ways of working as a qualitative researcher:

Method is my life partner.

I smile when I think of him

and his intricate complexity,

    grasping my hand firmly as I

    search for meaning.

He almost never leaves my mind.

Thinking poetically is analyzing and condensing large amounts of data into as few words as possible for the capture and evocation of core meanings—goals comparable to those of the methodologies of phenomenology and grounded theory. But this is not just about the quantity of words; it's also about the careful selection and arrangement of them to stimulate from readers and listeners powerful "wow" moments, or what is known among artists as **aesthetic arrest**. As you review text-based data from your study, find key words and phrases in your field notes, interview transcripts, documents, and so on that will serve the purposes of poetic composition. In vivo coding (using words or short phrases spoken by the participant) is one method to help get you there, but also rely on your intuitive capacity for determining what feels right artistically.

This thinking modality is not for everyone. I profiled poetic inquiry as a descriptive research method in one of my research methodology textbooks (Miles et al., 2014). A reviewer of the book's early manuscript questioned the inclusion of this approach with the critical comment, "Poetic inquiry—I just don't get it." I smiled and thought to myself, "Of course you don't." Researchers accustomed to more traditional conventions of quantitative and systematic qualitative data analysis (e.g., codes, categories, themes, theories) may find poetry a questionable approach to social investigation. Perhaps it is sometimes assumed that such inquiry is "fluff" or "less than" more rigorous analytic methods. You may be able to find receptive audiences among the poetically inclined, but, depending on your discipline, you may encounter strong resistance against and critical judgment of your work. Thus, poetic inquiry may serve as a viable method for the researcher's eyes only—a private data display for personal reflection that can stimulate later conventional forms of writing for public audiences.

> **For your mental Rolodex:** As you listen to participants in the field and review interview transcripts, remain vigilant for the organic poetry inherent in the data. Reformat some of your texts into poetic structures to explore how new meanings and understandings might be generated.

Thinking Proverbially

Aesop's fables have morals. Our research stories have theories. The classic tale of Aesop's "The Tortoise and the Hare" teaches readers that "Slow and steady wins the race." But a modern theory about achievement, developed from a case study of a university's unit reorganization, might propose that *Significant and sustained institutional change should occur by mandate from executive levels of power for initiation and transformation within limited time parameters.*

Our everyday lives are sometimes guided by folk wisdom in the form of **proverbs**—theories for productive living. When considering whether to indulge ourselves with a frivolous purchase, we might remember that "All that glitters is not gold." So we decide not to spend our hard-earned money carelessly because our reckless, "penny-wise and pound-foolish" buying experiences have taught us that "A fool and his money are soon parted." Having made a bad decision like this in our past makes us "Once bitten, twice shy." Instead, we refrain from making the purchase and take pride in our self-discipline, confident that "A penny saved is a penny earned." After all, "You never know what the future holds," so we should always "Set aside something for a rainy day" because "It's better to be safe than sorry."

Proverbs are theories about life and living. Recall from previous chapters that a theory (as it is traditionally conceived of in research) is a generalizable statement with an accompanying explanatory narrative that

- predicts and controls action through an if/then logic,
- explains how and/or why something happens by stating its cause(s), and
- provides insights and guidance for improving social life.

A proverb such as "If you lie down with dogs, you'll wake up with fleas" meets the criteria for a theory because it possesses an if/then logic, states the consequences of an action, and gives us insight into how we should conduct ourselves (i.e., we need to choose our companions and social settings cautiously to keep us out of trouble).

Different professions pass down insider knowledge or ways of working through aphorisms. Those in building construction teach their apprentices, "Measure twice, cut once." Veteran teachers share with novices, "Teachers don't always see what grows from seeds they've planted." A university professor of multicultural issues continually cautions his students, "This classroom will be safe, but it may not be comfortable." And a marriage counselor may regretfully advise clients, "Sometimes the best way to heal a relationship is to end it." Those who belong to Facebook might read friends' posts that share short quotes by famous people or nuggets of folk wisdom and motivational passages with accompanying pictures: "Do not judge by appearances: A rich heart may be under a poor coat" or "How others see you is not important; how you see yourself means everything."

Thinking proverbially succinctly phrases the life lessons heard during or suggested by your study. It works as a heuristic for collecting and analyzing the folk wisdom purported by your participants to discern the values, attitudes, and beliefs that may guide their actions. Your observations may also remind you of proverbs, pithy sayings, famous quotes, and the like from your own prior knowledge that are applicable to your study. One veteran teacher I observed reminded me that "All you need is love" for your students to get through difficult circumstances in the classroom. A bipolar, suicidal adolescent I interviewed said of himself (as his parents were recovering from drug and alcohol abuse), "What doesn't kill you makes you stronger."

If these pieces of folk wisdom are laypeople's informally phrased theories, then "Measure twice, cut once" might be expanded to read: *Significantly fewer errors will occur if the builder double-checks the measurements before cutting into construction materials.* But the simplicity and rhythm of "Measure twice, cut once" has more impact on one's memory. Kahneman (2011) advises that these proverbs or sayings have more staying power in our memories if they're elegant and especially if they rhyme ("An apple a day keeps the doctor away"). Hahn (2011, pp. 32–33) also suggests that we examine a proverb's opposing perspective to ensure that the first life lesson proposal for our study is not undercut by disconfirming evidence. We might posit that our participants confirm the adage, "You're never too old to learn." But is there anyone among the sample who supports, "You can't teach an old dog new tricks"? And don't forget to explore the canon of folk wisdom from other cultures, which offers unique insights on life. For example, we have these proverbs from Latin America: "The devil lurks even behind the cross," "Virtues all agree, but vices fight one another," and "He who speaks sows, and he who listens harvests" (Zona, 1996).

Many stage plays, teleplays, and screenplays are well known for their one-liners—memorable passages or quotable quotes that make an impact with their insight, irony, or poignancy (Trimble, 2006). Shakespeare's King Henry IV observed, "Uneasy lies the head that wears the crown." An adolescent character from the TV series *Boy Meets World* advises, "Life's tough; get a helmet." Dorothy from *The Wizard of Oz* film learns, "There's no place like home." These one-liners are comparable to proverbs, and in daily social life we should stay alert to such passages spoken by our participants that strike us as noteworthy nuggets of wisdom, for they have the potential to be built into a theory about our case. "Uneasy lies the head that wears the crown" begins a theoretical treatise on the emotional toll of responsibilities and hazards for those in leadership positions. In the everyday, real-life workplace, a disgruntled employee may observe about others, "Some people want all of the authority but none of the responsibility." This one-liner sets into motion an investigation of the validity of his assertion to further a study on power dynamics and relationships among an infighting staff.

The participants we interview or observe may occasionally say something offhandedly that strikes us as a profound insight. In my action research project with elementary school children to reduce bullying (Saldaña, 2005b), I was puzzled about why my efforts to teach peacekeeping and positive negotiation strategies were thwarted by young people's preferences for combative solutions. It all became clear when a fourth-grade girl told me, "Sometimes, you can't be nice to deal with oppression." That single quote became the through-line for the study's key assertion on power dynamics among youth. As another example, a university colleague and I once discussed how to achieve success in the entertainment industry, and I offered the legendary, "Well, it's not what you know but who you know." He countered with, "Wrong. It's not 'who you know'; it's *who knows you.*" And as I reflect on the invitations offered to me by others in influential positions, I realize he was right. I now offer his advice instead of my tired cliché—affirmation that not all proverbs should be accepted unquestioningly.

If you feel unable to develop a formal theory about your research, first listen for what types of proverbs, folk sayings, and folk wisdom might be used by participants in their everyday interactions or during interviews, and reflect on what classic proverbs might seem relevant to your particular case. Though it may seem pedantic, reflect on what moral, life lesson, or cautionary advice might be suggested by your study. Think about not what you learned, but what your participants learned. And always keep your ears open for those significant participant one-liners that seem to summarize what the study is all about.

For your mental Rolodex: As you investigate social life, attend to proverbs, folk wisdom, and significant quotes offered by participants. Use these as the basis for theory development from your study.

CLOSURE

Sometimes what separates a great piece of research from a mediocre one is its writing finesse. New ideas certainly make an impact on readers, but the literary accessibility of a journal article, chapter, or book comes from the author's ability to communicate ideas in an engaging manner. "The essence of persuasion, communication, and self-understanding has become the ability also to fashion a compelling narrative" (Pink, 2006, p. 66). Writing is all about choices; the genres, elements, and styles you select to represent and present your study embody the totality of your inquiry.

Writing is also thinking. Therefore, writing poetically necessitates thinking poetically. Writing theoretically means thinking theoretically. And writing well requires thinking well. What you type on a keyboard, what appears on a monitor screen documents the thoughts formulated in your mind. What you create is a product of your thinking. The past 10 chapters have offered various lenses, filters, and angles for your vision, in its broadest sense. It is now time to apply them on an as-needed, as-remembered, and as-inspired basis for your qualitative research studies.

EXERCISES FOR THINKING NARRATIVELY

1. Compose a one-page narrative monologue—a rant—about a social issue that easily angers you (e.g., economic disparity, ineffective government, gender inequality). Write your thoughts in everyday language and with uncensored honesty. Then privately voice out loud, nonstop, what you've written. Reflect on the experience of how verbalizing rather than just writing your thoughts may have impacted you.

2. Visit a field site where conversational exchanges are frequent (e.g., a restaurant, mall, social gathering). Listen to dialogic exchanges between people and focus not just on the content of the conversation but on the action, reaction, and interaction patterns they employ (e.g., turn-taking, question/answer, support, negation, disagreement, confirmation, laughter, verbal fluency).

3. Generate a two- to three-page selection from an interview transcript and apply in vivo coding to the text. (In vivo codes are words or short phrases spoken by the participant that the researcher interprets as significant; see Saldaña, 2013, pp. 91–96.) Use the in vivo codes as resources to create a found poem about the participant's experiences.

4. Brainstorm a list of folk sayings, folk wisdom, or proverbs from your particular discipline—for example, in education, "To teach is to learn twice"; in counseling, "You can't see the frame when you're in the picture"; in design, "Less is more." Write about or discuss with a peer the possible origins and bases of experience of one or more of these proverbs from your field. Critique the proverbs' legitimacy, credibility, and applicability to contemporary thought and practice in your discipline.

Closure

Thoughts About Thinking

LEARNING OBJECTIVES AND SUMMARY

- Your mind will consolidate the major principles of thinking qualitatively.
- Your mind will reflect on possible future applications of these methods in your research work.

This final chapter offers additional comments on thinking and guidance for your future qualitative research projects. Sections include

- Consolidation
- Questions and Answers
- Quality Thinking and Quality Presentation
- Closure: Thinking Qualitatively
- Exercises for Thoughts About Thinking

Consolidation

Most people remember only about 10% of what they read. And 70% to 90% of new classroom learning is forgotten within 18 to 24 hours of a lesson (Sousa, 2011, p. 76). Thus, educators and students should take time not just to review but to "cement" knowledge into mental storage where long-term memory can further process it. The brain can only hold information in working (short-term) memory for 15 to 20 seconds without elaborative rehearsal (Wolfe, 2010, pp. 126, 134). "The more fully we process information over time, the more connections we make, the more consolidation [joining together into a unified whole] takes place, and the better the memory will be" (p. 158). I use the analogy that good ideas, like good coffee and good tea, need time to brew and steep. Sleep, in fact, is a time of information consolidation when neural activity both strengthens long-term memories and makes connections. Consolidation leads not just to stronger memories but to understanding.

Out of curiosity, I asked several of my colleagues, "What happens in your mind as you think and transcend from problem to solution, from puzzlement to answer, from confusion to clarity?" Most responded that they deliberately take mental time away from the problem yet keep ruminating over it in their minds by placing it "on the back burner." What happens during that period of time differs, from sleeping and dreaming to taking a relaxing shower to working on unrelated yet necessary tasks. A few jot down their thoughts by hand or diagram as a way of working out the solution. And still others use the pressure of deadlines to force them to come up with a creative answer, so long as they remain calm within the storm. The solution eventually rushes toward them as a moment of clarity and awareness, as if something in the subconscious came together and pushed its way into conscious thought. Some refer to these instances as "Eureka!" or "Aha!" moments, but I have found myself verbally shouting "Yes!" when consolidation happens. Call them what you will, these are processes that most likely cannot be taught. They are circumstances for each individual to experience on his or her own terms and in his or her own time.

My personal problem-solving process entails imaginatively visualizing in my mind whatever is to be realized, exhausting the possibilities for its execution and choosing the most creative, and reflecting on how the process and product can be imbued with style. This is not only how I carry out my theatrical performances and conduct my studio classes, but also how I write academic articles and books. I don't just let it happen or hope it happens; I make it happen through deliberate choices. I'm messy and systematic at the same time. I'm neither linear nor holistic—I'm reverberative. I jump back and forth from one thing to another to produce a play, write a book, or analyze qualitative data.

Consolidation in qualitative inquiry occurs most often during the data analysis stages when the researcher attempts to construct both sense and meaning from the corpus. Consolidation continues when the researcher as writer organizes his or her thoughts into an appropriate presentational medium. These are not always easy tasks, for they require a mind that can both cognitively synthesize vast amounts of information and maintain an even emotional keel so as to focus and persevere. Answers to research problems emerge sometimes from systematic and persistent work, sometimes through long inward reflection, and sometimes through serendipitous discovery. These are the chances qualitative researchers must take—or, these are the options at their disposal—each time they proceed with a study.

Questions and Answers

If there are sometimes no easy answers, should we give up on them? I respectfully propose "no." I admittedly tire of research reports that ask a series of unanswered, rhetorical questions as their conclusion. Yes, this shows that the investigator knows that there is more work to be done, but unanswered questions suggest to me that the researcher has "timed out" or given up on the complexity of the issue at hand.

I advise throughout my writings that researchers should not pose unanswered questions in their write-ups' final sections. I have encountered resistance to that suggestion from a few colleagues, for they perceive questions as stimuli for reader reflection and collegial dialogue. Unanswered questions also serve as a mode of communication that documents the researcher's thinking about the challenges or intricacies of the topic. My objection to unanswered questions rests not with their content but with their phrasing. Imagine an excerpt from the conclusion of a report on school violence that reads as follows:

> Why do children continue to bully each other, despite adults' concerted efforts to educate them about the problem? Is it in their hardwired biological natures to dominate others? Is any intervention program an effective model? How many more children and teenagers must we tragically lose to suicide before society finds a remedy?

As I mentioned in Chapter 1, the honest thought that runs through my mind as I read a series of questions like this is, "Why are you asking *me* this? Don't *you* know?" I would rather read a passage that transforms the unanswered questions above into statements that offer me the writer's perspective:

> Sadly, children continue to bully each other, despite adults' concerted efforts to educate them about the problem. Some propose that domination over others is part of our hardwired, biological nature, suggesting we will continue to lose severely victimized youth through their tragic suicides.

Yet, even better is the writer's effort to propose possible solutions, albeit couched in terms of future research needs:

> Both victims *and* perpetrators of bullying need conscientious education on its destructive effects. Innovative intervention programs such as "Cooling Conflict" (O'Toole, Burton, & Plunkett, 2005) utilize a peer education model to lessen school violence through progressive techniques such as emotional intelligence training and role-play. This program could be explored beyond its pilot site to nurture safer school environments and to hopefully lessen the ever-growing number of bullying-related youth suicides.

The passage above offers a more proactive stance toward the issue than the first string of unanswered questions.

The ideal purpose of research is to increase knowledge and to find solutions to our problems. It is our duty to advance the world, not to continually push its pause button. I acknowledge that time for reflection is necessary for the formulation of good ideas. But we are living in an age when the speed of our solutions must catch up with the accelerated accumulation of our dilemmas. Anyone can ask a question; it takes a sharp thinker to construct a good answer. Researchers should begin their quest with many questions but hopefully end up with fewer than when they began, not more. Though it may seem rather aggressive, I challenge my students with the following: "If you ask tough questions, you better be damn ready to offer some tough answers."

Quality Thinking and Quality Presentation

If writing and creating are products of thinking, then the published report or presentation reflects the thinking processes of the researcher. The product embodies the mental ways of working of its creator. As a reader or member of an audience of a presentation, my own mind will uniquely perceive and interpret the research, since my personal knowledge, memories, emotions, values, attitudes, beliefs, and associations will influence and affect my responses.

I have attended conferences in which audiences for certain speakers seemed enthralled with the presentations they heard, while I was highly critical and skeptical of the reports and puzzled (admittedly, sometimes furious) about why others did not think and feel the same way I did. Of course, most people did not think and feel the same way I did because most people do not think and feel the same way I do. Hence, I choose to evaluate the quality and effectiveness of someone else's work by no one's standards but my own.

As I reflect on qualitative research studies that made me say to myself, "Wow" after I finished them, nine categories of criteria come to mind. These standards may or may not be compatible with your own, but I offer them for your consideration of what makes for quality qualitative research and reporting (adapted from Saldaña, 2011b, pp. 163–164). Through an artistic lens, these are not just evaluative criteria but aesthetic principles:

- **Rigor:** The author/creator persuades me that he or she has "done his (or her) homework" by providing a sufficient literature review and an exhaustive data analysis. There is evidence that ample time and careful thought went into all stages of the project.
- **Unity:** Good qualitative research maintains a sense of focus on its primary topic. The representation and presentation modalities chosen are consistent throughout and appropriate for the study.
- **Clarity:** The research report is written or presented in accessible, elegant, and/or evocative language. It is complex when necessary, yet told in such a way that I can follow it and absorb the ideas. Good thinking is clear thinking.
- **Utility:** The writing is unpretentious. The author/creator "keeps it real" by keeping theory to a minimum and emphasizing the pragmatic. Ideas are useful only if they hold relevance and applicability for others.

- **Priorities:** The researcher respects, honors, and emphasizes the participants' voices, especially marginalized groups such as people of color and children, when relevant to the study. Empathetic and ethical thought are interwoven throughout the report.
- **Engagement:** Regardless of the topic, good qualitative research keeps me intellectually interested and emotionally invested. Whether I'm reading a technical report or listening to a conference paper session, I am intrinsically motivated and attentive to what the author/creator has to share. In other words, the research is meaningful to me.
- **Relevance:** Regardless of the topic of the presentation or the author/creator's discipline, the research has some applicability and transferability to my own practice as a researcher or practitioner. I feel that the work has impacted me, become part of me, and even changed me.
- **Payoff:** I have been given new knowledge, fresh insights, keen awareness, personal discoveries, and deeper understandings—quite simply, things I didn't know before. My own ways of thinking have been positively altered.
- **Respect:** The author of a research report earns my respect because he or she presents the work with scholarly and/or artistic integrity. I now think highly of the researcher. A reputation is both made and earned, and this writer makes me want to experience more of what he or she has published or presented.

Consult with teachers and mentors in your field about what they consider to be outstanding works in qualitative inquiry. Read a variety of works, ranging from the traditional to the progressive, from grounded theory to phenomenology, from autoethnography to poetic inquiry, whether they are written from the standpoint of your own discipline or originate in fields outside your knowledge base. As time and funding permit, attend qualitative research conferences to hear from scholars firsthand and to network with peers across disciplines.

CLOSURE: THINKING QUALITATIVELY

One of my former students appreciated what she perceived as my ability to perceptively analyze qualitative data and told me, "I want to know how your mind works." I smiled and replied, "It would scare you." Early in my academic career, I was taught to speed read. Perhaps that intensive training also influenced and affected my mind to speed think. I like to present myself publicly as a laid-back yet very organized individual, but my mind is a chaotic maelstrom of intrapersonal mental processing and erratic emotional forays. "I can't turn my mind off" is a common saying several use to describe their thinking habits. I am one of those people. Memories, associations, new ideas, thought experiments, daydreams, fantasies, stream-of-consciousness images, to-do lists, projections, problem solving, task switching, earworms, emotional recall, empathic connections, and other mental operations flow rapidly through my brain in a dizzying array. I can switch to linear thought when needed for extended periods of time, but I can also let my emotions take over my body and become immersed in peak experiences (cf. Reinertsen, 2014).

Eisner (1998) posits, "How we think is influenced by what we think about and how we choose or are expected to represent its content" (p. 121). I am virtually always thinking about something qualitative. When I'm in a public setting such as a shopping mall, I observe customers and workers as they interact to study concepts such as transaction, persuasion, and role positioning. When I enter someone's home or office for the first time, my eyes rapidly scan and analyze the decor and environment to infer what the owner's personality or business ethic might be like. Though some become easily annoyed when forced to listen to other people's cell phone conversations, I eagerly eavesdrop on them and attune my ear to the speaker's words and vocal tones to sharpen my conversational awareness. As I drive on streets and highways, I consciously look for patterns in signage, vehicle movement, pedestrian dress, and so on. Even when I'm taking part in private, intimate, one-on-one dialogic exchanges with a close friend, part of my brain concurrently analyzes our discourse, subtexts, and presentations of self.

I enter a new city for business or leisure, and my mind thinks like an anthropologist as I examine the cityscape during a cab ride from the airport to the hotel. I walk through the city's streets and think like a sociologist as I observe tourists and residents clustered in crowds negotiating for space. I think categorically as I notice the types and numbers of downtown restaurants and their unique cuisine. I think historically as I take in the city's architecture and reflect on the buildings' original occupants and purposes. I think multiculturally when I observe how people of different races interact with each other in this particular part of the country. I think darkly about what kinds of things I might do as a stranger in the city's nightlife. I think intuitively as I walk alone in the evening and assess my personal safety on unknown streets. I think phenomenologically about what it means to experience this city. I think poetically as I text message my impressions about this new place to my friends.

We can never know exactly how another person thinks, much less whether that person thinks the same way we do. Neuroscience may, in the near future, develop methods for fully documenting the intricate thinking and emotive processes of a human being—as imagined in the 1983 science fiction film *Brainstorm*. For now, social researchers must rely on their knowledge, experiences, and imaginations to conceptualize how another person thinks and what he or she thinks about, feels, values, and believes. The methods of qualitative inquiry—interviews, participant observation, document and artifact review, visual materials, digital materials, participant-created artifacts, and so on—are the best tools we have for the instrumental functions of data collection. But it is our minds that must still systematically sort through and creatively analyze the corpus and reflect on its contents and meanings.

Cuzzort and King (2002) caution, "The more rigorously scientific we become in the social sciences, the more we remove ourselves from what we want to understand" (pp. 7–8). This warning was aimed at researchers who think quantitatively about the social world and how human behaviors can be seemingly reliably and validly measured. This book offers that statistics are just one way of constructing and interpreting knowledge about our lives. There are a repertoire of different lenses, filters, and angles for perceiving social action, reaction, and interaction in nonnumeric ways. Richards and Morse (2013) define *thinking qualitatively* as

> an exhausting process of being constantly aware and continually asking analytic questions of data, which, in turn, regularly address the questions asked. Qualitative inquiry constantly challenges assumptions, questions the obvious, reveals the hidden and the overt, the implicit, the taken-for-granted, and shows these in a new light. Without such an active mode of inquiry, you risk a shallow, descriptive study with few surprises, reporting the obvious. (pp. 218–219)

Pink (2006) proposes that we have transitioned from the information age to the conceptual age, where knowledge workers are now the creators and empathizers, whose tasks are "to create artistic and emotional beauty, to detect patterns and opportunities, to craft a satisfying narrative, and to combine seemingly unrelated ideas into a novel invention" (pp. 51–52). This is, for qualitative inquirers, not just our job description but our mission for understanding the connections between and among human relationships. It is my hope that *Thinking Qualitatively: Methods of Mind* has offered you some new and useful heuristics for active modes of inquiry.

There are approximately 1 trillion cells in your brain, with a possibility of up to 1 quadrillion synaptic connections to store memories and process data (Sousa, 2011, p. 22). Your brain is an analytic marvel. In the grand scheme of things, it's not always necessary to know when you're thinking musically or thinking inductively or thinking sociologically or even what the correct label is for the kind of thinking you're doing. What's important is that you simply *think*—multimodally, highdeeply, and qualitatively.

EXERCISES FOR THOUGHTS ABOUT THINKING

1. Reread all the *For your mental Rolodex* statements in Chapters 2 through 10 to review the summary principles of thinking qualitatively.

2. Reflect on how your thinking may (or may not) have been altered, impacted, transformed, or changed, or might change in the near future, after reading this book.

3. Not every possible type of thinking has been addressed in this text. Compose a profile comparable in length and purpose to those in Chapters 2 through 10 for one or more of the following (or a different lens, filter, and angle of your own choosing): Thinking Playfully; Thinking Technologically; Thinking Holistically; Thinking Metacognitively; Thinking _____ [base this modality on a discipline not addressed in Chapter 6, such as business, sport, journalism, or education].

4. Check various popular Internet sites on the brain, such as Brain Pickings (www.brainpickings .org) or a commercial site (e.g., www.lumosity.com or http://brainhq.positscience.com). Enter "brain" in an Internet search engine and explore selected sites.

5. This is a variation of an exercise from Chapter 1. Figure 11.1 is an outline of a human brain. Trace it onto your own sheet of paper and use colored pencils, crayons, and/or markers to creatively draw a representation of how to think qualitatively. Both words and illustrations can be used, but preferably more of the latter. Share your drawing with a partner who has also drawn the inside of his or her own brain and discuss the inferences and meanings of both drawings. If you completed this comparable exercise earlier after reading Chapter 1 and kept your brain drawing, compare your first drawing with this new thinking qualitatively drawing. Reflect on their similarities and differences.

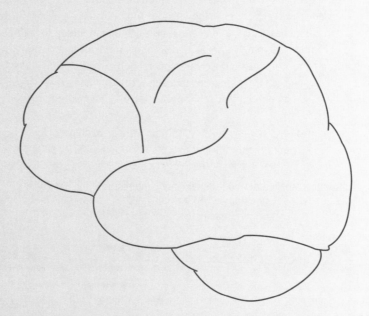

Figure 11.1.   Use this outline of a human brain to complete Exercise 5.

Glossary

abduction: examining an array of possibilities or explanations and selecting the most reasonable and credible one; explores the possible links or causation between phenomena.

action: a micro-unit of human activity consisting of a purposeful and meaningful behavior; speaking and mental activity, not just physical motion, are considered actions.

aesthetic arrest: an individual's powerful emotional response to a work of art or to participating in an artistic experience.

algorithm: a procedural, formulaic approach to solving a problem.

analysis: finding patterns and other essential features in data and articulating their interrelationships.

analytic induction: a process by which answers to research questions are emergently constructed as more data are collected and systematically examined.

angle: a cultural landscape position held by the researcher such as insider or outsider, intimate or distant, emotionally invested or objectively detached; also refers to micro-, meso-, and macro-perceptions of social life.

assertion: a statement of summative synthesis, supported by confirming evidence from the data corpus.

autoethnography: an account written in the first person about the researcher's personal lived experiences with an emphasis on the cultural or social domains of the experiences.

biparadigmatic: knowledge of and fluency in the respective vocabularies and heuristic and algorithmic grammars of both quantitative and qualitative inquiry.

bracket: to set aside one's own worldview in order to understand and respect another's.

capsule: a summative labeling device for important contents from the database.

CAQDAS: an acronym for "computer-assisted qualitative data analysis software"—programs for data storage, organization, and management during analysis.

case study: a focused research study on one unit of interest—for example, one person, one setting, one organization, one event.

category: a word or phrase labeling a grouped pattern of comparable codes and coded data; it condenses larger units of social action and phenomena for further analytic reflection.

causation: attributions of influences and affects (rather than cause and effect); examination of actions, reactions, and interactions to plot antecedent conditions, mediating variables, and outcomes.

code: a word or short phrase that symbolically assigns a summative, salient, essence-capturing, and/or evocative attribute to a portion of language-based or visual data.

codeweaving: an analytic technique of intentionally integrating several codes into a brief narrative to connect them in plausible ways.

cognitive dissonance: the mind's inability or unwillingness to process new information or contradictory perspectives when they conflict with established thinking patterns or personal values, attitudes, and beliefs.

complexity: acknowledgement and analysis of multiple interrelated factors involved with a phenomenon.

concept: a word or short phrase that symbolically represents a suggested meaning broader than a single item or action; an idea beyond the tangible and apparent.

conceptual framework: a set of epistemological, conceptual, and theoretical foundation principles for guidance throughout a research study.

connecting: joining disparate pieces of information into a coherent and more unified scheme.

consolidation: the mental process of joining things together into a unified whole to strengthen memories and understanding.

constructivist: pertaining to an epistemological approach to research that utilizes such methods as interviews and participant observation of natural social life to heuristically develop findings; an inductive and emergent approach to investigation.

creative nonfiction: qualitative research writing that employs the devices and conventions of fictional literature for the reportage of systematic investigation.

creativity: the enactment of original ideas, objects, and processes from the imagination; used for problem-solving as well as to produce artistic works.

critical thinking: evaluative reflection that examines the status quo in order to expose a social inequity or injustice that merits public knowledge and action for righting the wrong.

culture: a historically transmitted pattern of meanings embodied in symbols; knowledge learned and shared that people use to generate behavior and interpret experience.

cycle: a pattern of patterns; repetitive and sometimes cumulative sequences of an action series (such as phases and stages) within generally bounded time periods.

data corpus: the body of data; the total assembly of all empirical materials collected for a research study.

deduction: conclusion-making from evidence.

diagram: a summative visual representation and presentation of data analysis.

dialogue: conversational action, reaction, and interaction that influence and affect things into motion.

discipline: a major branch of academic study comprising related subject areas or fields.

duoethnography: a collaborative research methodology in which two (or more) researchers dialogue in print and juxtapose their life histories to provide multiple understandings of a social phenomenon.

elegance: simplicity; involves the perception and identification of core purposes or meanings, putting into as few words as possible what something "is."

emotion: "a feeling and its distinctive thoughts, psychological and biological states, and range of propensities to act" (Goleman, 1995, p. 289).

emotional intelligence: the capacity to understand one's own and others' emotions and to manage personal emotional states to enhance productive well-being, daily living, and interpersonal relationships; includes capacities such as self-awareness, empathy, self-disclosure, and stress management.

empathy: cognitive understanding and emotional reflection within oneself of what someone else is feeling.

epistemology: a theory of knowledge construction based on the researcher's worldview—that is, how her or his lens on the world and angled ways of knowing it focus and filter her or his perception and interpretation of it.

ethics: a set of personal and professional principles for intrapersonal action and interpersonal conduct, rooted in obligatory codes and the individual's value, attitude, and belief systems.

ethnotheatre: an arts-based research genre that employs the conventions of theatrical performance to stage for an audience a selected representation of fieldwork.

ethnography: a research methodology for the study of a group of people constituting a culture.

filter: a set of personal values, attitudes, and beliefs about the world, formed by one's unique personal biography, learned experiences, and individual thinking patterns; may also consist of particular theoretical perspectives or standpoints within a discipline.

grounded theory: a methodological approach to qualitative inquiry that inductively and systematically builds a theory through detailed coding and categorization of data.

hermeneutic: a theory and process of understanding and interpreting texts through multiple, layered readings.

heuristic: a method of problem-solving and self-discovery; a way of figuring out how to figure something out.

hierarchy: classification based on perceived level of importance.

highdeep: a compound of *higher* and *deeper*, suggesting both transcendence over and immersion in data and thinking.

hypothesis: a predictive statement field-tested or put through field experimentation to assess its reliability and validity.

induction: an open-ended investigation carried out with minimal assumptions, leaving the researcher open to emergent leads and new ideas; induction is exploratory and involves making discoveries and decisions as you go along.

inference: application of inductive, abductive, deductive, and retroductive thinking to partial evidence to determine or embellish what's currently happening, has happened, or may happen.

influences and affects: the qualitative construct of quantitative reasoning's "cause and effect"; acknowledges the multiple and interrelated attributes and outcomes of social action.

inquiry: a general term for the act of investigation.

interaction: the collective back-and-forth sequences of action and reaction between individuals or between an individual and something else.

interpretation: not necessarily a methodological approach as much as a highdeep level of understanding; reaches beyond the particular study to find application, meaning, and sense-making dimensions arising from the nature of what's been investigated.

intuition: a self-perception or feeling—a seemingly unexplainable cognition of that which is hidden or of something that is about to happen; a "recognition" skill that is developed over time.

intuitive inquiry: a cyclical, hermeneutic process of investigation; a holistic blending of the investigator's prior knowledge about the topic, the literature on the relevant subjects, the particular data at hand, and the reflexive interplay with one's imagination.

lens: a significant demographic attribute of the researcher, such as gender, age, ethnicity, sexual orientation, economic class, or occupation; might also consist of the particular research methodology or disciplinary approach employed for a study.

meaning-making: the individual's intertwined cognitive and emotional mental processing of something that stimulates personal interpretive relevance and generates personal understanding.

member checking: reviewing the researcher's data accuracy, analytic findings, and/or report in progress with participants as an ethics and trustworthiness tactic.

metacognition: cognitive awareness of one's own cognitive processes; thinking about thinking.

metaphor: a literary device that compares two things via their similarities, ignoring their differences (Miles, Huberman, & Saldaña, 2014, p. 281).

method: a way of doing something or solving a problem; often systematic in its approach.

methodology: the purpose or rationale for a particular method.

moments: a collection of short yet significant (as interpreted by the researcher) participant actions, reactions, and interactions in the data that merit focused analysis and discussion; micronarrative moments can be mundane, routine, conflict laden, or impactful.

monologue: an extended, one-person account told in the first person.

multidisciplinary: pertaining to the bringing together of two or more disciplines (areas of knowledge) for integrated study and application.

narrative: a storied account of events; a symbolic representation of knowledge and experiences.

narrative inquiry: a research methodology that utilizes story, in its broadest sense, as representation and presentation of the participants' experiences; also known as creative nonfiction.

paradigmatic corroboration: a mixed methods analytic comparison in which quantitative outcomes harmonize with qualitative outcomes.

participatory action research: an applied methodology in which the researcher and participants democratically coconstruct the investigation, formulation, implementation, and evaluation of solution strategies for a group's or community's local concerns.

pattern: an action, phenomenon, or content arrangement that occurs more than twice in the data and that the researcher establishes as repeated, and that thus possesses regularity; patterns serve as meaningful representations of participants' ways or habits of living.

personal significance: one's sense of self-worth and self-meaning through personal contributions, achievement, and deep relationships with significant others.

phenomenology: the study and description of lived experiences, the essences and essentials of experiential states, natures of being, and personally significant meanings of concepts.

poetic inquiry: a research methodology that utilizes the conventions of literary poetry for representation and presentation of participants' experiences or the researcher's personal reflections.

positivism: a research paradigm that applies logical and deductive methods, most often through quantitative measurement and hypothesis testing, to natural phenomena, including human behavior.

postpositivism: a reactionary research movement against positivism that rejects objective measurement of observable phenomena, intended originally for the sciences, for the study of natural social life.

poststructuralism: in qualitative inquiry, a research approach that meticulously examines the interpretations and meanings of texts through deconstruction and critique to investigate social understandings and complexity.

proposition: an evidence-based statement that puts forth a conditional event (if/then, when/then, since/that's why, etc.) of local and particular contexts.

proverb: a statement of folk wisdom, comparable to a theory.

qualitative data: documentation and evidence of the researcher's social investigation, usually but not exclusively nonquantitative in character; can include interview transcripts, field notes, documents, artifacts, photographs, video, written surveys, digital materials, and so forth.

qualitative research: an inclusive term for a wide variety of approaches to and methods for the study of natural social life; the data collected and analyzed are primarily (but not exclusively) nonquantitative in form and document the human experiences of others and/or of oneself in social action and reflexive states.

reaction: an individual's response to an action—either action from another person or thing or one's own action.

realism: a selective representation of everyday life through words and images for qualitative reporting.

reflection: the act of pondering various components of the research project to make sense of and gain personal understanding about their meanings; making sense of that which may be puzzling or confusing, and understanding the purpose or significance of something.

reflexivity: "conscious awareness of . . . cognitive and emotional filters comprising . . . experiences, worldviews, and biases that may influence [interpretations]" derived from social inquiry (O'Dwyer & Bernauer, 2014, p. 11).

refraction: tactical reflection for deliberately making things problematic or troubling; relishing the complexity of an issue and diverging into multiple mental pathways to account for and ponder various alternatives and possibilities.

research: systematic exploration, usually connected with a specific study's purpose and goals.

retroduction: a reconstruction of past events that describes and explains the history of a case; imaginative yet logical reconstruction of how a particular outcome may have come about.

schemata: procedural routines or "scripts" in the brain to cognitively process information and to respond or act.

simile: a literary device that compares two things using "like" or "as."

social intelligence: the ability and aptitude for nurturing constructive relationships, which requires facilities such as empathic accuracy, social cognition, concern for others, and the ability to positively influence the outcome of interactions.

subjectivity: one's personal feelings, opinions, biases, preferences, values, attitudes, and beliefs.

symbols: condensed attributions of specific associations, memories, and meanings; they consolidate various properties into a single representative entity.

theme: a sentence or extended phrase that identifies and functions as a way to categorize a set of data into a topic that emerges from a pattern of ideas; the topics generate extended narratives that unpack the statements and describe or explain their constituent elements.

theoretical construct: a phrase that serves as a category-like, abstract summation of a set of related themes.

theory: a generalizable statement with an accompanying explanatory narrative that predicts and controls action through an if/then logic, explains how and/or why something happens by stating its cause(s), and provides insights and guidance for improving social life.

thinking: the mind's ways of working—that is, the mental resources drawn upon to access, organize, and analyze information; make decisions; and solve problems.

transcendence: rising above initial analyses to reach highdeep levels of meaning; progressing from the particular and local of the study toward more general or universal aspects suggested by the case.

References

Abbott, A. (2004). *Methods of discovery: Heuristics for the social sciences.* New York, NY: W. W. Norton.

Adams, T. E. (2011). *Narrating the closet: An autoethnography of same-sex attraction.* Walnut Creek, CA: Left Coast Press.

Adler, P. A., & Adler, P. (1987). *Membership roles in field research.* Newbury Park, CA: Sage.

Agar, M. (1994). *Language shock: Understanding the culture of conversation.* New York, NY: Quill/William Morrow.

Alvesson, M., & Kärreman, D. (2011). *Qualitative research and theory development: Mystery as method.* London, UK: Sage.

Angrosino, M. V. (1994). On the bus with Vonnie Lee: Explorations in life history and metaphor. *Journal of Contemporary Ethnography, 23*(1), 14–28.

Auerbach, C. F., & Silverstein, L. B. (2003). *Qualitative data: An introduction to coding and analysis.* New York, NY: New York University Press.

Barone, T., & Eisner, E. W. (2012). *Arts based research.* Thousand Oaks, CA: Sage.

Bazeley, P. (2013). *Qualitative data analysis: Practical strategies.* London, UK: Sage.

Belcher, W. L. (2009). *Writing your journal article in 12 weeks: A guide to academic publishing success.* Thousand Oaks, CA: Sage.

Belli, R. F., Stafford, F. P., & Alwin, D. F. (Eds.). (2009). *Calendar and time diary methods in life course research.* Thousand Oaks, CA: Sage.

Berbary, L. A. (2011). Poststructural writerly representation: Screenplay as creative analytic practice. *Qualitative Inquiry, 17*(2), 186–196.

Berbary, L. A. (2012). "Don't be a whore, that's not ladylike": Discursive discipline and sorority women's gendered subjectivity. *Qualitative Inquiry, 18*(7), 602–625.

Bernard, H. R. (2011). *Research methods in anthropology: Qualitative and quantitative approaches* (5th ed.). Walnut Creek, CA: AltaMira Press.

Berk, L. E. (2009). *Development through the lifespan* (5th ed.). Boston, MA: Pearson.

Bettelheim, B. (1976). *The uses of enchantment: The meaning and importance of fairy tales.* New York, NY: Alfred A. Knopf.

Bogdan, R. C., & Biklen, S. K. (2007). *Qualitative research for education: An introduction to theories and methods* (5th ed.). Boston, MA: Pearson Education.

Booth, D., & Neelands, J. (1998). *Writing in role: Classroom projects connecting writing and drama.* Hamilton, ON: Calibum Enterprises.

Bresler, L. (2005). What musicianship can teach educational research. *Music Education Research, 7*(2), 169–183.

Bresler, L. (2013). The spectrum of distance: Empathic understanding and the pedagogical power of the arts. In B. White & T. Costantino (Eds.), *Aesthetics, empathy and education* (pp. 9–28). New York, NY: Peter Lang.

Brinkmann, S. (2012). *Qualitative inquiry in everyday life: Working with everyday life materials.* London, UK: Sage.

Butler-Kisber, L. (2010). *Qualitative inquiry: Thematic, narrative, and arts-informed perspectives.* London, UK: Sage.

Camic, P. M., Rhodes, J. E., & Yardley, L. (Eds.). (2003). *Qualitative research in psychology: Expanding perspectives in methodology and design.* Washington, DC: American Psychological Association.

Caswell, J., Jr. (2011). shots [sic]: a love story. In J. Saldaña (Ed.), *Ethnotheatre: Research from page to stage* (pp. 164–201). Walnut Creek, CA: Left Coast Press.

Chang, H. (2008). *Autoethnography as method.* Walnut Creek, CA: Left Coast Press.

Charmaz, K. (2009). The body, identity, and self: Adapting to impairment. In J. M. Morse, P. Noerager Stern, J. Corbin, B. Bowers, K. Charmaz, & A. E. Clarke (Eds.), *Developing grounded theory: The second generation* (pp. 155–191). Walnut Creek, CA: Left Coast Press.

Charon, J. M. (2013). *Ten questions: A sociological perspective* (8th ed.). Belmont, CA: Cengage Learning.

Clandinin, D. J., & Connelly, F. M. (2000). *Narrative inquiry: Experience and story in qualitative research.* San Francisco, CA: Jossey-Bass.

Clarke, A. E. (2005). *Situational analysis: Grounded theory after the postmodern turn.* Thousand Oaks, CA: Sage.

Coghlan, D., & Brannick, T. (2010). *Doing action research in your own organization* (3rd ed.). London, UK: Sage.

Collins, C. S., & Cooper, J. E. (2014). Emotional intelligence and the qualitative researcher. *International Journal of Qualitative Methods, 13.* Retrieved March 31, 2014, from http://ejournals.library.ualberta.ca/index.php/IJQM/index

Corbin J., & Strauss, A. (2008). *Basics of qualitative research: Techniques and procedures for developing grounded theory* (3rd ed.). Thousand Oaks, CA: Sage.

Corsaro, W. A. (2011). *The sociology of childhood* (3rd ed.). Thousand Oaks, CA: Pine Forge Press.

Coulter, C. A., & Smith, M. L. (2009). The construction zone: Literary elements in narrative research. *Educational Researcher, 38*(8), 577–590.

Creswell, J. W., & Plano-Clark, V. L. (2011). *Designing and conducting mixed methods research* (2nd ed.). Thousand Oaks, CA: Sage.

Cuzzort, R. P., & King, E. W. (2002). *Social thought into the twenty-first century* (6th ed.). Fort Worth, TX: Harcourt.

Denzin, N. K. (1995). *The cinematic society: The voyeur's gaze.* Thousand Oaks, CA: Sage.

Denzin, N. K., & Lincoln, Y. S. (2011). *The SAGE handbook of qualitative research* (4th ed.). Thousand Oaks, CA: Sage.

DeWalt, K. M., & DeWalt, B. R. (2011). *Participant observation: A guide for fieldworkers* (2nd ed.). Lanham, MD: AltaMira Press.

Dey, I. (1993). *Qualitative data analysis: A user-friendly guide for social scientists.* London, UK: Routledge.

Drew, P. (2008). Conversation analysis. In J. A. Smith (Ed.), *Qualitative psychology: A practical guide to research methods* (2nd ed., pp. 133–159). London, UK: Sage.

Dubinsky, J. M., Roehrig, G., & Varma, S. (2013). Infusing neuroscience into teacher professional development. *Educational Researcher, 42*(6), 317–329.

Duhigg, C. (2012). *The power of habit: How we do what we do in life and business.* New York, NY: Random House.

Edgerton, R. B. (1992). *Sick societies: Challenging the myth of primitive harmony.* New York, NY: Free Press.

Ehrenreich, B. (2001). *Nickel and dimed: On (not) getting by in America.* New York, NY: Henry Holt.

Eisenberg, N., & Strayer, J. (Eds.). (1990). *Empathy and its development.* New York, NY: Cambridge University Press.

Eisner, E. W. (1991). *The enlightened eye: Qualitative inquiry and the enhancement of educational practice.* New York, NY: Macmillan.

Eisner, E. W. (1998). *The kind of schools we need: Personal essays.* Portsmouth, NH: Heinemann.

Ensler, E. (2001). *The vagina monologues.* New York, NY: Villard.

Erickson, F. (1986). Qualitative methods in research on teaching. In M. C. Wittrock (Ed.), *Handbook of research on teaching* (3rd ed., pp. 119–161). New York, NY: Macmillan.

Erickson, F. (1997). Culture in society and educational practices. In J. A. Banks & C. A. M. Banks (Eds.), *Multicultural education: Issues and perspectives* (3rd ed., pp. 32–60). Boston, MA: Allyn & Bacon.

Ericsson, K. A., & Simon, H. A. (1993). *Protocol analysis: Verbal reports as data* (Rev. ed.). Cambridge, MA: Massachusetts Institute of Technology.

Fenstermaker, S., & Jones, N. (2011). *Sociologists backstage: Answers to 10 questions about what they do.* New York, NY: Routledge.

Finley, M. (2000). *Street rat.* Grosse Pointe, MI: Greenroom Press.

Finley, S., & Finley, M. (1999). Sp'ange: A research story. *Qualitative Inquiry, 5*(3), 313–337.

Florida, R. (2002). *The rise of the creative class.* New York, NY: Basic Books.

Flynn, R. (1991). The drama specialist: Controlled by . . . controlling by. . . *Youth Theatre Journal, 5*(3), 3–10.

Forrester, M. A. (Ed.). (2010). *Doing qualitative research in psychology: A practical guide.* London, UK: Sage.

Friese, S. (2012). *Qualitative data analysis with ATLAS.ti.* London, UK: Sage.

Gabler, J. (2011). *Sociology for dummies.* Hoboken, NJ: Wiley.

Gee, J. P. (2011). *How to do discourse analysis: A toolkit.* New York, NY: Routledge.

Geertz, C. (1973). *The interpretation of cultures.* New York, NY: Basic Books.

Geertz, C. (1983). *Local knowledge: Further essays in interpretive anthropology.* New York, NY: Basic Books.

Gibbs, G. R. (2007). *Analysing qualitative data.* London, UK: Sage.

Gibson, W. J., & Brown, A. (2009). *Working with qualitative data.* London, UK: Sage.

Giele, J. Z., & Elder, G. H., Jr. (Eds.). (1998). *Methods of life course research: Qualitative and quantitative approaches.* Thousand Oaks, CA: Sage.

Gilligan, C., Spencer, R., Weinberg, M. K., & Bertsch, T. (2006). On the Listening Guide: A voice-centered relational method. In S. N. Hesse-Biber & P. Leavy (Eds.), *Emergent methods in social research* (pp. 253–271). Thousand Oaks, CA: Sage.

Gobo, G. (2008). *Doing ethnography* (A. Belton, Trans.). London, UK: Sage.

Goffman, E. (1959). *The presentation of self in everyday life.* New York, NY: Anchor Books.

Goffman, E. (1963). *Stigma: Notes on the management of spoiled identity.* Englewood Cliffs, NJ: Prentice Hall.

Goleman, D. (1995). *Emotional intelligence.* New York, NY: Bantam Books.

Goleman, D. (2006). *Social intelligence: The new science of human relationships.* New York, NY: Bantam Books.

Goodall, H. L., Jr. (2000). *Writing the new ethnography.* Walnut Creek, CA: AltaMira Press.

Gordon, A. (2014, March 18). Killing pigs and weed maps: The mostly unread world of academic papers. *Pacific Standard.* Retrieved April 5, 2014, from http://www.psmag.com/navigation/books-and-culture/killing-pigs-weed-maps-mostly-unread-world-academic-papers-76733/

Gray, R., & Sinding, C. (2002). *Standing ovation: Performing social science research about cancer.* Walnut Creek, CA: AltaMira Press.

Gregoire, C. (2014). *18 things highly creative people do differently.* Retrieved March 9, 2014, from http://www.huffingtonpost.com/2014/03/04/creativity-habits_n_4859769.html

Gutkind, L. (Ed.). (2008). *Keep it real: Everything you need to know about researching and writing creative nonfiction.* New York, NY: W. W. Norton.

Hacker, K. (2013). *Community-based participatory research.* Thousand Oaks, CA: Sage.

Hahn, D. (2011). *Brainstorm: Unleashing your creative self.* New York, NY: Disney Editions.

Hakel, M. (1968). How often is often? *American Psychologist, 23*(7), 533–534.

Hammersley, M., & Atkinson, P. (2007). *Ethnography: Principles in practice* (3rd ed.). London, UK: Routledge.

Hesse-Biber, S. N. (Ed.). (2012). *Handbook of feminist research: Theory and praxis* (2nd ed.). Thousand Oaks, CA: Sage.

Hesse-Biber, S. N. (Ed.). (2014). *Feminist research practice: A primer* (2nd ed.). Thousand Oaks, CA: Sage.

Hitchcock, G., & Hughes, D. (1995). *Research and the teacher: A qualitative introduction to school-based research* (2nd ed.). London, UK: Routledge.

Hochschild, A. R. (2003). *The managed heart: Commercialization of human feeling* (2nd ed.). Berkeley, CA: University of California Press.

Holstein, J. A., & Gubrium, J. F. (Eds.). (2012). *Varieties of narrative analysis.* Thousand Oaks, CA: Sage.

hooks, b. (1994). *Teaching to transgress: Education as the practice of freedom.* New York, NY: Routledge.

hooks, b. (2003). *Teaching community: A pedagogy of hope.* New York, NY: Routledge.

hooks, b. (2010). *Teaching critical thinking: Practical wisdom.* New York, NY: Routledge.

Huff, D. (1954). *How to lie with statistics.* New York, NY: W. W. Norton.

Humphreys, L. (1970). *Tearoom trade: Impersonal sex in public places.* Chicago, IL: Aldine.

Jackson, A. Y., & Mazzei, L. A. (2012). *Thinking with theory in qualitative research: Viewing data across multiple perspectives.* New York, NY: Routledge.

Janesick, V. J. (2010). *Oral history for the qualitative researcher: Choreographing the story.* New York, NY: Guilford Press.

Jensen, E. (2001). *Arts with the brain in mind.* Alexandria, VA: Association for Supervision and Curriculum Development.

Jones, E., Gallois, C., Callan, V., & Barker, M. (1999). Strategies of accommodation: Development of a coding system for conversational interaction. *Journal of Language and Social Psychology, 18*(2), 123–152.

Jones, S. H., Adams, T. E., & Ellis, C. (Eds.). (2013). *Handbook of autoethnography.* Walnut Creek, CA: Left Coast Press.

Kahneman, D. (2011). *Thinking, fast and slow.* New York, NY: Farrar, Straus and Giroux.

Kaufman, M., & Members of the Tectonic Theater Project. (2001). *The Laramie project* (acting ed.). New York, NY: Dramatists Play Service.

Kelin, D. A., II (2005). *To feel as our ancestors did: Collecting and performing oral histories.* Portsmouth, NH: Heinemann.

Kelling, G. L., & Wilson J. Q. (1982). Broken windows: The police and neighborhood safety. *The Atlantic.* Retrieved August 2, 2013, from http://www.theatlantic.com/magazine/print/1982/03/broken-windows/304465/

Kendell, D. (2013). *Sociology in our times* (9th ed.). Belmont, CA: Wadsworth Cengage Learning.

Kirchner, L. (2014, January 7). Breaking down the broken windows theory. *Pacific Standard Newsletter.* Retrieved January 23, 2014, from http://www.psmag.com/navigation/politics-and-law/breaking-broken-windows-theory-72310/

Knowles, J. G., & Cole, A. L. (2008). *Handbook of the arts in qualitative research: Perspectives, methodologies, examples, and issues.* Thousand Oaks, CA: Sage.

Knowlton, L. W., & Phillips, C. C. (2013). *The logic model guidebook: Better strategies for great results* (2nd ed.). Thousand Oaks, CA: Sage.

Kozol, J. (1991). *Savage inequalities: Children in America's schools.* New York, NY: Crown.

Krippendorff, K., & Bock, M. A. (Eds.). (2009). *The content analysis reader.* Thousand Oaks, CA: Sage.

Kuckartz, U. (2014). *Qualitative text analysis: A guide to methods, practice & using software* (A. McWhertor, Trans.). London, UK: Sage.

Kvale, S., & Brinkmann, S. (2009). *Interviews: Learning the craft of qualitative research interviewing* (2nd ed.). Thousand Oaks, CA: Sage.

Lakoff, G., & Johnson, M. (1980). *Metaphors we live by.* Chicago, IL: University of Chicago Press.

Landy, R. J. (1993). *Persona and performance: The meaning of role in drama, therapy, and everyday life.* New York, NY: Guilford.

Langer, S. K. (1977). *Feeling and form.* New York, NY: Longman.

Leavy, P. (2009). *Method meets art: Arts-based research practice.* New York, NY: Guilford Press.

Leavy, P. (2011). *Oral history.* New York, NY: Oxford.

Lévi-Strauss, C. (1978). *Myth and meaning.* Abingdon, UK: Routledge.

Liebow, E. (1967). *Tally's corner: A study of Negro streetcorner men.* Boston, MA: Little, Brown.

Lincoln, Y. S., & Guba, E. G. (1985). *Naturalistic inquiry.* Newbury Park, CA: Sage.

Lindlof, T. R., & Taylor, B. C. (2011). *Qualitative communication research methods* (3rd ed.). Thousand Oaks, CA: Sage.

Lupton, D. (2012). *Medicine as culture: Illness, disease and the body* (3rd ed.). London, UK: Sage.

Mack, P. (2012). *Inside artist/teacher burnout.* Unpublished doctoral dissertation, Arizona State University.

Madden, R. (2010). *Being ethnographic: A guide to the theory and practice of ethnography.* London, UK: Sage.

Manovski, M. P. (2012). *Finding my voice: (Re)living, (re)learning, and (re)searching becoming a singer in a culture of marginalization.* Unpublished doctoral dissertation, Oakland University.

Margolis, E., & Pauwels, L. (Eds.). (2011). *The SAGE handbook of visual research methods.* London, UK: Sage.

Maxwell, J. A. (2012). *A realist approach for qualitative research.* Thousand Oaks, CA: Sage.

Maxwell, J. A. (2013). *Qualitative research design: An interactive approach* (3rd ed.). Thousand Oaks, CA: Sage.

McCammon, L., Saldaña, J., Hines, A., & Omasta, M. (2012). Lifelong impact: Adult perceptions of their high school speech and/or theatre participation. *Youth Theatre Journal, 26*(1), 2–25.

McCurdy, D. W., Spradley, J. P., & Shandy, D. J. (2005). *The cultural experience: Ethnography in complex society* (2nd ed.). Long Grove, IL: Waveland Press.

McIntyre, M. (2009). Home is where the heart is: A reader's theatre. *International Journal of the Creative Arts in Interdisciplinary Practice.* Retrieved September 15, 2009, from http://www.ijcaip.com/archives/CCAHTE-Journal-7-McIntyre.html

McKnight, K. S. (2010). *The teacher's big book of graphic organizers.* San Francisco, CA: Jossey-Bass.

McKnight, K. S. (2013). *The elementary teacher's big book of graphic organizers.* San Francisco, CA: Jossey-Bass.

Mears, C. L. (2009). *Interviewing for education and social science research: The gateway approach.* New York, NY: Palgrave Macmillan.

Miles, M. B., Huberman, A. M., & Saldaña, J. (2014). *Qualitative data analysis: A methods sourcebook* (3rd ed.). Thousand Oaks, CA: Sage.

Moore, L. C. (2010). Learning in schools. In D. F. Lancy, J. Bock, & S. Gaskins (Eds.), *The anthropology of learning in childhood* (pp. 207–232). Walnut Creek, CA: AltaMira Press.

Morgan, D. L. (2014). *Integrating qualitative and quantitative methods: A pragmatic approach.* Thousand Oaks, CA: Sage.

Morrison, K. (2009). *Causation in educational research.* London, UK: Routledge.

Munton, A. G., Silvester, J., Stratton, P., & Hanks, H. (1999). *Attributions in action: A practical approach to coding qualitative data.* Chichester, UK: Wiley.

Murray, M. (2008). Narrative psychology. In J. A. Smith (Ed.), *Qualitative psychology: A practical guide to research methods* (2nd ed., pp. 111–132). London, UK: Sage.

Norris, J. (2009). *Playbuilding as qualitative research: A participatory arts-based approach.* Walnut Creek, CA: Left Coast Press.

Norris, J., Sawyer, R. D., & Lund, D. E. (2012). *Duoethnography: Dialogic methods for social, health, and educational research.* Walnut Creek, CA: Left Coast Press.

Obenhaus, P. (Director). (1985). *Einstein on the beach: The changing image of opera* [videorecording]. Direct Cinema.

O'Dwyer, L. M., & Bernauer, J. A. (2014). *Quantitative research for the qualitative researcher.* Thousand Oaks, CA: Sage.

O'Toole, J., Burton, B., & Plunkett, A. (2005). *Cooling conflict: A new approach to managing bullying and conflict in schools.* Frenchs Forest, Australia: Pearson Education.

Ownings, A. (2002). *Hey, waitress! The U.S.A. from the other side of the tray.* Berkeley, CA: University of California Press.

Packer, M. (2011). *The science of qualitative research.* New York, NY: Cambridge University Press.

Park, H.-Y. (2009). Writing in Korean, living in the U.S.: A screenplay about a bilingual boy and his mom. *Qualitative Inquiry, 15*(6), 1103–1124.

Pascoe, C. J. (2007). *Dude, you're a fag: Masculinity and sexuality in high school.* Berkeley, CA: University of California Press.

Paulus, T., Lester, J. N., & Dempster, P. G. (2014). *Digital tools for qualitative research.* London, UK: Sage.

Peshkin, A. (1986). *God's choice: The total world of a Fundamentalist Christian school.* Chicago, IL: University of Chicago Press.

Pink, D. H. (2006). *A whole new mind: Why right-brainers will rule the future.* New York, NY: Riverhead Books.

Poulos, C. N. (2009). *Accidental ethnography: An inquiry into family secrecy.* Walnut Creek, CA: Left Coast Press.

Prendergast, M., Leggo, C., & Sameshima, P. (Eds.). (2009). *Poetic inquiry: Vibrant voices in the social sciences.* Rotterdam, Netherlands: Sense.

Rapley, T. (2007). *Doing conversation, discourse and document analysis.* London, UK: Sage.

Ravitch, S. M., & Riggan, M. (2012). *Reason & rigor: How conceptual frameworks guide research.* Thousand Oaks, CA: Sage.

Reich, S. (1989). *Different trains.* Elektra/Asylum/Nonesuch Records.

Richards, L., & Morse, J. M. (2013). *Readme first for a user's guide to qualitative methods* (3rd ed.). Thousand Oaks, CA: Sage.

Reinertsen, A. B. (2014). Welcome to my brain. *Qualitative Inquiry, 20*(3), 255–266.

Riessman, C. K. (2008). *Narrative methods for the human sciences.* Thousand Oaks, CA: Sage.

Rosenbaum, M. S. (2011). From theoretical generation to verification using structural equation modeling. In V. B. Martin & A. Glynnild (Eds.), *Grounded theory: The philosophy, method, and work of Barney Glaser* (pp. 283–295). Boca Raton, FL: BrownWalker Press.

Roy, D. F. (1959). "Banana time": Job satisfaction and informal interaction. *Human Organization, 18*(4), 158–168.

Royce, A. P. (2004). *The anthropology of the performing arts: Artistry, virtuosity, and interpretation in a cross-cultural perspective.* Lanham, MD: AltaMira Press.

Rubin, H. J., & Rubin, I. S. (2012). *Qualitative interviewing: The art of hearing data* (3rd ed.). Thousand Oaks, CA: Sage.

Saldaña, J. (1997). "Survival": A white teacher's conception of drama with inner city Hispanic youth. *Youth Theatre Journal, 11*, 25–46.

Saldaña, J. (1998). Ethical issues in an ethnographic performance text: The "dramatic impact" of "juicy stuff." *Research in Drama Education, 3*(2), 181–196.

Saldaña, J. (2003). *Longitudinal qualitative research: Analyzing change through time.* Walnut Creek, CA: AltaMira Press.

Saldaña, J. (Ed.). (2005a). *Ethnodrama: An anthology of reality theatre.* Walnut Creek, CA: AltaMira Press.

Saldaña, J. (2005b). Theatre of the oppressed with children: A field experiment. *Youth Theatre Journal, 19*, 117–133.

Saldaña, J. (2009). Popular film as an instructional strategy in qualitative research methods courses. *Qualitative Inquiry, 15*(1), 247–261.

Saldaña, J. (2010). Writing ethnodrama: A sampler from educational research. In M. Savin-Baden & C. H. Major (Eds.), *New approaches to qualitative research: Wisdom and uncertainty* (pp. 61–69). London, UK: Routledge.

Saldaña, J. (2011a). *Ethnotheatre: Research from page to stage.* Walnut Creek, CA: Left Coast Press.

Saldaña, J. (2011b). *Fundamentals of qualitative research.* New York, NY: Oxford University Press.

Saldaña, J. (2013). *The coding manual for qualitative researchers* (2nd ed.). London, UK: Sage.

Saldaña J. (2014). Coding and analysis strategies. In P. Leavy (Ed.), *The Oxford handbook of qualitative research* (pp. 581–605). New York, NY: Oxford University Press.

Saldaña, J., Finley, S., & Finley, M. (2005). Street rat. In J. Saldaña (Ed.), *Ethnodrama: An anthology of reality theatre* (pp. 139–179). Walnut Creek, CA: AltaMira Press.

Salkind, N. J. (2013). *Statistics for people who (think they) hate statistics* (3rd ed.). Thousand Oaks, CA: Sage.

Sandelowski, M., Trimble, F., Woodard, E. K., & Barroso J. (2006). From synthesis to script: Transforming qualitative research findings for use in practice. *Qualitative Health Research, 16*(10), 1350–1370.

Sawyer, R. D., & Norris, J. (2013). *Duoethnography.* New York, NY: Oxford.

Schreier, M. (2012). *Qualitative content analysis in practice.* London, UK: Sage.

Seidman, I. (2013). *Interviewing as qualitative research: A guide for researchers in education and the social sciences* (4th ed.). New York, NY: Teachers College Press.

Smith, A. D. (2000). *Talk to me: Listening between the lines.* New York, NY: Random House.

Smith, J. A. (2008). *Qualitative psychology: A practical guide to research methods* (2nd ed.). London, UK: Sage.

Smith, J. A., Flowers, P., & Larkin, M. (2009). *Interpretative phenomenological analysis: Theory, method and research.* London, UK: Sage.

Sousa, D. A. (2011). *How the brain learns* (4th ed.). Thousand Oaks, CA: Corwin.

Spradley, J. P. (1979). *The ethnographic interview.* Fort Worth, TX: Harcourt Brace Jovanovich.

Spradley, J. P. (1980). *Participant observation.* Fort Worth, TX: Harcourt Brace Jovanovich.

Spry, T. (2011). *Body, paper, stage: Writing and performing autoethnography.* Walnut Creek, CA: Left Coast Press.

Stake, R. E. (1995). *The art of case study research.* Thousand Oaks, CA: Sage.

Stilgoe, J. R. (1998). *Outside lies magic: Regaining history and awareness in everyday places.* New York, NY: Walker.

Strauch, B. (2010). *The secret life of the grown-up brain: The surprising talents of the middle-aged mind.* New York, NY: Penguin Books.

Stringer, E. T. (2014). *Action research* (4th ed.). Thousand Oaks, CA: Sage.

Sullivan P. (2012). *Qualitative data analysis using a dialogical approach.* London, UK: Sage.

Sunstein, B. S., & Chiseri-Strater, E. (2012). *FieldWorking: Reading and writing research* (4th ed.). Boston, MA: Bedford/St. Martin's.

Tashakkori, A., & Teddlie, C. (Eds.). (2010). *The SAGE handbook of mixed methods in social & behavioral research* (2nd ed.). Thousand Oaks, CA: Sage.

Terkel, S. (1972). *Working: People talk about what they do all day and how they feel about what they do.* New York, NY: New Press.

Thompson, J., Windschitl, M., & Braaten, M. (2013). Developing a theory of ambitious early-career teacher practice. *American Educational Research Journal, 50*(3), 574–615.

Trimble, E. (2006). *Quote unquote volume 4: Movie quotes for unscripted moments.* Sherman Oaks, CA: Autumn Leaves.

Toth, J. (1993). *The mole people: Life in the tunnels beneath New York City.* Chicago, IL: Chicago Review Press.

Turnbull, C. M. (1972). *The mountain people.* New York, NY: Simon & Schuster.

Umoquit, M., Tso, P., Varga-Atkins, T., O'Brien, M., & Wheeldon, J. (2013). *Diagrammatic elicitation: Defining the use of diagrams in data collection.* Retrieved August 12, 2013, from http://www.nova.edu/ssss/QR/QR18/umoquit60.pdf

Urquhart, C. (2013). *Grounded theory for qualitative research: A practical guide.* London, UK: Sage.

van Maanen, J. (2011). *Tales of the field: On writing ethnography* (2nd ed.). Chicago, IL: University of Chicago Press.

Van Manen, M. (1990). *Researching lived experience.* New York, NY: State University of New York Press.

Wagner, J. (1986). *The search for signs of intelligent life in the universe.* New York, NY: HarperCollins.

Waite, D. (2014). Teaching the unteachable: Some issues of qualitative research pedagogy. *Qualitative Inquiry, 20*(3), 267–281.

Wales, P. (2009). Positioning the drama teacher: Exploring the power of identity in teaching practices. *Research in Drama Education, 14*(2), 261–278.

Wertz, F. J., Charmaz, K., McMullen, L. M., Josselson, R., Anderson, R., & McSpadden, E. (2011). *Five ways of doing qualitative analysis.* New York, NY: Guilford Press.

Wheeldon, J., & Åhlberg, M. K. (2012). *Visualizing social science research: Maps, methods, & meaning.* Thousand Oaks, CA: Sage.

White, M. (2013). *How did our brains get so brilliant? Pacific Standard.* Retrieved September 17, 2013, from http://www.psmag.com/science/brains-get-brilliant-smart-evolution-65825/

Wilson, D. (2010, May 18). College graduates to make global economy more productive. *Bloomberg News.* Retrieved February 2, 2014, from http://www.bloomberg.com/news/2010-05-18/college-graduates-to-make-global-economy-more-productive-chart-of-the-day.html

Winkelman, M. (1994). Cultural shock and adaptation. *Journal of Counseling and Development, 73*(2), 121–126.

Wolcott, H. F. (1973). *The man in the principal's office: An ethnography.* Prospect Heights, IL: Waveland Press.

Wolcott, H. F. (1994). *Transforming qualitative data: Description, analysis, and interpretation.* Thousand Oaks, CA: Sage.

Wolcott, H. F. (2002). *Sneaky kid and its aftermath: Ethics and intimacy in fieldwork.* Walnut Creek, CA: AltaMira Press.

Wolcott, H. F. (2009). *Writing up qualitative research* (3rd ed.). Thousand Oaks, CA: Sage.

Wolfe, P. (2010). *Brain matters: Translating research into classroom practice* (2nd ed.). Alexandria, VA: Association for Supervision and Curriculum Development.

Wright, D. (2004). *I am my own wife.* New York, NY: Faber and Faber.

Zona, G. A. (1996). *Eyes that see do not grow old: The proverbs of Mexico, Central and South America.* New York, NY: Touchstone.

Index